Mass Communications and Media Studies

2

ᆌ

Mass Communications and Media Studies

An Introduction

Peyton Paxson

continuum

2010

The Continuum International Publishing Group Inc
80 Maiden Lane, New York, NY 10038

The Continuum International Publishing Group Ltd
The Tower Building, 11 York Road, London SE1 7NX

www.continuumbooks.com

Library of Congress Cataloging-in-Publication Data
Paxson, Peyton.
Mass communications and media studies : an introduction /
by Peyton Paxson.
   p. cm.
Includes bibliographical references and index.
ISBN-13: 978-1-4411-0895-1 (pbk. : alk. paper)
ISBN-10: 1-4411-0895-5 (pbk. : alk. paper) 1. Mass media. I. Title.

P90.P357 2010
302.23–dc22
                                                    2010003641

ISBN: 978-1-4411-0895-1

Typeset by Newgen Imaging Systems Pvt Ltd, Chennai, India
Printed and bound in the United States of America
   by Sheridan Books, Inc

Contents

Acknowledgments

To Katie Gallof at Continuum, who made it happen.

To my dean, Clea Andreadis, and my program chair, Michelle Bloomer, for letting it happen.

To my old pal Francine Taylor, for keeping it real.

To my wife and best friend Karen L. Muncaster.

To my family in El Paso.

And to my brother-in-law, Bob Muncaster, who will read this book in a big brown truck.

Thank you all.

A Note to the Reader . . .

Nearly 20 years ago, a 10-year-old asked me what I thought about "The Crisis in the Gulf." I thought it was odd that a child would use such an expression. I later discovered that he had learned the term from CNN, which used it as its "branding" of its coverage of the first Gulf war.

Mass communications are more than a source of entertainment and information. They affect how we see the world and how we see ourselves. Yet because they are so embedded in our lives, it is easy for us to take mass communications for granted. This book doesn't do that. Chapter 1 looks at the cultural, social, and economic roles that mass communications serve. Chapter 2 discusses the need for each of us to be media literate, and provides a framework for thinking critically about the media.

The mass communications industry arose in the United States in the 1800s, as the Industrial Revolution generated the need for mass marketing and mass media. For two centuries, mass communications was essentially a one-way process, with information and entertainment created and delivered by the mass media to individuals. Chapters 4 through 8 examine "traditional" media: television, radio, print media, and movies. These chapters look at how each communications medium arose and discuss the current industry structure of each.

Most traditional media are essentially advertising delivery vehicles. This should be obvious for broadcast and print media, and advertising plays a larger role in movies than you may realize. The structure of the advertising industry is discussed in Chapter 3, and the role advertising plays in each medium is examined in the chapters devoted to those media.

Chapters 8 and 9 focus on the Internet and what are commonly referred to as "new" media. New media include social networking, mobile communications devices, and video games. The interactivity of these media and their ability to let users view media whenever and wherever they want are posing serious threats to traditional media.

Chapter 10 examines the disaggregation of audiences and the convergence of media. We will see that these relatively recent phenomena provide new opportunities to consumers and new challenges to the media industry. The role that law and government regulation play in shaping and controlling the mass communications industry is the topic of Chapter 11. We know that globalization is an increasingly important process. The book concludes with a discussion of how mass communications both affect globalization and are affected by it.

Each chapter ends with thoughts about the future of each topic, as well as a discussion of career opportunities that these topics present. There are also a handful of questions at the end of each chapter that ask you to engage in critical thinking and discussion of the topics presented.

This book provides a condensed introduction to mass communications. Its brevity and lack of color illustrations serve to make this book an accessible and affordable alternative to other books in the field.

Mass Communications and Contemporary Culture

1

Chapter contents

Issues and trends in mass communications and contemporary culture

- Interpersonal communications have existed as long as humanity; mass communications are a relatively recent development.
- Mass media in the past lacked the ability to quickly receive feedback from their audiences, but new communication technology provides increased interactivity.
- Just as interpersonal communications allow people to establish relationships with each other, mass communications serve a role in building and maintaining communities.
- Mass communications are distributed through mass media, which arose during the American Industrial Revolution of the 1800s to provide mass marketing for firms that mass manufactured products.
- Mass markets are segmented into numerous characteristics, including people's age, income, and attitudes.
- Half a dozen firms control many of the major media channels in the United States.

"For the first time in human history, most of the stories about people, life, and values are told not by parents, schools, churches, or others in the community who have their own stories to tell but by a group of distant media conglomerates that have something to sell. This is a radical change in the way we employ creative talent, the way we cast the symbolic environment, and the way we learn our roles in life."

George Gerbner[1]

Mass communications

This book looks at mass communications as a source of entertainment and information, as a process, and as a business. *Communication* means the practice of encoding information through sounds, symbols, and actions in order to transmit that information to others. Communication also includes decoding that information and interpreting it to give it meaning. Wilbur Schramm, a key figure in communication studies, developed one of the best-known models of communication in 1954[2] (see Figure 1.1).

Note that Schramm's model is cyclical, with both parties involved in encoding and decoding each other's messages. It may help you to understand Schramm's model by labeling the bottom message as feedback, which the sender of the original message uses to determine whether the message was decoded and interpreted as intended. Interpersonal communications, whether one-on-one or in groups, is as old as humanity. However, mass communications have existed for only a few hundred years. By *mass*

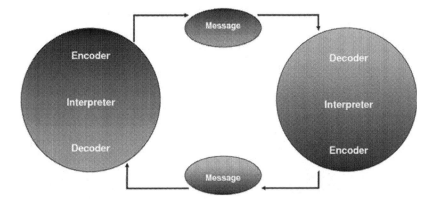

Figure 1.1 Schramm's communication model.

communications, we mean communicating with many people, perhaps millions of people, often simultaneously. Mass communications are messages: the means of communicating these messages is through the *mass media.* (Note: media is the plural of medium. Therefore, the correct usage is to say, "the media are ..." not "the media is." Even people who work in mass media often get this wrong.)

In many ways, mass communications rely more on quantity than quality, while interpersonal communications rely more on quality than quantity. Mass communications can reach more people at one time (a greater quantity) than interpersonal communications can. For example, the January 20, 2009 presidential inauguration of Barack Obama drew 37.8 million television viewers in the United States.[3] A few days later, over 95 million U.S. viewers watched the Super Bowl. Millions of people in other countries also watched these events, either live or recorded. Today, nearly any event can be transmitted around the globe instantaneously. Global electronic communications also allow newspapers and news magazines to print stories as they occur, although the distribution of print media creates a time lag in delivery of this information. The potential viewership, readership, or listenership for an event can approach nearly all of the world's population.

However, the quality of mass communications rarely attains the quality of effective interpersonal communication. Interpersonal communications can occur one-on-one or within a group. One of the key differences between interpersonal communications and mass communications is that we are much more likely to have feedback in interpersonal communications than we are in mass communications. As we saw in Schramm's model of communication, feedback is part of a loop: we encode messages and transmit them to others; they decode our message, encode their response, and transmit that response back to the original sender, who begins the decoding, encoding, and transmitting process again. Even when we silently look at the other person who has just spoken to us and walk away, we are sending a message.

If necessary, someone involved in interpersonal communication can repeat or rephrase something that another person did not hear, did not hear correctly, or did not understand. Based on the verbal or nonverbal reaction of the other person or persons during interpersonal communications, we can see if our message is being interpreted the way we want it to be (or not) and whether it is being accepted the way we want it to be (or not). As part of the feedback process, the other person may display nonverbal communications (such as smiling with delight or looking away with disinterest) while we are communicating with them. They can reply to our questions or ask questions of their own. Based on this feedback, we can adjust the message as necessary.

Though lacking the level of feedback that interpersonal communication possesses, the mass media still attempt to assess their ability to connect with audiences. For example, print publications collect readership figures and television networks collect viewership numbers. Newspapers and magazines also solicit letters from readers and publish some of them. However, unlike many forms of interpersonal communications, these efforts to measure the effectiveness of mass communications often occur after the fact.

Advertisers receive feedback for their advertisements both directly and indirectly. A particularly successful advertisement may result in increased sales of the advertised product or service. Similarly, unsuccessful advertising may lead to diminished sales. This success, or lack of it, is a form of consumer feedback. Consumers may also take it upon themselves to communicate with an advertiser. For example, *Ms.* Magazine maintains a "No comment" section that presents advertisements that have run in other publications, which the *Ms.* staff finds objectionable for their portrayal of females. *Ms.* includes the address of the advertiser, to whom many readers of *Ms.* write complaining about the advertisement.

Another form of negative feedback is the boycott, or refusal to do business with certain advertisers. The boycott may originate from an advertisement that some people find offensive. For example, an advertisement perceived to be racist may lead to an organized effort to avoid buying the advertised product. Another form of negative feedback results from *channel effect*. The medium in which an advertisement is placed affects how consumers perceive the advertisement. In this case, if the medium is viewed as unacceptable, the advertisement placed in that media is also viewed unfavorably. For example, the editors of the *Penthouse* magazine, competing against Internet pornography, decided to make the magazine more sexually explicit. This resulted in several advertisers pulling their advertisements from the publication.

Mass communications and communities

An important question about the quality of mass communications is whether they help build and maintain communities or whether they, in fact, hurt our sense of community and connection to others. While we may be able to enjoy talking with others about recent movies and television shows or articles that we have read, we also talk with others less while we are consuming media. (How many times have you been told "Shhh!" by someone watching television or listening to the radio?)

Some people defend mass communications as a means of reconfiguring our sense of community, away from a sense of shared physical space, to one that is based on shared interests. For example, someone with an interest in skydiving may live in an area where there are few other skydivers. However, there are magazines and Internet websites targeted at skydivers. Still, the one-sidedness of mass media, with the advertising-supported medium as sender and consumers as receivers, means that most mass media are driven by profits, rather than a social exchange.

In an era when new social media such as Facebook and Twitter have been so energetically embraced by consumers, more traditional forms of mass media have had to adjust. The lack of quality of communication among traditional mass media stands in sharp contrast to the interactivity of new communication media. Traditional media now encourage their audiences to use the Internet, text messaging, and social media to comment on the articles or programs that these media distribute.

Mass communications and technology: Gutenberg

Mass communications require technology. Today, many forms of mass communications rely on electronics. However, the first important event in mass communications was movable type and the printing press, which was originally operated by hand. The German printer Johannes Gutenberg (1398–1468) (see Figure 1.2) often is credited with inventing movable type around 1440. While many scholars today believe that movable type originated in China about 600 years earlier, Gutenberg did popularize it in Europe. Movable type was a significant improvement over earlier forms of book-making, which involved either handwritten manuscripts or the use of carved woodblocks. Movable type made printing faster and easier, as a printer could quickly set up lines of type and quickly print documents. This new efficiency in printing reduced the cost of printing documents and the cost of the documents themselves. When books became less expensive, more people could buy books.

Figure 1.2 Johannes Gutenberg. *Source*: iStockphoto

The first important book that Gutenberg published was the Bible in 1455. Prior to this time, few people owned the Bible. Few people could read, as there was little reading material, and there was little need to read. Even if one could read, printed documents were quite expensive. As a result, rich people and some officials within the Roman Catholic Church were among the few Europeans who could read prior to Gutenberg's work.

Movable type not only expanded the market for reading material; it led to the spread of discoveries and ideas. Thus, the printing press helped advance the European Renaissance, which saw startling new advances in the arts between the fourteenth and seventeenth centuries, as well as the Scientific Revolution, which began in the mid 1500s. The printing press also fostered the Reformation, a religious movement that began in Germany in the early 1500s. The Reformation, an effort by some members of the Roman Catholic church to change what they saw as wrongful beliefs and activities within the church, resulted in many followers leaving the Roman Catholic Church in protest (thus, they were "Protestants") and forming new Christian sects. One of the key figures in the Reformation was Martin Luther

(1483–1546) a Catholic monk in Germany who distributed printed documents to promote his religious arguments.

You have probably heard the expression that information is power. It is typical among those who hold power not to want to give up any of that power. The aristocracy of Europe understandably felt threatened by the changes that the printing press brought to the continent. However, as we will see, most mass communications became the property of the mass media, which often control which messages we are exposed to (or not).

Mass communications and technology: the Industrial Revolution

Our quick look at the history of mass communications jumps from the 1500s to the 1800s. The nineteenth century saw the beginning of the Industrial Revolution in the United States. Borrowing technology and techniques from the British, whose Industrial Revolution began earlier, the first American industrial factories, built in New England in the 1810s and 1820s, produced textiles. Other factories producing consumer goods and commercial equipment soon followed throughout the United States.

To explore the relationship between mass manufacturing and mass media, we use the chocolate industry as an example. Beginning in the 1840s, Baker's Chocolate of Dorchester, Massachusetts is believed to be the first branded, packaged grocery item in the United States. Once a product has a brand name (as opposed to being a generic item) the owner of that brand is motivated to advertise the product. It would do little good for a chocolate maker to advertise for chocolate in general, as that advertising would help the advertiser to only a small degree, while also helping its competitors in the chocolate-making business. With a brand name on a product or its package, advertising that product by name helps boost the sales of that particular brand.

Years after the Baker's Chocolate brand was introduced, Milton Hershey created an inexpensive way of producing milk chocolate, and built what was then the largest chocolate factory in the world, producing the first molded chocolate bar at the turn of the early twentieth century.[4] The Hershey chocolate bar exemplifies two conditions for the rise of the mass media in the nineteenth century. The Hershey bar has a brand name, and the product is mass manufactured. If a firm manufactures 100,000 branded candy bars a day (or cans of paint, computer monitors, and so on) it needs to sell 100,000 of those items every day. This requires *mass marketing*. In order to mass market an item, the advertiser needs mass media for placing advertisements. Thus, the rise of mass manufacturing in America led to the emergence of mass media. Figure 1.3 shows the timeline for developments in communication.

Mass media and mass markets

Although we are all consumers, we are not all the same type of consumers. A variety of factors affects our consumption habits and preferences. One method of categorizing people is by *demographics*. Demographics are measurable statistics of people based on such factors as age, gender, income, education, and geographic location (usually identified by zip code). For example, the 22-year-old who makes $3 million a year as a professional athlete has very different consumption habits than the 22-year-old who has just started a career selling insurance.

Another categorization of people is by *psychographics*, which examines consumers' attitudes, beliefs, and habits (including buying habits). For instance, a consumer who is concerned about global warming is more likely to buy a Toyota Prius than is the driver of a Hummer, who may believe that global warming is a myth propagated by liberals.

The demographics and psychographics of consumers play a large part in determining what types of mass media they consume. Few young people read *Reader's Digest*; few old people listen to Jay-Z. Although both poor people and rich people use the Internet, few poor people use the Internet to search for vacation ideas, and few rich people use the Internet to learn about unemployment benefits. Because our differences as people determine which mass media we consume, different forms of mass media aim themselves at different groups of people.

The effort by the mass media to identify and attract increasingly specialized demographic and psychographic groups leads to *disaggregation* among the mass media. While your parents can probably remember when there

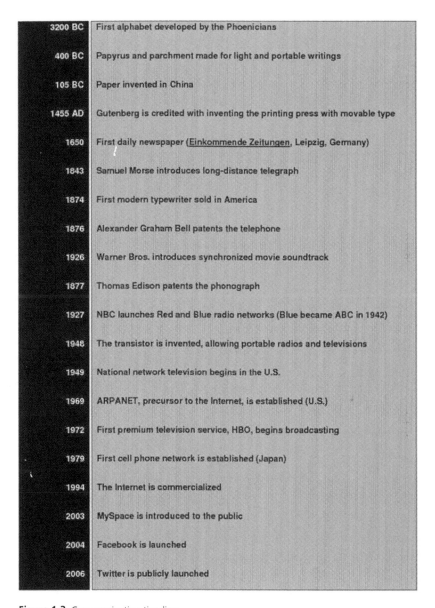

3200 BC	First alphabet developed by the Phoenicians
400 BC	Papyrus and parchment made for light and portable writings
105 BC	Paper invented in China
1455 AD	Gutenberg is credited with inventing the printing press with movable type
1650	First daily newspaper (Einkommende Zeitungen, Leipzig, Germany)
1843	Samuel Morse introduces long-distance telegraph
1874	First modern typewriter sold in America
1876	Alexander Graham Bell patents the telephone
1926	Warner Bros. introduces synchronized movie soundtrack
1877	Thomas Edison patents the phonograph
1927	NBC launches Red and Blue radio networks (Blue became ABC in 1942)
1948	The transistor is invented, allowing portable radios and televisions
1949	National network television begins in the U.S.
1969	ARPANET, precursor to the Internet, is established (U.S.)
1972	First premium television service, HBO, begins broadcasting
1979	First cell phone network is established (Japan)
1994	The Internet is commercialized
2003	MySpace is introduced to the public
2004	Facebook is launched
2006	Twitter is publicly launched

Figure 1.3 Communication timeline.

were only three or four television channels, there are now at least a hundred, and this does not include the thousands of choices for viewing television programs on the Internet. Today, relatively few broadcasters try to appeal to the entire population. Instead, we have television for women (Lifetime) and television for men (Spike). We also have music television aimed at college students (MTV) and people who have been out of school for a while (VH1). There are also cable networks aimed at different ethnic groups, such as BET and Telemundo. Magazines cater to different interests, occupations, and hobbies. The Internet allows mass media to reach groups that are even more segmented.

A key factor driving disaggregation is the desire among advertisers to identify specific media vehicles that attract highly defined groups of customers. For example, many of the millions of people who watch television are not interested in the services of investment firms. Accordingly, investment firms want to advertise only in those media that their prospective customers are most likely to consume. Disaggregation has led to the rise of media conglomerates that own a wide variety of different media brands. Figure 1.4 shows an abbreviated list of just a sampling of the media brands owned by the so-called Big Six. You are probably familiar with some of these "family trees," while some may surprise you.[5]

Five of these firms were founded in the United States. The News Corporation, originally headquartered in Australia, was founded by Rupert Murdoch, who has since become a U.S. citizen. Three foreign-based firms also need to be mentioned: Sony (Japan), Vivendi (France), and Bertelsmann (Germany). These firms maintain a strong presence in the United States and engage in partnerships with American firms. Sony, well known for its electronics goods, is also one of the major movie and television studio owners in the United States and an important music label. Vivendi owns several American music labels and several major American video game firms, and owns part of movie and television firms in partnership with GE. Bertlesmann owns American book and magazine publishing firms and together with Sony owns several American music labels.

These media firms create products that we consume. These products are entertaining and informative, but they are all created for the primary purpose of generating a profit for their owners. Because we spend so much of our time consuming media, they have become an important part of our culture.

General Electric
Broadcast Television: NBC Networks, Telemundo
Cable: CNBC, MSNBC, Bravo, Sci Fi Channel, USA, Oxygen
Film: Universal Pictures

Time Warner
Broadcast Television: CW Network (50% with CBS)
Cable: HBO, Cinemax, TruTV, TBS, Cartoon Network, Turner Classic Movies, TNT, CNN
Internet: AOL, MapQuest, Moviefone, NASCAR.com, PGA.com
Film: Warner Bros. Pictures, New Line Cinema, Castle Rock
Comics: DC Comics, MAD magazine
Book Publishing: Time Warner Book Group, Little, Brown and Company, Books-of-the-Month Club
Magazines: *People, Time, Sports Illustrated, Fortune*, over 100 others

Walt Disney
Broadcast Television: ABC
Cable Networks: ESPN, ESPN2, ESPN Classic, Disney Channel Toon Disney, SOAPnet
Radio Programming: ESPN Radio, "Imus in the Morning"
Magazines: *Family Fun, ESPN the Magazine, Jetix, Wondertime, Bassmaster, Disney Adventures*
Music: Walt Disney Records, Hollywood Records, Buena Vista Records, Lyric Street Records,
Disney Music Publishing Worldwide
Comics: Marvel Comics
Books: Hyperion Books, Hyperion Books for Children, Disney Press
Film Production and Distribution: Walt Disney, Touchstone Pictures, Miramax Films, Pixar
Animation Studios, Hollywood Pictures, Buena Vista
Online: Go Network

News Corporation
Television Networks: Fox, MyNetworkTV
Cable: Fox Business Channel, Fox Movie Channel, Fox News Channel, Fox College Sports, Fox
Regional Sports Networks
Magazines: *Barron's, TVGuide*
Newspapers: *The Wall Street Journal, The New York Post, MarketWatch, Dow Jones Newswire*,
many community newspapers
Film: 20th Century Fox
Online: MySpace.com, RottenTomatoes, photobucket.com

CBS
Television Networks: CBS, CW Network (50% with Time Warner)
Cable: CBS College Sports Network, the Smithsonian Channel, Showtime, the Movie Channel, Flix
Radio: 140 radio stations in 31 markets
Books: Scribner, Simon & Schuster, Touchstone, Fireside

Viacom (shares ownership ties with CBS)
Cable: MTV, Nickelodeon/Nick-at-Nite, TV Land, VH1, Spike TV, CMT, Comedy Central, BET
Film: Paramount, Dreamworks, National Amusement theaters
Online: RatemyProfessors.com, Addicting Games

Figure 1.4 Big Six media firms.

Contemporary culture

Describing "contemporary" is relatively easy. It means of the current time. *Culture* proves to be a more problematic term. Sociologist Raymond Williams described it as including the "variable cultures of different nations and periods, and also variable cultures of social and economic groups within a nation."[6] (Yes, Williams violates the rule that says one should not use the word being defined within the definition.) Williams tells us that when archeologists and anthropologists discuss culture, they often mean material production. Material production is a fancy way of referring to the "stuff" that different groups of people make. Why do we dress the way we do? How do we determine what is in style and what is not? The media play a significant role in these decisions.

Williams says that for those who study history, literature, and art history, culture means the signifying or symbolic systems that different groups of people use. These systems include language and nonverbal communication. We communicate ideas not only through words, but also by how those words are presented and by whom. For example, when we see an advertisement for medicine, the advertisement often features an actor dressed to look like a doctor. Even though she is not really a doctor, the message is more believable because the actor *looks like* a doctor.

Many people believe that the mass media have no impact on our lives, but are merely forms of entertainment. George Gerbner, quoted at the beginning of this chapter, was one of many communications scholars who believe otherwise. The fact that mass media often present themselves to us as entertainment means that we are more willing to pay attention to them, as we perceive mass media as informative and entertaining. When we tell ourselves that the mass media are "only entertainment," we consume media carelessly.

Mediated culture

Why do college students in Tallahassee and Seattle tend to wear pretty much the same types of clothes? Why do they tend to listen to the same types of music? Enjoy the same movies or television shows? Drink the same brands of beer or cola? Because they are exposed to many of the same media messages and images! No matter where you live, you probably recognize the icons in the chart shown in Figure 1.5.

Figure 1.5 Cultural icons.

It seems simplistic to say that the media (plural noun) mediate (verb). For our purposes, mediate means that the mass media serve as an intermediary, or go-between, for people and reality. This does not mean that the mass media create reality; rather, they create a value system for how we look at and interpret reality.

Mass media provide us with reproductions of moving images, still images, and sounds. We are able to view performances and sporting events that we cannot attend in person. We are able to see landmarks and works of art from all around the world. We are able to watch historic events, such as presidential inaugurations and wars. It is easy to take this for granted today, but this ability to observe or witness from a distance is a relatively recent phenomenon in the thousands of years of human existence.

However, observing or witnessing an event through the media should not be confused with being there. As media scholar David Buckingham tells, "The media do not offer us a transparent window on the world. They provide channels through which representations and images of the world can be communicated *indirectly*. The media *intervene*; they provide us with selective versions of the world, rather than direct access to it."[7] For some, the difference between experiencing events in person and experiencing events through communication media has become blurred. It is common to be at a sporting event and see fans spend most of the game watching the broadcast of the game on the scoreboard's jumbotron. You probably know at least one person who finds romantic movies (or perhaps pornography) more interesting than actual relationships.

However, not all of mass media's effects on contemporary culture are harmful. Mass media allow us to learn about the ideas and activities of people around the world. They allow us to witness the work of some of the world's most creative artists. They can cheer us up when we are sad or stressed and keep us company when we are alone.

In this book, we will briefly examine the history of the most significant forms of mass media in order to provide the social and economic context for

Figure 1.6 Communications technology has advanced significantly since Gutenberg's day.
Source: iStockphoto

the current state of the media. For example, how did sound recording change the movie industry? How did the rise of television in the late 1940s and 1950s affect the radio and movie industries? What has digital downloading meant to the recorded music industry? Having this historical context can help us predict future shifts in the mass media. Figure 1.6 shows how far mass communications have come since Gutenberg.

Mass communications and careers

Because you are reading this book, it is likely that you are considering either a career in mass media, or a career in which communications are an important part of the job. You are not alone. According to the U.S. Department of Labor's Bureau of Labor Statistics, more than 1,500 higher education institutions offer educational programs in communication, journalism, and related fields.[8] The need for people and businesses to communicate with others remains an important aspect of contemporary culture.

The U.S. Department of Labor estimates that between 2006 and 2016, there will be double-digit increases in employment for the following occupational categories:

- Advertising, marketing, promotions, public relations, and sales managers (11.7 percent)
- Arts, design, entertainment, sports, and media occupations (11.4 percent)
- Media and communications occupations (10.8 percent)
- Media and communications equipment occupations (13.0 percent)[9]

The Bureau of Labor Statistics tells us that there are about 313,000 people working in radio, television, and cable broadcasting in the United States today,[10] about 370,000 people working in the motion picture, video and sound recording industries,[11] and about 850,000 people working in the newspaper, magazine, and book publishing industries.[12] There are also about 500,000 people working in the advertising and public relations fields.[13]

As we will see in later chapters, the mass media are currently in flux, with some media growing rapidly, some relatively static, and some in serious decline. Certain types of print media, particularly newspapers, are contracting, as people increasingly rely on electronic media for information and entertainment. Thus, the Bureau of Labor Statistics estimates there were will be a seven percent decrease in publishing jobs between 2006 and 2016.[14]

Understandably, many of those who have had careers in print communications will attempt to follow the market, and move into jobs in electronic media. The Bureau of Labor Statistics predicts a 44 percent increase in Internet publishing and broadcasting jobs during the same period.[15]

Questions for critical thinking and discussion

1. Although some countries decided to have the government operate radio and television stations, many countries, such as the United States, rely instead on privately owned radio and television stations. Government-owned stations rely on government subsidies to operate. Private-owned broadcasting companies rely on selling commercial time to advertisers for their revenue. Private-owned radio and television stations must broadcast content that is attractive both to advertisers and the people who buy advertised goods and services.

   • How does the reliance on advertising revenue affect the content of privately owned radio and television stations?

2. Estimate how many hours you spend using media on the average day.

   • Do you think you use media more than the average person or less? Explain.
   • Do you think that ten years from now you will use media more than you do now or less? Explain.

3. Americans love freedom of choice. However, there are only three American automakers, and there are only two major brands of cola.

   • Should we care that only half a dozen companies control a large share of American mass media? Explain why or why not.

4. Imagine that you are taking three courses. One is taught in a small classroom with no more than a dozen students seated around a table. One is taught in a large lecture hall with about 150 students. One is being taught online.

   • Using Schramm's model on p. 2, describe how the communication would vary in each of these class settings.
   • In which class setting(s) would you prefer to learn? Why?

5. We discussed the demographics and psychographics of people in this chapter. Take Strategic Business Insights' VALS survey to see what type of consumer group you fall into: The survey is available at http://www.strategicbusinessinsights.com/vals/presurvey.shtml

   You will notice that most of the questions are psychographic in nature—they ask about your beliefs and attitudes. Only a few questions toward the end of the survey ask for demographic information about you, such as age, gender, and income. (Remember that this survey attempts to categorize you as a consumer, nothing more.)

   • Were the results about you accurate? Why or why not?
   • How do you feel about such surveys? Explain.

Additional resources

Abercrombie, Nicholas, and Brian Longhurst, *The Penguin Dictionary of Media Studies* (New York: Penguin, 2007).

Adbusters Media Foundation at https://www.adbusters.org/

Brooke, Erin Duffy, and Joseph Turow, eds., *Key Readings in Media Today: Mass Communication in Contexts* (New York: Routledge, 2008).

Durham, Meenakshi Gigi, and Douglas Kellner, eds., *Media and Cultural Studies: Keyworks*, rev. ed. (Malden, MA: Blackwell, 2006).

Ms. magazine's "No Comment" archives at http://www.msmagazine.com/nocommentarchive.asp

Stokes, Jane, *How to do Media and Cultural Studies* (London: Sage Publications, 2003).

2 Media Studies and Media Literacy

Chapter contents

Issues and trends in media studies and media literacy

- Because the media greatly affect our lives, it is important to be media literate.
- All media messages are constructed.
- The media have a distinct language or code.
- Audience responses to media vary and are based on individual characteristics and belief systems.
- The media have embedded values that reflect their cultural setting.
- The media have an agenda; the media affect our lives in part because that is what media owners want to do.

Media studies

Communications as a course of study originally focused on interpersonal communication between individuals. For example, Alexander Graham Bell invented the telephone as part of his research on hearing and speech among deaf people. Many schools today offer courses in interpersonal communications and group dynamics, as well as other courses that examine how we communicate directly with others. As mass communications technology has allowed large media firms to arise; many courses and programs now examine various aspects of communications in the context of mass media industries.

Even among those not interested in careers in the media, it is important to understand how the media function, and what roles they serve in society. Similarly, most students who take economics courses do not plan to become economists, yet they need to understand how economics affect our lives. The media affect economic issues and social and political issues as well.

Media studies typically begin by looking at the structure of the media. The media are types of industries with owners who seek a profit. One needs to know not only who owns what and the prevailing business model for each medium. There are emerging media that have yet to establish a business model. For instance, Twitter is popular with millions of users, but its owners tell us that their business model is still "in the research phase."[1] Media studies also examine the media's messages. In order to understand those messages, one must become media literate. Media literacy requires you to do something that you may have never done before: think critically about the mass media.

Media literacy

We learned how to speak a language (or several languages) before we began attending school. Children around the age of three are often frustrated, as they understand that we use language to communicate our thoughts and feelings, but they still lack the sufficient vocabulary to share their thoughts and feelings. Even three-year-olds understand the importance of effective communication.

Once we begin school, we learn to read and write. Literacy is a powerful skill, of which those who control a society are sometimes fearful. During the days of the killing fields of Cambodia (1975–1979) the Khmer Rouge regime sought to exterminate all literate Cambodians, identified as those who wore eyeglasses or owned a writing pen. The Khmer Rouge destroyed the books in Cambodia's National Library and turned the building into a stable. More recently, the Taliban regime in Afghanistan (1996–2001) prohibited the education of girls and provided only limited educational access to boys. As a result, 90 percent of females and over 60 percent of males in Afghanistan cannot read.[2]

In the twenty-first century, many people consider computer literacy to be a basic skill that every member of society needs to acquire. Most of us take this for granted, but we need to remember that computers did not exist a few generations ago. Similarly, media literacy includes knowledge of new and emerging types of media (see Figure 2.1).

The Media Awareness Network of Canada describes media literacy as, "The process of understanding and using the mass media in an assertive and non-passive way. This includes an informed and critical understanding of the nature of the media, the techniques used by them and the impact of these techniques."[3] Because many of us consider the media to be primarily a form of entertainment, relatively few people care to incorporate critical thinking when discussing mass media. Unfortunately, this is exactly how

Figure 2.1 Media literacy must begin at an early age. *Source*: iStockphoto

the mass media want consumers to think about them: with an uncritical eye and ear, refusing to consider the media seriously, receiving media messages passively.

But critical thinking about the media does not mean refusing to believe in anything the media present us. Although many people confuse the two, there is an important difference between cynicism and skepticism. One commentator, Josh Ozersky, has argued that the cynical presentation of conventional values in the media helps "advertisers in their perennial quest for credibility by creating a supersaturated atmosphere of irony, which atrophies our ability to believe in anything."[4] Ozersky warns against cynicism, which means not really believing in anything—not having a value system at all. Skepticism requires carefully choosing and examining what one decides to believe in. If the media promote cynicism, media literacy promotes skepticism.

Some media critics argue that the media want us to rely on them to tell us how to think. Or to not think much at all! Ford recently ran a television advertisement that asked viewers, "Are you tough enough to drive a Ford truck?" The fact that the advertisement aired for many months indicates that it may have helped Ford sell trucks. That many viewers did not crack up in laughter while watching the advertisement says a lot about us. Many consumers claim that advertising affects others but not themselves—a phenomenon that media scholars call the *third-person effect*. Each of us needs to recognize the power that the media hold in our lives.

Numerous organizations foster media literacy and critical thinking skills. The United Nations Educational, Scientific, and Cultural Organization (UNESCO) states that, "The proliferation of mass media has brought about decisive changes in human communication processes and behaviour. Media education aims to empower citizens by providing them with the competencies, attitudes and skills necessary to comprehend media functions."[5]

One U.S. organization, the National Association for Media Literacy Education (NAMLE) arose in 2001 to help students develop media literacy. NAMLE states that, "Media literacy is an essential life skill for the 21st century. As communication technologies transform society, they affect our understanding of ourselves, our communities, and our diverse culture."[6] NAMLE says that media studies should include a critical analysis using a basic set of concepts.[7] Another educators' group, the Center for Media Literacy (CML) says that its mission, "is to help children and adults prepare

National Association for Media Literacy Education's Core Concepts	Center for Media Literacy's Core Concepts
All media messages are constructed	All media messages are constructed
Each medium has different characteristics, strengths, and a unique language of construction	Media messages are constructed using a creative language with its own rules
Media messages are produced for particular purposes	Different people experience the same media message differently
All media messages contain embedded values and points of view	Media have embedded values and points of view
People use their individual skills, beliefs and experiences to construct their own meanings from media messages	Most media messages are organized to gain profit and/or power.
Media and media messages can influence beliefs, attitudes, values, behaviors, and the democratic process	

Figure 2.2 Core concepts of media literacy. *Source*: National Association for Media Literacy Education and Center for Media Literacy

for living and learning in a global media culture . . ."[8] CML has five core concepts, quite similar to NAMLE's guiding principles for media education.[9] Figure 2.2 displays the core concepts of NAMLE and CML.

In this book, we will use a framework that borrows from and combines the two frameworks already mentioned.

All media messages are constructed

We will consider each item, distributed through mass media, as a message. The first question is the following: Who made the message? Do we see the message as that of an individual, a team of people, or a "faceless" corporation? If the message seems to have an anonymous source, what is the source's reason for trying to remain anonymous? Why was the message made? There is usually an economic agenda—somebody is trying to make money. The content itself may be sold or rented, such as a book, a movie, or recorded music. Or the content may be free or almost free, as the purpose of the content is to attract an audience for advertisers. Who is the target audience, and how do you know? While most rap/hip-hop music is made by African American artists from urban areas, the largest consumer group of this type of music is white suburban teenaged males. Similarly, many advertisements for men's cologne are targeted toward women, who buy men's cologne as a gift.

We will see throughout this book, with a special focus in Chapter 10, that many media messages today are created by consumers. We want to connect with others, or share our ideas or artistic work without seeking monetary benefits. So another important question is, who paid for the message? It costs money to produce media, and that money originated somewhere. We will see that some of the most popular new media today have yet to generate a profit for their owners despite large audiences.

The media have a distinct language or code

"We look to Los Angeles for the language we use."

Morrissey, "Glamorous Glue"

The media are intensely segmented. For instance, most major movie releases are based on a set group of *genres*, or formats, as we will see later. Movies typically are 100 to 120 minutes long. We will also examine the established formats that popular music tends to fall within, and discuss why the average popular song is between three to four minutes long.

Daily newspapers have the same sections—generally in the same order, no matter which city you live in. Television programs generally fall within a few set categories: situation comedies running for 30 minutes; dramas and reality shows running for an hour.

In addition to standard formats, there are often standard characterizations. If you are watching a television show or a movie that shows an actor playing a mugger in a big city, how likely is it that the actor will be handsome, with blond hair and blue eyes? Not very! Similarly, if a character wears glasses, that character is likely old, intelligent, or geeky.

Media coding: themes and icons

Icons are symbols that represent *themes*. Themes are ideas or ideals that can be communicated through words or through icons. The relationship between an icon and the theme that it represents can be obvious: the Statue of Liberty represents liberty. Marilyn Monroe remains an icon of sexuality, a pickup truck represents masculinity, and a cell phone connotes mobility and connectivity. The theme of freedom of choice is highlighted in the numerous versions of Coke and Pepsi that are available, even though these choices come from only two firms.

Media coding: local television news

To help understand how media messages are coded, we will look briefly at local television news. Your local newscast likely shares similar *production values* with newscasts elsewhere. To start, it is a safe bet that your local newscast has two anchors—two people seated at a desk ("talking heads") most likely one male and one female. They may occasionally make small talk between themselves or with the sports announcer and weathercaster when they transition into/from the sports or weather. How do we know? Because this is how local newscasts are coded in nearly every American television market.

The language of television news attempts to create a sense of urgency. This has become especially true as television must now compete with the Internet and news feeds on mobile texting devices. The Internet has no news cycle—a news story can be posted while the event is still occurring. Except for a few 24-hour news stations, television newscasts must share time with other television programming. Thus, a newscast must seem timely, even if the event being reported has already taken place (neither a car accident nor a robbery will wait until 6:00 p.m.). The sense of urgency or timeliness is communicated with terms such as "breaking news." Reporters will tell us what is happening "at this hour." The reporter will typically be "on the scene," even if the fire, accident, robbery, etc., happened many hours earlier, and there really is nothing much to see. If a victim of a crime or accident is a child, the child's age will be repeated, and the adjective "little" may be used consistently before the victim's name. If a newscast is recycling a story that was previously reported, this is a "developing story."

During the evening's programming between the early news and the late news broadcasts, we see several "tease" advertisements for the late newscast that highlight top stories. Throughout the newscast itself, there will be teases that tell us about what other news will be discussed in that newscast. These occur during all newscasts, but are most common during the late news, as broadcasters do not want viewers to turn off the television and go to sleep.

When it is time for the weather report, if there is any chance that the weather will be bad, that is emphasized. Storms are more interesting to viewers than pleasant weather. If there is a major snowstorm or hurricane, the weather announcer may be outside in the elements, while urging viewers to be smart and stay inside.

The newscast is labeled something similar to Eyewitness News or Newscenter. This creates the *brand* for the newscast. One needs a package in order to sell a brand, and the local television news is, like other mass media forms, essentially a packaged product.

Media coding: celebrity endorsements

Another common code is the use of celebrity endorsements. Many professional athletes, including LeBron James and Maria Sharapova, make far more money from product endorsements than they do from playing their respective sport. Of course, the income that celebrity endorsers receive from advertisers ends up being paid for by consumers. Endorsement contracts typically contain morals clauses. This clause allows the advertiser to void the contract if the celebrity engages in conduct seen as diminishing the value of the product. Thus, when photographs of swimmer Michael Phelps smoking marijuana were published in 2009, Kellogg refused to renew his endorsement contract, saying that Phelps's behavior was "not consistent with the image of Kellogg."[10] Later that year, Tiger Wood's marital infidelity cost him several sponsorship agreements.

For some products, the fact that a celebrity endorser has led a less than saintly life can actually help. For example, Curtis James Jackson III, better known as 50 Cent, who has engaged in significantly more controversial activity than Michael Phelps, profits from product endorsements and licensing deals with a variety of products including clothing, sports water, and condoms.

Why are endorsements so critical to the marketing of consumer products? The answer to that question may be that consciously or subconsciously, consumers want to imitate celebrities however possible. As emphasized in a Gatorade advertisement that featured Michael Jordan, drinking the advertised product allows the consumer to "Be like Mike." Even if we are not athletic and will never be a movie star or famous, we can still consume the same products that the famous claim to consume.

Audience responses to media vary

You may already be familiar with the concepts of selective exposure, selective perception, and selective retention. If people consider themselves politically liberal, they are unlikely to listen to Rush Limbaugh's radio program, as they are unlikely to share his conservative views. Limbaugh's listeners are most likely those people who agree with what Limbaugh says. This is an example of *selective exposure*.

Selective perception refers to how we process the information to which we are exposed. Imagine that baseball fans are watching a televised game between the Red Sox and the Yankees. A close play at home plate has the umpire call the Red Sox runner out. Yankee fans and Red Sox fans alike see the slow-motion replay. Yankee fans are most likely to perceive the umpire's call as correct; Red Sox fans are likely to disagree, even though each set of fans watched the same slow-motion replay.

We demonstrate *selective retention* by what information we choose to remember and what we decide to forget. We are most likely to remember things that support our view of others, the world, and ourselves. Similarly, we are most likely to forget things that conflict with those views. For example, if a famous movie star whom we admire gets caught committing a minor crime, we are more likely to forget that crime than a similar one committed by a movie star that we dislike.

Our exposure to, perception of, and retention of a media message may vary based on our demographics and psychographics, discussed in the previous chapter. Interpretations of messages also depend on how success-ful the creator of the message was. Many media creators use *focus groups* to test their messages. Media researchers gather groups of people together that fall within the target market for the message they are testing. For example, if a television program is intended for a primarily female audience in their twenties, the focus group will be comprised of females in that age group. The focus group may be asked to watch an episode of the program. They will then be asked to comment on the characters, the plot line, and so on.

The interactivity of new media such as the Internet and mobile texting devices allow media creators to receive feedback, often instantly. Just as we individually use feedback when communicating with others to determine how our message is being received (or whether it is being received) mass media outlets solicit our comments in order to determine the effectiveness of their messages. Today, the mass media ask us to e-mail or text-message them, or to post comments at their websites. In essence, this is free market research for those media outlets as they collect audience data without paying for it.

Audience response also depends on the degree to which members of the audience are involved with the media message. Some types of media are *high involvement* while others are *low involvement*. A video game is a high involvement medium on which the audience must focus. This is one reason why in-game advertising has become a hot industry. However, radio is low involvement—many of us play the radio as background noise. Thus, radio advertisements are frequently repeated, as they require repetition of the message in order for us to retain that information.

Audience response: NASCAR

An interesting intersection of consumers and producers occurs in NASCAR racing. The appeal of NASCAR to advertisers is rather obvious. The cars themselves are moving billboards, crammed full of product names, as are the drivers' uniforms. To watch a NASCAR race is to watch speeding billboards turning left for several hours. More importantly, fans of particular drivers actively choose the products of those advertisers who support the drivers' incomes. One study found that almost two-thirds of those who call themselves avid fans of NASCAR racing are more likely to consume a product or service regularly if it is an official sponsor of their favorite driver.[11]

The media have embedded values

Most mass media want to maintain a certain comfort level for their audiences. As a result, most mass media shy away from challenging common assumptions about the social and economic order of the world. Because audiences tend to be the most comfortable with what they already perceive and know, the mass media tend to enforce the status quo.

Consider the presentation of African Americans in the media. Most commonly, we see black people in the roles of entertainers: musicians, athletes, performers. Rarely do we see African Americans cast as executives or leaders, even at a time when the U.S. president is African American. Stereotypes that conform to how the majority of the audience perceives the world are common in the mass media; these stereotypical presentations continue to reinforce those stereotypes. Such stereotypes may not necessarily be negative, but they are unrealistically limited.

Another issue is who is seen in the media, and who is not. For example, many Asian American people complain about being absent from most American media, except for situations when a computer geek or martial arts character is depicted. Other groups are also missing or underrepresented in the media; how often do we see characters with disabilities?

Embedded value: it's all about us

One noteworthy display of the media's embedded values occurred soon after the events of September 11, 2001 (9/11). The Reuters news service declined to use the term "terrorism" to describe the events of that day, as part of its policy to avoid the use of "emotive words." Many American journalists criticized Reuters, and CNN's website ran an announcement in October 2001, stating, "There have been false reports that CNN has not used the word 'terrorist' to refer to those who attacked the World Trade Center and Pentagon. In fact, CNN has consistently and repeatedly referred to the attackers and hijackers as terrorists, and it will continue to do so."

That same month, CNN's chair, Walter Isaacson, "ordered his staff to balance images of civilian devastation in Afghan cities with reminders that the Taliban harbors murderous terrorists, saying it 'seems perverse to focus too much on the casualties or hardship in Afghanistan.'"[12] One embedded value in American mass media is that the United States is the "good guy" in the world, as that is what most American consumers want the media to tell them.[13]

The media have an agenda

For most media owners, the agenda is simple: to make money. The media generate content that attracts audiences for the advertisers who support those media. Thus, many media are essentially advertising delivery vehicles. These media strive to maintain an advertiser friendly environment.

Take for example, WHDH, a television station in Boston. In 1990, WHDH ran an advertisement by an organization called Neighbor to Neighbor that associated Folgers coffee with right-wing death squads financed by coffee growers in El Salvador. Procter & Gamble, makers of Folgers Coffee, responded by withdrawing its advertising from WHDH, which earned an estimated $1 million annually from Procter & Gamble advertising.[14] Three years later, Neighbor to Neighbor wanted to buy time from WHDH for an advertisement that advocated single-payer healthcare. WHDH had learned its lesson and rejected the advertisement. A spokesperson for WHDH explained, "[M]any of our advertisers are health insurers, and we don't want to take any hits from the health insurance companies."[15]

Today, consumers create an increasing amount of media content. Many of those who maintain web logs (blogs) or have pages on social networking sites have little or no desire to earn a profit from those sites, although the sponsors of those sites intend to profit from them, usually by selling advertising. Why would someone want to create content without intending to make a profit? Many of us use social networking sites in order to communicate with friends. Some of us want to share our opinions and beliefs with others, perhaps in an effort to affect others' opinions and beliefs, or simply to be heard. (In this sense, a web site may be little more than the cyberspace version of a bumper sticker.) Some of us want to share our creative work, such as music, videos, and graphics, with others. In essence, then, much of the content available in the so-called new media that includes texting, tweeting, Facebooking, and blogging, is generated by those seeking intrinsic rewards such as recognition, a sense of belonging, or a sense of accomplishment, rather than extrinsic rewards such as money. This is a very different agenda from that of most media creators in the past.

Media studies, media literacy and careers

Media literacy educators work as teachers in both primary and secondary schools as well as at colleges and universities. The U.S. Bureau of Labor Statistics predicts that there will be the need for 479,000 additional teaching positions between 2006 and 2016.[16] Of course, media studies and media literacy teaching positions are a very small percentage of the total. Similarly, the Bureau anticipates 23 percent growth in college teaching positions during the same period, with a small percentage of those positions in media studies and media literacy.[17]

Questions for critical thinking and discussion

1. Visit the web sites for two groups that argue that the mainstream media are biased. Media Matters, a liberal site, criticizes what it sees as media's conservative bias. It can be accessed at mediamatters.org. Accuracy in Media, a conservative group, argues exactly the opposite. It can be accessed at www.aim.org.

   • Try to find a news topic that both web sites discuss, preferably one about which you do not already have strong feelings.
   • Does one of these web sites present the topic more persuasively than the other does? Explain why or why not.

2. You probably know of at least one household that chooses not to have a television.

   • Regardless of your personal feelings, provide a good argument for not owning a television set.
   • Now, provide a good argument to support owning a television set.

3. Do the media have any responsibility to society?

   • If you believe they do, describe the nature of that responsibility.
   • If you believe that they do not, explain why not.

4. Do you believe that you were media literate before you began reading this book?

   • Do you believe that most members of your family are media literate?
   • Explain your answers.

5. This chapter describes a skeptic as someone who is carefully about what s/he believes in, and a cynic as someone who believes in nothing.

   • Why does the education system attempt to make people skeptical?
   • Why do the entertainment media (and the advertisers who support them) attempt to make people cynical?
   • Who do you think is more successful in their efforts—educators or advertisers? Explain your answer.

Additional resources

Accuracy in Media, www.aim.org

Buckingham, David, *Media Education; Literacy, Learning and Contemporary Culture* (Cambridge, England: Polity, 2003).

Center for Media Literacy, www.medialit.org

De Zengotita, Thomas, *Mediated; How the Media Shapes Your World and the Way You Live in It* (New York: Bloomsbury, 2005).

Fairness& Accuracy in Media Reporting, www.fair.org

Media Alliance, www.media-alliance.org

Media and Democracy Coalition, media-democracy.net

Media Awareness Network, www.media-awareness.ca

Media Education Foundation, www.mediaed.org

Media Matters, mediamatters.org

Media Watch, www.mediawatch.com

National Association for Media Literacy, www.namle.net

PBS Teachers: Media Literacy, www.pbs.org/teachers/media_lit

UNESCO Information and Media Literacy Portal, portal.unesco.org/ci/en/ev.php-URL_ID=15886&
URL_DO=DO_TOPIC&URL_SECTION=201.html

3

Advertising

Chapter contents

Issues and trends in advertising

- Advertising is everywhere and cannot be avoided.
- Advertisers in the United States spent approximately $285 billion on advertising in 2008 or about $900 per person.
- Advertisers attempt to create a sense of dissatisfaction among consumers in order to generate demand for their products and services.
- Because advertising is the primary source of revenue for most media, the media offer a friendly environment for advertisers.
- Advertisers and advertising agencies engage in both qualitative and quantitative research to identify and reach their target markets.
- New media create new opportunities for advertisers.

Those who try to evaluate our exposure to advertising disagree on how many advertisements we see or hear daily.[1] One source of disagreement lies in describing exactly what an advertisement is. Certainly, it includes the 30-second advertisements that run during television programming as well as the display advertisements in magazines and newspapers. Does the meaning of advertisement include a car company's logo on the trunk lid of the car in front of us on the highway? What about the label on the soft drink can on our desk? What an advertisement is may not be so simple. The other issue in quantifying exposure to advertisements is deciding what exposure means. Did we pay any attention to the advertisement? Did it somehow register in our conscious or subconscious? Figure 3.1 showcases a billboard; can you recall how many billboards you passed yesterday?

Some of us consume more media than others do. College students spend more time out of the house than other adults do and are more likely to use mobile media. Older adults are more likely to read a print edition of a daily newspaper than college students.

There are those who pay more attention to advertisements than other people. For example, while you may get up from the television to get a snack

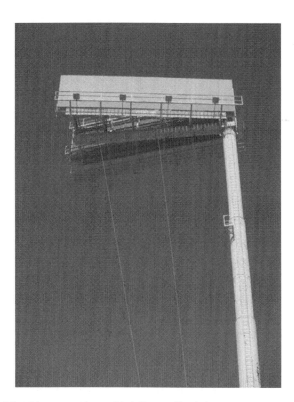

Figure 3.1 Advertising cannot be avoided. *Source*: iStockphoto

during a commercial break, young children have trouble distinguishing between television programming and television advertising and may give each equal attention. We are also exposed to advertisements for products that we do not use ourselves; a nonsmoker will typically ignore a cigarette advertisement.

Regardless of what the actual exposure figures are, advertising is a multibillion dollar industry that stimulates consumption of the goods and services advertised. While some of us are more susceptible to advertising messages than other people, advertising affects all of us whether we are willing to admit it or not.

A brief history of the advertising industry

If you look up from this book, you will likely see brand names, trademarks, and logos for any number of branded products around you. Advertising historians cite branding as a precondition of advertising. Branding is not as old as you may think, as it did not become common until the American Industrial Revolution in the mid 1800s. Before this period, individuals or small firms produced products in small lots and often sold them generically. A shopper would ask the general store merchant for a pound of flour or a quart of cooking oil, and the merchant would draw those items from unbranded sacks, boxes, or barrels. Services were offered by individuals rather than by corporations.

As discussed in Chapter 1, the Industrial Revolution brought mechanization, which allowed for the mass manufacturing of both products and packaging. New machines allowed companies to make hundreds of items in the same time it took to make a single item only a few years earlier. The ability to mass-produce products generated the need to mass market those products. If, for example, a company could make 50,000 bars of soap daily, it needed to sell 50,000 bars of soap a day.

Early advertisements were relatively simple and did little selling. Manufacturers frequently created their own advertisements; they knew their product but did not always know how to sell it. They often simply told consumers that a product existed and asked consumers to try it. By the early 1900s, advertisers realized that they had to compete more aggressively against each other, and instead of creating their own advertising, many began to seek the help of advertising agencies. Advertising agencies themselves evolved from firms that merely placed advertisements in publications to full-service firms that provide a full range of creative and strategic services.

From the beginning of the Industrial Revolution through the early twentieth century, most advertising appeared in print media, such as newspapers and magazines, along with billboards where local governments allowed them. This is because those were the only mass media available. The first electronic advertising medium, commercial radio, arose in the 1920s, and television followed twenty years later. This combination of electronic and print media remained unchanged until the commercialization of the Internet in the 1990s. The Internet's power as a mass communication medium continues to evolve. While a few firms such as Google and Amazon have been able to create successful business models based on the Internet, many other firms have failed. In particular, newspaper and magazine publishers that have created web presences have yet to capture sufficient advertising revenue from their online publications to offset declining advertising revenue from their print publications.

For a timeline of advertising history, visit *Advertising Age* magazine's Historical Timeline at http://adage.com/century/timeline/index.html.

The advertising industry today

> *"Historians and archaeologists will one day discover that the ads of our time are the richest and most faithful reflections that any society ever made of its entire range of activities."* [2]
>
> *Marshall McLuhan*

Today, advertising agencies create most of the advertisements that you see or hear. Do not confuse *advertising agencies* with *advertisers*. Advertisers are the clients of advertising agencies. Advertisers pay advertising agencies to create advertisements and place them in various media. Four global firms—Interpublic, Omnicom, France's Publicis Groupe, and Britian's

WPP—control most of the world's largest advertising agencies. In addition, there are many smaller full-service agencies. The traditional form of advertising agency income was the receipt of a commission (15 percent, but now often less) from the media outlets in which agencies place advertisements for their clients. However, as advertising and marketing have evolved, full-service firms have begun to offer a range of services for which they charge a fee directly to their clients. There are also *boutique firms* that specialize in certain aspects of the advertising business, such as direct marketing through mail or e-mail, or special events promotions.

Typically, advertising agencies will obtain an *advertising kit* from various media outlets—television stations, web sites, magazines, newspapers, radio stations, and so on. The advertising kit provides technical specifications for creating advertisements, publication schedules and deadlines, and perhaps a *rate card*, which provides a price list for different types of advertisements.

The media charge advertisers for advertising based on space or time. This means that print and Internet advertising prices are based on how large the advertisement is, and where it is located; television and radio advertising prices are based on how long the advertisement is, and when it is broadcast. The price of advertising is also based on how many people will see the advertisement. Two concerns for advertisers are reach and frequency. *Reach* is a measurement of how many people are exposed to an advertisement. *Frequency* is the number of times an advertisement is communicated. An advertiser who advertises during the Super Bowl or "American Idol" will pay for the reach of those popular television programs. Those who advertise on radio tend to emphasize frequency. Advertisers that lack consumer loyalty for their products tend to emphasize frequency as well. For example, it is likely that advertisements appear in your daily newspaper every day for wireless telephone providers. This is because most consumers are willing to consider a new wireless provider when their current contract expires.

The total number of people who are likely to see or hear an advertisement is measured in thousands, using the abbreviation M, from the Roman numeral for thousand. Advertisers look at *CPM*, or cost per thousand impressions. The media in which those advertisements appear measure RPM or revenue per thousand impressions.

Because the stated CPM that media firms offer advertisers drives media revenue, media firms are tempted to inflate the size of their claimed audiences. Advertisers are quite aware of this. To measure the number of readers of print media (readership), number of listeners of radio (listenership), number of viewers of television (viewership), or number of visitors of a web site, independent organizations has been established to provide reliable information to advertisers. The first of these organizations was the Audit Bureau of Circulations (ABC) founded in 1914 (http://www.accessabc.com). The ABC consists of representatives from major advertisers, advertising agencies, and the publications industry. The ABC checks that the readership numbers that magazines and newspapers claim for themselves are true. Nielsen (http://www.nielsen.com) measures viewership of television programs, Internet sites, and mobile media such as phone texting. Arbitron (http://www.arbitron.com) monitors radio listenership. Media firms and advertising firms pay for subscriptions to these organizations to track how many people consume each medium.

Top advertisers

Procter & Gamble (P&G) has dominated the list of the nation's top advertisers for many years. P&G's brands include Pantene, Cover Girl, Gillette, Crest, Charmin, and Pringles. As you can see in Figure 3.2, P&G spends nearly $5 billion a year on advertising in the U.S.[3]

Notice that the very troubled General Motors ranks among the top ten advertisers; if GM were to fail, the media would be among the industries that would be adversely affected. The U.S. Government ranks thirty-first among American advertisers, spending nearly $1.2 billion in 2008, much of that on advertising that recruits for the armed forces.[4] This use of taxpayers'

Advertiser	U.S. Advertising Spending (2008)
Procter & Gamble	$4,838.1 million
Verizon	$3,700.0 million
AT&T	$3,073.0 million
General Motors	$2,901.1 million
Johnson & Johnson	$2,529.2 million
Unilever	$2,422.6 million
Walt Disney	$2,217.6 million
Time Warner	$2,207.7 million
General Electric	$2,019.3 million
Sears Holding	$1,864.9 million

Figure 3.2 Top advertisers. *Source: Advertising Age*

dollars places the government ahead of firms such as General Mills and Nestlé in annual advertising expenditures.

To see the 100 firms that spend the most money on advertising in the United States, visit *Advertising Age*'s rankings at http://adage.com/marketertrees09.

Advertising's target: consumers

Numbers alone do not tell the whole story. Advertisers and advertising agencies divide consumers into *demographics* and *psychographics*, as discussed in Chapter 1. College students are among the favorite demographic groups for advertisers. This is because this age group spends a lot of money on discretionary items such as clothing and entertainment. Advertisers also want to help young adults establish lifelong buying habits, because this age group has many years of consumption ahead of it.

Sometimes, advertisers will run different types of advertisements at the same time, to see which type of advertisement gets the most response. This is a question of *quantitative research*, because it examines the number of people who respond to an advertisement. In their analysis of this research ("data mining") advertisers will examine the information they collect and then see how different types of people respond to different types of advertisements. This is called *qualitative research* because it examines types of people rather than simply the number of people who respond to an advertisement.

Certain goods and services meet basic human needs and are advertised to a broad range of consumers. For example, advertisements for chewing gum or toilet paper are aimed at many millions of consumers. Other goods and services are used by relatively small groups of people; these smaller groups are called *niches*. Advertisements for investment banks and luxury cars target niches. It would not make any sense for an advertiser for a niche product to pay to advertise in a medium consumed by millions of people who are not in the market for that product or service. Therefore, Cadillac will probably not advertise during "American Idol," which is one of the most popular television programs in the United States. However, Cadillac would likely advertise during a golf broadcast, because the smaller group of people who watch golf tend to be older and wealthier and more likely to drive Cadillacs.

Advertising's message

Professional advertising agencies do not merely announce that a product is for sale; they try to give us a "reason why" we should buy the advertised item. Some of these reasons seem obvious, such as when a dishwasher detergent is advertised as getting your plates and glasses clean. Some of these reasons are more subtle.

Advertisers typically seek to create a greater sense of psychological need for their product than the product itself may suggest. You may already be familiar with Abraham Maslow's Hierarchy of Needs if you have taken a course in psychology. Maslow's theory states that all humans share similar sets of psychological needs, which he groups in a hierarchy, visually represented by a pyramid (see Figure 3.3).[5]

Atop the pyramid is self-actualization, which Maslow stated is difficult to achieve. What is self-actualization? To quote from a long-running advertising campaign for the U.S. Army, it is the ability to "Be all that you can be."

Most advertisements target the needs below self-actualization on Maslow's hierarchy. Returning to the subject of dishwasher detergent, it meets the physiological need of cleaning one's plates and glasses and serves a safety need by sanitizing those items. However, advertisements for dishwasher detergents also offer the product as a means of gaining or maintaining the esteem of others by helping consumers successfully host

Figure 3.3 Maslow's Hierarchy of Needs.

others in their homes. The advertisements tell us that the right brand of dishwasher detergent will show your guests how well you manage your household and your social engagements. Advertisements often present mundane products or services as serving some heroic role in consumers' lives. In fact, an old saying in advertising is "let the product be the hero."

Even though many of us know that these messages are suspect, these messages are so frequent and widespread that it is almost impossible to ignore them. Exposure to advertising begins at an early age, even before we learn to read. Of course, young children rarely view advertising critically. Instead, they accept advertising's messages as both truthful and realistic. Consequently, we are likely to grow up using advertising as a reference for how things are in the world, and how they are supposed to be.

Advertisers want people to buy things. They do this by portraying a world without their product as one of deprivation and lost opportunities. Advertisers emphasize how unhappy we should be without their product. After all, if we were content with our lives, there would be little incentive to buy new things.

As discussed in the previous chapter, many of us claim that, although advertising is a powerful force in society, it has little effect on us personally. Ironically, we tend to acknowledge the power of the mass media, but only as it applies to other people. This *third-person effect* is exactly what advertisers and advertising agencies want us to believe. Consumers' willingness to view or listen to advertisements with a casual attitude means that we are not thinking about those advertisements in a critical manner. This makes it even easier for advertisements to influence our attitudes about the products and services advertised, as well as influence our attitudes about ourselves.

Ethical issues in advertising

Many advertisements rely on *puffery* and make a claim that sounds good, but cannot really be evaluated. For example, if an insurance company tells you that its automobile policy is "your best choice," how does one evaluate or measure that claim? If a product is advertised as "America's favorite," what does that mean? Many advertisements use comparative terms ("better than ever") or superlative terms ("hottest deal in town") without offering an objective basis of measurement. Advertisements also offer information that sounds impressive, but does not really tell us much. For example, the advertisements for a brand of beer tell us that it is "triple hop brewed." That sounds good, but what does that mean?

When thinking about advertising's message, one also needs to think about the media that those messages appear in. The media rely heavily on advertising revenue for their profits. Although we pay for cable television and subscriptions to magazines and newspapers, the cost of these media are heavily subsidized by the advertisers who place their advertisements in those media. Understandably, then, these media try to make themselves attractive to advertisers by creating a friendly environment for those advertisers.

It also is common to see advertisements masquerading as news events. Historian Daniel J. Boorstin coined the term *pseudo-event* for an event that is staged primarily for marketing purposes. For example, many of the award shows broadcast on television today are primarily publicity vehicles for celebrities and advertisements for various movies, television shows, and other entertainment media.

Generating hype around such events is one form of *stealth marketing*. There is so much advertising clutter that we pay little attention to much of it. As a result, some advertisers produce advertising that is sneakier than it seems. One of the many forms of stealth marketing is product placement in television programs, movies, and video games. (Anybody who watches "American Idol" likely knows what brand of beverage the judges consume during the show.) No matter how hard we may try to avoid it, we are exposed to advertising and its messages.

Of course, placing advertising nearly everywhere is expensive. American firms spent approximately $285 billion on advertising in 2008.[6] With a total U.S. population of about 304 million, that figures to over $900 per capita on advertising spending annually.

Advertising by medium

One major expense for advertisers is buying space in the media. According to *Advertising Age*, advertisers spent over $142 billion on advertising space in the mass media in 2008.[7] Among the major media, that spending was apportioned as the chart shown in Figure 3.4 indicates.

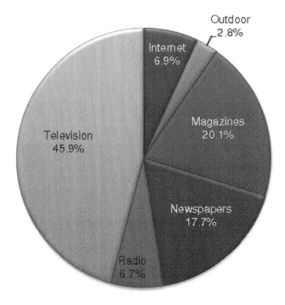

Figure 3.4 Advertising expenditures by medium. *Source:* Data from *Advertising Age*

Print and outdoor advertising today

Print advertising can (but does not always) provide more information than most other advertising formats. Print advertising is static. It does not move, although people are attracted to movement. To compensate, print advertising uses various techniques to get our attention. For example, the advertisements on the right hand page (the *recto* side) of a newspaper or magazine usually cost more than the same-sized advertisement on the left-hand (*verso*) side, as our eyes tend to focus first on the right-hand page. Because sentences in English and other languages that use the Roman alphabet move from left to right, our eyes naturally move toward the right when we go through the simple motion of turning through a newspaper or a magazine. Similarly, our eyes usually will take us to the top left side of the page and continue down to the bottom right hand side of the page. As a result, the major elements of most newspaper and magazine advertisements tend to be arranged in the form of the letter Z.

Advertisements in print media rely on visual elements to get our attention. We tend to skip over pages that contain advertisements, and many print media are cluttered with hundreds of advertisements. It is important to advertisers that an advertisement contain something that causes us at least to pause at that advertisement. This may be through clever writing, or *copy*, whether funny, shocking, or seemingly incongruent. Photographs and illustrations are carefully composed to transmit as much information in a manner that does not ask the consumer to work too hard to gather meaning. Photographs are usually digitally edited. Although we should know better, being repeatedly exposed to images of seemingly flawless professional models causes many of us to have esteem issues about our own appearance.

About 60 percent of a typical newspaper is devoted to advertising. Newspapers typically contain advertisements for local stores and services, although they contain some national advertising as well. Different readers favor different sections of the newspaper. Advertisements aimed primarily at men often appear in the sports section; advertisements aimed primarily at women often appear in the section titled (depending on the newspaper) living, life, lifestyle, or home.

In 2008, advertisers spent $6.99 billion on outdoor advertising, including billboards.[8] In some ways, billboards require advertisers to use the opposite approach of what is used in much print advertising. While magazine and newspaper advertisements can provide a lot of information, billboards must be succinct. Billboards are typically along major roadways, designed to get the attention of motorists and their passengers as they drive by. For a billboard to be effective, it must communicate its information within just a few seconds. Accordingly, billboard advertising try to communicate as much information in as few words as possible and rely on photography or graphic images that are simple yet distinctive.

Radio and television advertising today

There are over 4,700 commercial radio stations on the AM band and over 6,000 stations on the FM band in the United States. The great majority of these radio stations rely on advertising for their income. According to the Radio Advertising Bureau, advertisers spent over $19 billion on radio on advertising in 2008.[9]

Most radio advertising is purchased by local businesses, such as stores, restaurants, and clubs, although national advertisers also purchase radio advertising time. Radio advertising is inexpensive relative to most other media. Production costs are low with only the need for one or two "voice talents" (speakers) and perhaps some sound effects. The price charged by radio stations to run an advertisement is also relatively cheap; in some markets, a 30-second advertisement may cost as little as $20. Because the advertisements are inexpensive, those who advertise on radio can afford to emphasize frequency—a listener may hear many advertisements for the same advertiser or may hear the same advertisement repeatedly.

This emphasis on frequency can also be explained by the fact that many of us pay very little attention to the advertisements we hear on the radio. Advertisers know this. Although one or two advertisements for a particular product may not get our attention, frequent advertisements for the same product aired dozens of times over the course of a week helps get the advertiser's message across.

Many people listen to the radio in their cars, on the way to and from work or school. The highest radio listenership occurs during so-called *drive time* in major metropolitan markets—during the morning and evening rush hours (7 a.m. to 9 a.m. and 4 p.m. to 6 p.m.). Because so many radio listeners are motorists, many advertisements target impulsive decisions by people who are on the road—these advertisements may be for a fast food restaurant, a gas station, a convenience store, and so on.

Unlike radio, television—the other broadcast medium—provides visual images for a society that seems to be increasingly visually oriented. There are over 1,300 commercial broadcast television stations in the United States in addition to numerous cable channels. Just as most radio stations do, most television stations (with the exception of premium channels, such as HBO, and pay per view) rely on advertising to make a profit. Television rates vary greatly, depending on the size of the audience watching a particular program at a particular time. For example, a 30-second advertisement on a local television station in a small town might cost the advertiser only a few hundred dollars. Yet, consider that Fox, home of "American Idol," earned an *average* of $254,852 per 30-second advertisement in 2008.[10] NBC charged $3 million for some 30-second advertisements during the 2009 Super Bowl.[11] Altogether, advertisers spent $71.6 billion on television advertising in 2008.[12]

Internet and new media advertising today

Because their audiences are watching less television, reading fewer newspapers, and listening to less radio, advertisers are also moving away from older forms of advertising media and turning to new media. These new media include the Internet, particularly social networking sites such as MySpace and Facebook, video games and virtual worlds, and cell phones and text messaging (referred to in the industry as SMS or short message service) devices. In the near future, consumers are also expected to embrace electronic forms of newspapers and magazines. These new electronic publications will be available not just on computers, but also on cell phones and other wireless devices.

Internet advertising first became a widespread practice around 1996. A key reason that commercial advertisers became excited about the Internet is its interactivity. Instead of advertising being a one-way street with information coming only from the advertiser, the Internet facilitates advertisers' ability to receive feedback from consumers. This interactivity allows advertisers to find out quickly which advertising messages work and which ones do not. More importantly, it helps advertisers to learn *why* these messages did or did not work.

The interactive nature of new media, as well as the ability to mass-customize these media, will allow advertisers to pinpoint their consumers more effectively in the future. Advertisers will be better able to measure whether their advertisements are effective in attracting our attention. This is because they will know if we click on their on-screen advertisements, or respond to a text message an advertiser sends us. In virtual worlds such as Second Life, advertisers are using avatars that interact with others who participate in virtual worlds.

While interactivity helps advertisers evaluate their effectiveness, it also threatens advertisers. An advertiser can spend a lot of money developing an advertising campaign and placing advertisements online. Yet an "ordinary" consumer may be able to do serious damage simply by posting negative comments about an advertisement, the product or service advertised, or the advertiser itself. New media portals must find a balance, providing a comfortable environment for advertisers while at the same time allowing consumers to maintain a voice.

The Internet also allows advertisers to create sites that are promoted only in a particular magazine or in a particular television advertisement. When surfers go to those web sites, the advertiser is then able to measure which advertisements and which media generate the best consumer response.

Many advertisers use a combination of traditional media and new media to both communicate with their target markets and test the effectiveness of those communications.

The future of advertising

With the increase in the number of advertisers and advertising media over time, it has become harder for individual advertisers to break through the clutter and get (and keep) our attention. This is why advertisers are constantly looking for and experimenting with new ways to get us to buy their products and services. For example, a 30-second television advertisement today may consist of a series of 20 to 30 different images. A television advertisement from the early 1960s may consist of exactly one shot and would seem dull and boring to viewers today.

Each new advertising medium creates new possibilities for advertisers. For instance, General Mills was the only new company able to enter the breakfast cereal market successfully after the industry had been established several decades earlier. This was because General Mills aggressively pursued the then-new medium of commercial radio before the older cereal companies did. More recently, the Internet helped create new companies such as Amazon and new services such as iTunes.

New media also provide new opportunities for advertisers to identify and target different segments of consumers. For example, teens and those in their early twenties tend to watch less television than most other age groups do. Yet, this age group is a heavy user of the Internet and mobile media devices. Understandably, youth-oriented companies such as Abercrombie and Fitch do no television advertising, relying instead on the types of media that their target markets are more exposed to. In Chapter 9, we will look at new media forms that are emerging.

Advertising and careers

Advertising agencies are composed of specialized professionals; some agencies have thousands of employees. Advertising agency personnel include copywriters, who write the words that are read in a print or online advertisement or spoken in a radio or television advertisement. Commercial artists design the look of advertisements and choose the type of lettering and the colors that are used and so on. Advertising researchers try to determine what types of messages and images are most effective in selling the different types of products advertised. Advertising buyers decide which publications and broadcast media to advertise in, and negotiate prices for that advertising. Because advertising agencies are a business, they also have employees who handle administrative and financial tasks.

Large advertisers typically have employees who supervise the marketing functions of the firm. These employees select the advertising agencies that will develop and place their advertising campaigns, and supervise the advertising agencies' work on behalf of their firm. Media outlets such as television stations and newspapers employ salespeople to work with advertising agencies to sell advertising time or space in their medium.

Questions for critical thinking and discussion

1. As private citizens, we enjoy freedom of speech, protected by the First Amendment of the U.S. Constitution. The courts have generally held that ideological speech, which is comprised primarily of political and religious speech, is highly protected. The courts have ruled that commercial speech, including advertising, enjoys some First Amendment protection, but not to the same degree as ideological speech. Thus, commercial speech can be subject to more governmental regulations and restrictions than ideological speech is.

   - Should commercial speech have the same degree of First Amendment protection as ideological speech? Explain why or why not.

2. The third-person effect describes how many of us recognize that advertising has a powerful effect on many other people, but not on ourselves.

   - Why do you think that so many people, although recognizing the power of advertising, do not believe that advertising affects them personally?

3. Some people argue that the market itself is the best way to regulate advertising. They say that if a product or service does not perform as advertised, the advertiser risks alienating its customers. As a result, advertisers are motivated to produce advertisements that are accurate and not misleading. Other people argue that there are too many unsophisticated consumers who will be victimized by misleading advertising. This group supports government regulation of advertising as a means of protecting consumers.

   - Which argument do you find the most persuasive?
   - Why did you answer the way you did?

(Continued)

Questions for critical thinking and discussion—Cont'd

4. Stealth marketing is an effort by advertisers and other marketing firms to create material that is advertising, while attempting to disguise the advertising as something else.

    - Visit the web site http://www.teen.com and look around.
    - Discuss how the site uses "stealth marketing" to sell products and services.
    - What are some of the ways that the site tries to gather data about its visitors?
    - Why do you think that the site wants to gather this data?
    - In your opinion, is this site ethical? Explain your answer.

5. Review Maslow's Hierarchy of Needs pyramid on p. 39. Advertisers commonly present their products or services as meeting a need higher on the pyramid than one would normally assume. Find a magazine advertisement that offers a product or service as meeting one of these needs.

    - Does the need associated with the advertised item seem logical to you? Or has the advertiser presented the item as meeting a need that is higher on the pyramid? Explain.

Additional resources

Adbrands, www.adbrands.net

Adbusters, www.adbusters.org

Advertising Age, www.adage.com

Advertising Resources (University of Iowa), www.warc.com

Advertising World "The Ultimate Marketing Communications Directory", advertising.utexas.edu/world.

American Advertising: A Brief History, historymatters.gmu.edu/mse/ads/amadv.html

American Advertising Federation, www.aaf.org

Cable Television Advertising Bureau, www.thecab.tv

Danesi, Marcel, *Brands* (New York: Taylor & Francis, 2006).

John W. Hartman Center for Sales, Advertising & Marketing History, library.duke.edu/specialcollections/Hartman

Internet Advertising Bureau, www.iab.net

Kilbourne, Jean, *Can't Buy My Love: How Advertising Changes the Way We Think and Feel* (New York: Touchstone, 2000).

Magazine Publishers of America's Consumer Marketing Page, www.magazine.org/consumer_marketing/index.aspx

Marchand, Roland, *Advertising the American Dream: Making Way for Modernity, 1920–1940* (Berkeley: University of California Press, 1986).

Mierau, Christina B., *Accept No Substitutes: The History of American Advertising* (Minneapolis: Lerner, 2000).

Outdoor Advertising Association of America, www.oaaa.org

Radio Advertising Bureau, www.rab.com

Sivulka, Juliann, *Soap, Sex, and Cigarettes: A Cultural History of American Advertising* (Belmont, CA: Wadsworth, 1997).

Television Bureau of Advertising, www.tvb.org

World Advertising Research Center, www.warc.com

4 Television

Chapter contents

Issues and trends in television

- Television was the dominant medium in the United States in the second half of the twentieth century, but faces significant challenges today.
- The first few decades of television were dominated by three broadcast networks, but television narrowcasting today provides hundreds of choices to viewers.
- Despite the range of choices, the most popular types of television programs fall within only a few well-defined genres.
- Most television programming is directed toward the types of viewers that are most attractive to advertisers.
- New technology allows viewers to decide where and when they watch television content.

> *"When television is good, nothing—not the theater, not the magazines or newspapers— nothing is better. But when television is bad, nothing is worse. . . . I invite you to sit down in front of your television set when your station goes on the air . . . and keep your eyes glued to that set until the station signs off. I can assure you that you will observe a vast wasteland."[1]*
>
> Federal Communications Commission Chairman Newton Minow, in his address to the National Association of Broadcasters on May 9, 1961

Minow's "Vast Wasteland" speech remains a legendary criticism of television half a century later. Yet many observers say television has only gotten worse. Regardless of how one feels about the quality of television programming, television's importance as a source of entertainment and information continued to grow during the second half of the twentieth century. Today, however, we are witnessing significant changes and challenges, as new forms of media arise to compete with television.

A brief history of broadcast television

As is discussed in Chapter 5, commercial radio arose during the 1920s. Even though commercial radio was still young, radio network executives were aware of the potential of television's success and spent millions of dollars developing television technology in the 1930s. However, this was the period of the Great Depression, when few consumers had the financial ability, and even fewer the confidence in the nation's economy, to invest in television sets. While the industrial buildup during World War II led to virtual full employment in the United States, the telecommunications industry focused on meeting the military's needs while federal laws rationed many civilian goods. When the war ended in 1945, the nation witnessed the confluence between tremendous consumer demand and electronics manufacturers who wanted to maintain the levels of production that they had during the war.

The dominant radio networks CBS, NBC, and ABC (a spin-off of NBC under a court order in 1943) shifted their focus to television after World War II. Their previous experience as radio networks proved advantageous. Accordingly, the lack of an existing network proved a competitive

Figure 4.1 A television set was a prestigious item in post-World War II homes. *Source:* iStockphoto

disadvantage for the DuMont network, which also rose during the 1940s, only to fail in the next decade. Figure 4.1 shows an old television set that would have been a prized possession in many post-World War II homes.

Because the commercial television broadcast band was limited to 12 stations in any single market, there was a tremendous clamor for relatively scarce television licenses. Government officials realized that the growing demand for television broadcast licenses would soon mean the depletion of licenses in the nation's largest markets. The Federal Communications Commission (FCC) responded with a moratorium on granting licenses in 1948. When the moratorium was lifted in 1952, the FCC had expanded the available television band, adding channels on the Ultra High Frequency (UHF) band in addition to the existing Very High Frequency (VHF) band. VHF station signals were received through "rabbit ears," indoor antennae placed on top of the television, while indoor UHF antennae were

Figure 4.2 Television antenna. *Source:* Image from the Internet

hoop-shaped, as shown in Figure 4.2. UHF broadcasting proved to be inferior in many markets, with weaker signals and poorer reception than VHF stations, and UHF licenses have been considered much less valuable than VHF licenses.

Efforts to design color television technology began in television's earliest days. One of the many challenges that faced those involved in providing color television broadcasting to consumers was the cost. It was relatively expensive to produce color broadcasts and quite expensive to receive color broadcasts because color television sets were sold at prohibitive prices for most Americans. CBS made the first significant effort to popularize color television, producing its own television sets for a short period in the early 1950s. RCA followed with a different type of color technology, but sold so few sets that *Time* magazine called color television, "the most resounding industrial flop of 1956."[2] RCA continued its efforts, however, and in 1960 began broadcasting its entire prime-time schedule in color. By 1965, CBS and ABC were also broadcasting all their prime-time programs in color, and color television sets outsold black and white sets for the first time that year.[3]

The ownership structure of local television stations combines *owned and operated* (O&O) stations that the networks themselves own and *affiliates*, which are owned by other firms. Rule changes by the FCC over the years, under considerable pressure from the networks, have steadily increased the number of local television stations that the networks can own.

As discussed in Chapter 1, many of the major media are owned by only a few firms. In 1943, the FCC ordered NBC to sell one of its two networks, the government claiming that NBC had too much control of the broadcasting industry. NBC sold the Blue Network to the creator of Lifesavers candy, and it became ABC. Ownership of the three largest networks remained relatively stable for four decades, with CBS often enjoying the highest audience share, and ABC usually in third place behind NBC.

The mid-1980s marked the beginning of two decades of change in network ownership and dominance. In 1985, RCA, which had created NBC in 1926, was acquired by General Electric, the largest non-oil-related merger in U.S. history at the time. (In early 2010, General Electric was in negotiations to sell NBC to cable operator Comcast, subject to FCC approval.) The following year, the broadcasting firm Capital Cities bought ABC. Capital Cities/ABC was sold to the Walt Disney Company in 1996, the largest media merger in the United States at the time.

The manufacturing firm Westinghouse purchased CBS in 1995. Westinghouse changed its name to CBS two years later, with existing manufacturing operations treated as subsidiaries. In 1999, CBS merged with Viacom, which owned MTV and numerous other cable networks. Viacom and CBS split in 2006, with Viacom retaining control over its cable holdings and CBS focusing on radio and television broadcasting, as well as outdoor advertising and book publishing. CBS and Time Warner share ownership of the CW Network.

Although NBC, CBS, and ABC essentially ruled television for the first four decades of its existence, Rupert Murdoch's Fox Television, created in 1986, rose to become a formidable competitor. Murdoch began as a newspaper publisher in his native Australia, becoming a U.S. citizen in 1985 to comply with FCC media ownership regulations. Fox's first network hit was "The Simpsons," which began airing in 1989 and remains in prime-time today. The 2009–2010 season of "The Simpsons" made it the longest-running scripted series in television history.

Fox's biggest risk, which turned out to be a profitable one, was bidding over $1 billion in 1993 for the rights to broadcast National Football League games. This gamble helped Fox develop a higher profile among television viewers and strengthen its network of local affiliates, especially in those markets with NFL teams. Many observers initially scoffed at what they saw as foolishness on Fox's part, noting that 120 of the 139 local Fox affiliates were on the still relatively obscure UHF broadcast band.[4] Many of these critics failed to appreciate the fact that those local affiliates were also available on local cable television.

A brief history of cable television

Cable television originated as Community Antenna Television (CATV) in Pennsylvania in 1948. In rural communities with poor television reception from nearby cities, large antennae were built and the television signals they received were transmitted to local homes by cable. Over time, companies brought cable television broadcasting into the cities. Cable programming as we know it today began in 1972, with the launch of Home Box Office (HBO), the first premium television network. Unlike previously free broadcast television, viewers paid for HBO subscriptions in order to watch recently released movies without commercial interruptions. (This was before the widespread availability of home video players.)

The National Cable and Telecommunications Association estimated in November 2009 that there were 104.6 million basic and digital cable subscribers to cable television in the United States, up from 2 million in 1975.[5] Comcast enjoys the greatest market share, with 24.1 million basic subscribers, followed by Time Warner (13.1 million) and Cox (5.3 million). Among cable networks, Discovery, Turner Network Television, ESPN, CNN, and USA Network are the five most widely available networks, each accessible by about 98 million subscribers.[6]

For many years, cable television programming relied primarily on movies and sports events, as well as reruns of sitcoms and dramatic programs that had originally aired on broadcast networks. Over the past decade or so, however, cable networks have begun investing more in original programming. Until rather recently, the broadcast networks enjoyed both higher viewer ratings and higher critical acclaim for their programming than did cable networks. While broadcast networks continue to draw the largest audiences, cable is now challenging broadcasting in terms of program quality. In 2004, HBO's "The Sopranos" was the first cable-based program to win an Emmy award for outstanding drama series, an award the program won again in 2007. In 2008, "Mad Men," airing on AMC, was the first program available in most markets on basic cable (HBO is a premium channel in most markets) to win an Emmy award for outstanding drama series.

"The Daily Show" with John Stewart, which airs on Comedy Central, has achieved a significant level of cultural importance, particularly among viewers between the ages of 18 to 34, the demographic that is so attractive to advertisers. You are probably aware that many viewers consider "The Daily Show" to be an important source of information about contemporary political events, even though the program is clearly intended to be satirical.

The television industry today

For several decades, many Americans had a choice of only three networks (ABC, CBS, and NBC) with occasional independent broadcasters that relied primarily on syndicated reruns of network programs. Because broadcasters were originally striving to attract a general audience, broadcasting tended to be mainstream and highly formulaic. In the 1990s, the virtually unlimited number of channels available through cable television allowed television firms to embrace the process known as *narrowcasting*.

Narrowcasting is the development of different types of programming for different types of audiences. Thus, today we have Lifetime television for women and Spike television for men. There are Nickelodeon and the Disney Channel for children. MTV aims for a younger age demographic that does VH1, both of which are owned by the same firm. Television for Spanish speaking audiences includes Univision and Telemundo, and BET targets African American viewers. In 2005, Viacom's MTV Networks introduced LOGO, designed to appeal to viewers who are lesbian, gay, bisexual, or transgender. The trend toward identifying distinct niches in the market correlates to the *disaggregation* of American media markets.

Recent technological developments will likely lead to further changes. Through the Digital Television Transition and Public Safety Act of 2006,

Figure 4.3 The recent trend is larger televisions and smaller audiences per channel. *Source*: iStockphoto

Congress required television broadcasters to switch to digital broadcasting in 2009. The original deadline for broadcasters to switch from analog to digital transmissions was originally set for February 17 and then postponed to June 12, 2009. All televisions sold in the United States as of March 1, 2007 are required to have a digital tuner. This move freed up commercial band space, which the FCC auctioned to cellular telephone companies, wireless broadband providers, and other telecommunication firms. The television set shown in Figure 4.3 probably has a digital tuner.

Because the Telecommunications Act of 1996 gave the firms that held existing analog broadcasting licenses the exclusive right to digital licenses, many of those within government as well as critics outside of government labeled Congress's actions as a form of corporate welfare. These critics argued that the federal government should have sold rather than given away the digital licenses. Instead, Congress budgeted up to $1.5 billion of taxpayers' money to provide coupons for digital converter boxes in the households that did not have digital television service. By September 2009, nearly 35 million coupons, worth $40 each, had been redeemed.[7]

Television programming

Many of the first generation of television programs that began airing in the 1940s had migrated from radio. Sporting events also provided a significant amount of television programming in the early days because they were relatively inexpensive to produce (they merely recorded events that were going to take place anyway) and they consumed several airs of broadcast time during an era in which many television stations simply did not have enough programming to fill their broadcast schedules. In addition to sporting events, the most popular forms of television programming today fall within a few genres.

Sitcoms

Situation comedies, or sitcoms, tend to be half an hour in length (without advertisements, they are actually about 22 minutes long). The humor, of course, is based on the situation in which the characters find themselves. The structure of most sitcoms is usually formulaic. After an establishing shot (a brief view of the outside of the home, office, or business where the interior action is set) we are introduced to some sort of dramatic tension. One or more of the characters finds themselves in a difficult situation, often brought on by that character's personality or idiosyncrasies. The plot of the show centers on the character resolving this difficulty, often through plainly illogical means. This counterintuitive approach to the problem creates much of the humor of the situation. For example, the protagonist (main character) is a young man who finds that he has accidentally scheduled two dates for the same evening. Rather than break one of the dates, as the viewer knows he should, he (perhaps aided by his friends) tries to concoct a way to go out on both dates that evening. Toward the end of the program is the climax, at which point the protagonist typically succeeds in spite of himself— or fails entirely. The denouement (day-NOO-mon) which translates to "unwinding" in French follows, with the protagonist reflecting on what has happened. Of course, he has not learned his lesson, leaving the viewer wanting to watch the following week to see in what new predicament the protagonist will find himself.

Many of the situation comedies of the 1950s through 1970s featured the traditional nuclear family, which included a mother, father, and children. Today, situation comedies are more likely to focus on a nontraditional family, or on a group of people who are all roughly the same age, whether teenagers or folks in their late twenties. Children and seniors typically will say something uncharacteristic for their age, with particularly mature statements delivered by child characters and childlike statements uttered by elderly characters. This incongruence provides another humorous element.

Dramas

Another common prime-time program is the drama. These hour-long programs typically feature a particular profession. Most commonly, these professions are not deskbound, but involve people in active roles, perhaps in multiple settings. Many of these dramas involve lawyers, doctors, firefighters, police officers and detectives, or, of course, crime scene investigators. Dramas today often have ensemble casts, featuring a number of primary characters, unlike older dramas, which had a star or two with a supporting cast. In order to convey a sense of urgency and excitement, several different story lines may be contained within a single show, with the action shifting from one scene to another, in an effort to keep viewers' attention throughout the program.

Contests and reality shows

You are probably not surprised that among the most popular program types today are talent/endurance contests and reality shows, as it is hard for a television viewer to avoid "American Idol," "Survivor," "The Biggest Loser," and similar programs. This type of programming is not only popular with viewers, but with the television industry as well. These programs are relatively cheap to produce compared to comedies and dramas. Few of the people who appear on these shows receive large salaries. Set designs and stage property costs are also relatively low, and there is usually little need for screenwriters to develop scripts. (Crime and medical dramas, with expensive actors, settings, special effects, and screenwriters, can cost as much as $3 million an episode to produce.) As a result, many observers believe that we will continue to see a continuing stream of contests and reality programs for as long as they remain even moderately popular with viewers.

News

Ted Turner introduced the Cable Network News (CNN) in 1980. CNN was the first television channel devoted exclusively to news, an alternative to traditional news programming on television, which typically only aired early in the morning and in the early and late evening. Two years later, CNN added Headline News, which cycled through breaking news and the top stories of the day in 30-minute segments. Time Warner acquired Turner's cable networks in 1996, the same year that Rupert Murdoch's News Corporation launched Fox News, and Microsoft and NBC collaborated to offer MSNBC. To establish its niche in the television news industry, Fox News has adopted a politically conservative tone to its reporting, although it states its coverage is "fair and balanced." Similarly, many observers claim that MSNBC's presentation of the news tends to favor the liberal political agenda. Regardless of a news agency's particular political or social bias, the point here is that even the presentation of "facts" is subject to interpretation. In addition to the choices of words or images used to report the news, the bias of the news media determines which events they cover and which facts they present. The process of selective exposure often determines which news station a viewer chooses to watch. It is more likely that a viewer whose political views are conservative will watch Fox News and that a politically liberal viewer will choose MSNBC.

Just as 24-hour news stations have changed the timing practices of television news, the rise of the Internet has created new demands for timeliness from television news broadcasters. Headline News responded by reducing its 30-minute news cycles to 15-minute segments. Many television news broadcasts use crawls, brief written synopses of news stories that move across the screen. This allows the simultaneous presentation of breaking news stories and recaps of earlier news stories, providing a sense of timeliness to viewers.

Local television stations rely heavily on their local newscasts as a source of revenue, as all of the advertising time during those newscasts is purchased from local stations rather than national networks. This economic incentive places significant pressure on local television news directors to appeal to the largest number of viewers. The trend for the last decade or more has been to incorporate more sensationalism into local news coverage. The unofficial motto for many local television news agencies is "if it bleeds, it leads;" the first story on many local newscasts will often be a homicide or tragic accident that horrifies viewers at the same time it titillates them. Likewise, television weather reporters hope for bad weather rather than good weather, as viewers are more likely to watch television when storms threaten.

Syndicated programming

First-run *syndicated programming* is sold to network affiliates and independent local stations, rather than to broadcast networks. Some of the most popular syndicated programs are daily programs, called *strip programs*. Top-rated strip programs include game shows such as "Wheel of Fortune" and "Jeopardy." Other popular syndicated programs are "Judge Judy" and "Dr. Phil." It is common today for local stations to receive the syndicated program free or at a significant discount with the syndicator relying on advertising sales as the primary revenue source, as part of a barter agreement (the local station barters its advertising time in exchange for programming from the syndicator).

Television casting

One common source of criticism of television throughout much of its history is that it portrays females and members of minority groups in ways that are stereotypical, limited, and inaccurate. This criticism reached a peak in the fall of 1999, when the television networks introduced 26 new prime-time programs, none of which had a minority group member in a leading role. Many civil rights and media organizations expressed outrage, including organizations that advocate on behalf of African Americans, Hispanic Americans, and Asian Americans. The concern among many media observers was that white writers so dominated television programs' creative staffs that they did not know how to include nonwhite characters in their productions. Perhaps in an effort to avoid offending members of minority groups, those minority groups were rendered virtually invisible on prime-time television.

Stung by this criticism, television program producers vowed to include more minority group members in major roles. For example, ABC aired "The George Lopez Show," the first network program in which all the major characters were Hispanic, from 2002 to 2007. In a study released at the end of 2008, however, the National Association for the Advancement of Colored People (NAACP) found that "African-American actors' share of all television and theatrical roles was 13.8 percent, down from 15.3 percent the previous year. In 2004, Hispanic actors were cast in 5.5 percent of all such roles, Asian-American actors were cast in 2.9 percent of all roles and

Native-American actors were cast in only 48 roles, representing a less than 1 percent share."[8] In the United States, minority groups continue to comprise an increasingly larger percentage of the population. This reality has yet to be reflected accurately in television programming. For example, Hispanics represent more than 14 percent of the population in the Unites States while Hispanic characters occupy less than six percent of television and theatrical roles.

Sex and violence on television

Sexual and violent program content presents another cause for concern among some critics of television. In response to some of the criticism about televised content that some viewers find inappropriate for themselves or children, Congress asked the television industry to develop a voluntary rating system for program content. Preferring firmly suggested voluntary compliance among its members to the possibility of government mandated compliance, the National Association of Broadcasters and the National Cable Television Association produced the rating system as seen in Figure 4.4.

In tandem with the television industry's release of its new content rating system, the FCC stipulated that all television sets with a 13-inch or larger screen manufactured after January 1, 2000 must have V Chip technology. (The "V" stands for either violence control or viewer control, depending on whom you ask.) This relatively inexpensive technology, which detects coded signals combined in television signals, combined with the voluntary television rating system, allows users to block programs based on their content rating. While some claim that the V Chip represents censorship, others argue that this technology helps parents control the types of programs that their children watch, especially at those times when parents are not at home to supervise their children's television viewing.

Television and audience

We begin our look at television viewers by taking a snapshot of one television market. Boston is the nation's seventh largest television market with 2.4 million television households. Note that a television market does not

THE TV PARENTAL GUIDELINES

THE RATINGS

Audience: indicates the audience for which a television program is appropriate. ⟶
Content Label: indicates a show may contain violence, sex, adult language, ⟶
or suggestive dialogue.

The Content Labels

TV Parental Guidelines may have one or more letters added to the basic rating to let parents know
when a show may contain violence, sex, adult language or suggestive dialogue.

D – suggestive dialogue (usually means talks about sex)
L – coarse or crude language
S – sexual situations
V – violence
FV – fantasy violence (children's programming only)

 All Children

This program is designed to be appropriate for all children.
Whether animated or live-action, the themes and elements
in this program are specifically designed for a very young
audience, including children from ages 2-6. This program
is not expected to frighten younger children.

 Directed to Older Children

This program is designed for children age 7 and above. It
may be more appropriate for children who have acquired
the developmental skills needed to distinguish between
make-believe and reality. Themes and elements in this
program may include mild fantasy violence or comedic
violence, or may frighten children under the age of 7.
Therefore, parents may wish to consider the suitability of
this program for their very young children.

 Directed to Older Children –
Fantasy Violence

For those programs where fantasy violence may be more
intense or more combative than other programs in this
category, such programs will be designated TV-Y7-FV.

 General Audience

Most parents would find this program suitable for all ages.
Although this rating does not signify a program designed
specifically for children, most parents may let younger
children watch this program unattended. It contains little
or no violence, no strong language and little or no sexual
dialogue or situations.

 Parental Guidance Suggested

This program contains material that parents may find
unsuitable for younger children. Many parents may want
to watch it with their younger children. The theme itself
may call for parental guidance and/or the program may
contain one or more of the following: some suggestive
dialogue (D), infrequent coarse language (L), some sexual
situations (S), or moderate violence (V).

 Parents Strongly Cautioned

This program contains some material that many parents
would find unsuitable for children under 14 years of age.
Parents are strongly urged to exercise greater care in
monitoring this program and are cautioned against letting
children under the age of 14 watch unattended. This
program may contain one or more of the following:
intensely suggestive dialogue (D), strong coarse language
(L), intense sexual situations (S), or intense violence (V).

 Mature Audience Only

This program is specifically designed to be viewed by
adults and therefore may be unsuitable for children under
17. This program may contain one or more of the following:
crude indecent language (L), explicit sexual activity (S), or
graphic violence (V).

Figure 4.4 The TV parental guideline ratings. *Source:* tvguidelines.org

follow political borders like city limits and state lines, as many television households are beyond those borders. For example, the Boston television market includes much of Massachusetts, part of New Hampshire, and a county in Vermont. (The market you live in probably coincides with the city where most of the local newscasts that you can view in your home originate.) According to Nielsen, between September 22, 2008 and March 17, 2009, the members of an average household in Boston watched a combined 8.35 hours of television per day.[9] The daily viewing by age group in Boston during this period reflects similar patterns of viewing by these groups in other television markets:

- Age 2–18: 4.73 hours
- Age 18–34: 4.01 hours
- Age 25–54: 4.75 hours
- Age 55+: 6.34 hours.

Figure 4.5 symbolizes the programming choices available to different audiences. As is the case with many other types of media, teenagers and people in their twenties are among the most attractive viewers to television broadcasters. This is because this age group is quite attractive to advertisers. However, due to the active lifestyles of most teens and twenty-somethings and because of the many other types of communications and entertainment media that this age group relies on, teens and twenty-somethings are one of the age groups that watch the least amount of television. One of the two age groups that watch the most television is young children (many of whom are not yet in school or not yet in school all day). Young children are attractive to many advertisers as a conduit of pull marketing; they do not actually buy products but have significant influence on their parents' purchasing decisions regarding toys, breakfast cereals, and snacks. As a result, there are many television programs targeted at young children, especially in the daytime (including, of course, Saturday morning cartoons).

The other age group that watches the most television is the elderly. The reason that older people tend to watch more television than other groups is due primarily to their often sedentary lifestyle. In 1970, CBS canceled "The Red Skelton Show," which at the time was the seventh highest rated program in the country. Many believed that this was because Skelton's audience was considered too old by many advertisers. Similarly, CBS cancelled "Dr. Quinn, Medicine Woman" in 1998, when it was among the 20 highest

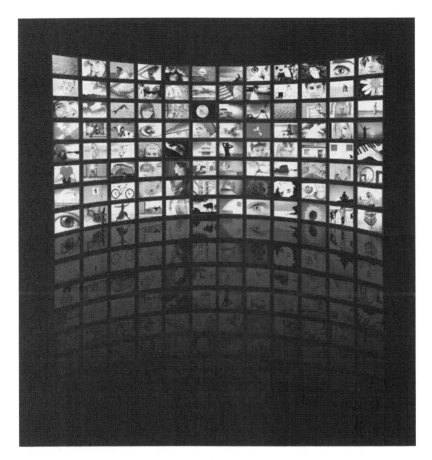

Figure 4.5 There are different types of television programming for different audiences. *Source*: iStockphoto

rated programs. The show aired on Saturday evening, which tends to have a smaller (and older) audience. Advertisers' disregard for older viewers is usually attributed to the belief that older consumers are "set in their ways," with strong likes and dislikes and well-established buying habits that cannot be changed by advertising.

Television and audience measurement

For decades, Nielsen Media Research (formerly A. C. Nielsen) has provided the most significant measurement of television audiences. These measurements are crucial to networks, local television stations, and advertisers. The price that networks get for national advertising time and the price that local stations get for local *spot* advertising time depend primarily on the size of the audience that a television program collects for the firms that will advertise during that program. In 2009, Nielsen estimated that there were 114.5 million television households.[10] Of course, Nielsen cannot possibly monitor the daily viewing of each of those households. Thus, Nielsen does what automobile manufacturers do when they crash-test cars: they sample. Currently, each household that agrees to compile data for Nielsen represents around 4,000 households. Nielsen uses a combination of electronic metering devices and written diaries to sample television viewing throughout the country.

Nielsen's two key measurements are "rating" and "share." A "rating" point represents one percent of all U.S. households with television, or about 1.145 million households. If a program had a rating of 12, for example, that means that 12 percent of U.S. television households were believed to have watched that program, based on the Nielsen sample. If for example, "The Mentalist" had a rating of 10.3, that means that Nielsen estimates that about 11.8 million households (10.3 × 1.145 million) watched that program. "Share" is the percentage of households who were watching television during the time segment in which a particular program was on. For example, if a program has a share of 11/4, Nielsen estimates that 11 percent of television households were watching television during a particular period. Nielsen also estimates that the program drew four percent of those households who were watching television during that period. Thus, share is not merely a function of the popularity of a particular program; it is also based on the popularity of a particular time of day for television viewing.

As is true with most sampling methods, there are complaints that Nielsen's sampling does not provide an accurate measurement of the public's viewing habits. Today, with so many choices of television channels available to the average viewer, it becomes increasingly likely for some programs to fail to register viewers in Nielsen's surveys. The math is simple: Nielsen estimates that the average household has 109 choices of channels to watch, and Nielsen is sampling only a fraction of the households who own televisions. As a result, some programs can fall through the cracks. The increasing interactivity of digital television may provide a remedy for this in the future because it is possible for the digital television service provider to track exactly how many households are tuned to each channel that service provider offers. However, it remains difficult to ascertain which members of a household are actually watching a particular program in a measured household;

although we may know that a particular household watched a "Seinfeld" rerun last night, we are uncertain whether it was the 13-year-old male who lives in that household, his 39-year-old mother, or both. Nielsen attempts to gather this demographic data by issuing paper diaries to its sample households during the four annual periods known as sweeps in November, February, May, and July.[11] Understandably, broadcasters beef up their programming schedules during sweeps periods.

The future of television

The shift in 2009 from analog to digital broadcasting hastens media *convergence*, as it becomes increasingly difficult to identify distinct media and distinct media firms. (Media convergence is examined in detail in Chapter 10.) For many Americans today, the firm that is their cable television provider is also their Internet Service Provider (ISP) and may be the provider of their telephone service (landline or wireless or both). Convergence facilitates time shifting, as many of us now watch television programming at some time other than when it was originally broadcast, and we no longer need a television to watch those programs. Many viewers watch entire programs or selected portions of programs on Internet websites such as Hulu, Blinkx, and YouTube, as well as websites associated with television networks. Although some television content providers have resisted such sites, others have cooperated, as these sites can add another source of advertising revenue.

The increasing mobility of devices for watching television has caused many of those in the television and advertising industries to reconsider whether measuring programs' popularity by the percentage of households tuned to a particular program at a particular time reflects contemporary viewing habits. As a result, Nielsen has begun measuring other communication platforms, including cell phones, iPods, and computers.

Ironically, even though Americans are watching more television today than ever before—an average of 151 hours a month—the size of the audience share for any particular program or television channel is declining. The television industry expects this trend to continue. Viewers will have even more choices of what to watch and more choices of media on which to watch it. As media analyst Alan Gould says, "With more than 500 channels, and linear and nonlinear viewership, we're far from the three networks that captivated 90 percent of the viewership 30 years ago."[12]

The highest rated single television program in total number of U.S. viewers was Super Bowl XLIV (between the New Orleans Saints and Indianapolis Colts) in 2010. The football broadcast gathered an audience of 106.5 million Americans. The highest rated single television program in terms of audience share was the final episode of "M*A*S*H" in 1983, with a share of 77. Although *more people* watched the 2010 Super Bowl than the conclusion of "M*A*S*H" (due partly to the fact that there were more Americans in 2010 than in 1983) a *larger percentage* of Americans watched "M*A*S*H"—the 2010 Super Bowl's share was 68. This should not be surprising. With so many other media forms competing against television, and with so many choices of what to watch on television, audiences for a particular program in the future will unlikely reach the audience shares seen in the twentieth century.

Should the television networks be afraid of their diminishing share of the media market? Some of the top television executives disagree with each other on the issue. Jeff Zucker, the head of NBC Universal, said in February 2009 that, "broadcast television is in a time of tremendous transition, and if we don't attempt to change the model now, we could be in danger of becoming the automobile industry or the newspaper industry."[13] Leslie Moonves, chief at CBS, remains optimistic, saying, "I'm here to tell you—the model ain't broken."[14]

Television and careers

For those interested in what many consider the most glamorous jobs in television—actors, producers, and directors, the U.S. Department of Labor's Bureau of Labor Statistics predicts that there will be an 11 percent increase in jobs between 2006 and 2016.[15] This is equal to the average for job growth in all occupations. The Bureau estimates that job growth for careers in television camera operating and editing will about 12 percent.[16]

The outlook for television announcers, including news, sports, and weather reporters, is not encouraging; the Bureau of Labor Statistics anticipates a moderate decline in these jobs through 2016. As the Bureau tells us, "Increasing consolidation of radio and television stations, the advent of new technology, and growth of alternative media sources, such as satellite radio, will contribute to the expected decline."[17] In other words, the bureau recognizes what many in the television industry have also recognized: television, the dominant medium in the United States for half of the twentieth century, faces significant competition today.

Questions for critical thinking and discussion

1. In *The Image: Or What Happened to the American Dream*, the late Daniel Boorstin described a celebrity as "a person who is well-known for his well-knownness." Boorstin wrote this in 1961.

   - Has the definition of a celebrity changed since then?
   - Would you want to be a celebrity? Why or why not?

2. Assume that you work for Time Warner, the large media and entertainment conglomerate. Time Warner wants you to develop a new cable television station.

   - First, you must identify a viewing group that is underserved by the current cable television lineup. (Remember, most currently underserved viewing groups are unattractive to advertisers, but this does not mean that all underserved groups are.) Describe why you think this group would be an attractive market for Time Warner and its advertisers.
   - Next identify at least three types of programming that this group will be attracted to, and explain why.
   - Finally, identify at least three types of advertisers who would be interested in using your channel to reach that group, and explain why.

3. Timothy McVeigh was executed on June 11, 2001, for the murder of 168 people at the Murrah federal building in Oklahoma City. A Gallup poll revealed that about 23 percent of Americans would have watched the execution if it was broadcast.

   - Assume that Osama Bin Laden is taken into custody, tried and convicted for the events of 9/11. He is to be executed. The government is interested in allowing Bin Laden's execution to be televised.
   - Imagine that you are an executive at one of the major television networks. Would you pay for the rights to broadcast Bin Laden's execution? Why or why not?
   - Regardless of your decision, which advertisers do you believe would buy commercial time during the broadcast? Explain why.

4. In a 2002 *New York Times* article entitled, "The Remote Controllers," Marshall Sella wrote: "With the aid of the Internet, the loftiest dream for television is being realized: an odd brand of interactivity. Television began as a one-way street winding from producers to consumers, but that street is now becoming two-way. A man with one machine (a TV) is doomed to isolation, but a man with two machines (TV and a computer) can belong to a community."[18]

   - What benefits does Internet-based interactivity between television programmers and television viewers bring to viewers?
   - What benefits does this interactivity bring to television programmers?

(Continued)

Questions for critical thinking and discussion—Cont'd

5. As discussed in this chapter, television viewers have an expanding range of choices of where they watch television programs. This is due to the variety of technologies available to television viewers today. Television viewers also have the ability to time-shift programming: watching programs when the viewer decides to rather than when the programming is broadcast. Television executives are not sure what this means for the future of program content that has proven to be popular in the past.

   • What effect, if any, will the increasing mobility of television viewing have on television content? Explain.
   • What effect, if any, will the ability to time-shift television viewing have on television content? Explain.

Additional resources

Academy of Television Arts & Sciences' Emmy Award at www.emmy.tv

Blumenthal, Howard J., and Oliver R. Goodenough, *This Business of Television*, 3rd ed. (New York: Billboard Books, 2006).

Carter, Bill, *Desperate Networks* (New York: Broadway Books, 2006).

Edgerton, Gary, *The Columbia History of American Television* (New York: Columbia University Press, 2007).

Marc, David, *Demographic Vistas: Television in American Culture*, revised edition (Philadelphia: University of Pennsylvania Press, 1996).

Mittell, Jason, *Television and American Culture* (New York: Oxford University Press, 2009).

National Association of Broadcasters, www.nab.org

Newcomb, Horace, ed., *Television: The Critical View*, 7th ed. (New York: Oxford University Press, 2006).

Television Bureau of Advertising, www.tvb.org

Time Magazine's 100 Best TV Shows of All-Time, www.time.com/time/specials/2007/article/0,2880 4,1651341_1659188,00.html

Radio and Music ![5]

Issues and trends in radio and music

- Radio's reliance on music for its programming arose from necessity after the introduction of television.
- Traditional broadcast radio must now compete with satellite and Internet radio.
- The music industry is less reliant on radio, leading to increased diversity of musical styles.
- Music in physical form sold at bricks and mortar retailers is being replaced by digital versions of music available through downloads.
- Professional musicians are relying less on recorded music sales and more on touring and commercial licensing agreements.
- The long tail effect allows consumers to listen to more choices of music than ever before.

Every culture has music. The U.S. is a diverse nation, and its various cultures have infused American music with a wide variety of styles. For much of the last century, radio was the primary means of transmitting recorded music.

A brief history of radio

The early days

Inventors began making significant progress with radio technology in the 1890s and early 1900s. Pittsburgh's Westinghouse Electric Company was among the first firms involved in developing radio technology. KDKA aired the U.S.'s first commercial radio broadcast in 1920 from a shack at the Westinghouse plant. Because the station had very little content available, it played records to fill its broadcast time. American Telephone & Telegraph (AT&T) began connecting a group of radio stations in 1923, and KDKA joined as an original member. The first true radio network was the National Broadcasting Company (NBC), a subsidiary of the Radio Corporation of America (RCA), which like Westinghouse was active in developing commercial radio for the public. In 1926, NBC operated two networks, called the Red and Blue Networks. The Red network feature music and other types of entertainment, while the Blue network focused on news and information broadcasts. Figure 5.1 shows an old radio.

Figure 5.1 Early radios were considered furniture in many homes. *Source:* iStockphoto

Soon after the creation of the two NBC networks, the U.S. government grew concerned that a few corporations could monopolize the relatively scarce locations on the AM (amplitude modulation) part of the radio spectrum. In order to better allocate a scarce resource, Congress established the Federal Radio Commission in 1927. The Commission was responsible for awarding radio licenses in each identified radio market (city or metropolitan area). Anticipating the need to regulate television and other forms of telecommunications, Congress changed the name of the Radio Commission to the Federal Communication Commission (FCC) in 1934.

In 1939, the FCC determined that NBC's Red and Blue networks were too dominant in the radio market. The FCC ordered RCA to sell one of the two networks to create more competition in the industry. Although RCA fought the FCC's order in the courts, the FCC prevailed. RCA sold its Blue Network in 1943 to the creator of Lifesavers candy, and the Blue Network changed its name to the American Broadcasting Corporation (ABC) two years later.

The predecessor of the Columbia Broadcasting System (CBS) began in 1927, soon after the creation of NBC's two radio networks. The other major radio network to be created during this period was the Mutual Broadcasting System. Although Mutual had the largest number of affiliates among the four national radio networks, the company was loosely organized, relying on a cooperative system of program development among its member stations.

The advent of radio provided advertising opportunities that allowed new producers of consumer goods to enter the market. For example, the breakfast cereal industry, although only a few decades old, had already become dominated by a handful of companies, such as Kellogg and Post. Breakfast cereal makers were among the nation's top advertisers at that time, focused largely on newspaper and magazine advertising. Thus, it was almost impossible for a new company to enter this very profitable field, as the cost to advertise to gain a foothold in the field was prohibitive. However, General Mills, based in Minneapolis, purchased a local radio station in 1924, which it renamed WCCO, with a powerful signal that carried its programming into several states. Besides regular entertainment programming, the station broadcast advertisements for its products, which included Cheerios and Wheaties. In 1933, Wheaties began sponsoring broadcasts of professional baseball games, eventually growing to a network of 95 stations. General

Mills sponsored other radio programs during the 1930s and 1940s, a period known as the Golden Age of Radio. General Mills' aggressive entry into radio advertising helped it become the last major entrant in the breakfast cereal industry.

Another innovator in the use of radio was Franklin Delano Roosevelt (FDR), who served as U.S. president from 1933 until his death in 1945. Not only was FDR the nation's longest serving president, his time in office was among the most difficult in American history, as the nation endured the Great Depression through the 1930s, followed by World War II. Roosevelt used radio to broadcast a series of what he called "Fireside Chats." Roosevelt gave 31 of these broadcasts between 1933 and 1944. Although Roosevelt had been educated at Harvard and came from a family with great wealth and an impressive pedigree, he purposely used simple language to address the nation; 80% of his broadcasts were spoken in the 1,000 most commonly used words in American English.[1] While this use of the media by a political figure is commonplace today, Roosevelt was the first to engage the public effectively through use of the mass media.

Roosevelt died a few weeks before World War II ended in 1945. The end of the war also ended the Golden Age of Radio. Although television technology had been under development during the 1930s, the Great Depression meant that few consumers could afford a television. Research and development of telecommunications equipment flourished during World War II, but the focus of this work was on military applications. Although Americans easily found employment during the war, there were few consumer goods available on which to spend their paychecks. The end of the war led to a confluence of consumer demand and the availability of television.

Radio in the television era

The FCC adopted rules for the current configuration of the FM (frequency modulation) radio band after World War II. This, however, was not the greatest postwar change for the radio industry. Once the war was over, telecommunication manufacturers and broadcast companies could turn their attention to television in earnest. NBC, CBS, and the new ABC began developing television networks. Many of the old radio comedies and dramas moved to television. Radio station owners were understandably concerned. Fortunately for the radio industry, although new television technology posed a threat, new transistor technology soon came to the rescue.

During the earlier part of the twentieth century, radios were relatively large and costly. The invention of the transistor in 1947 by Bell Labs allowed radios to be made much smaller and much less expensively, which also made them portable. The post–World War II youth movement, and increased mobility thanks to the spread of automobiles and roads after the war, generated significant demand for portable radios. However, many American firms focused on military and other government applications of transistors. This allowed Sony of Japan, which purchased a license from Bell Labs in the early 1950s, to develop the first "pocket radio." Another important development in commercial radio was the FCC's adoption of FM stereo technology in 1961, which allowed for better quality sound.

The years following World War II were the peak of the Baby Boom, with over 78 million children born in the United States between 1946 and 1964. This increase in young people created a substantial youth movement in the country, and young people like music. Todd Storz, owner of radio stations in the Midwest, noticed that young people liked to listen to certain popular songs repeatedly. Storz responded by creating Top 40 radio, for which a broadcaster identifies the 40 most popular songs of the day and plays them repeatedly. Originally, the list of songs drew from the sales of single records in stores. Not all radio stations could compete for the same listeners, so broadcasters began experimenting with different music formats. Today, Top 40 is more commonly known as *contemporary hit radio*, as many stations play a song rotation that is closer to 20 songs than 40.

Radio introduced many Americans to rock and roll in the 1950s. One of the most influential disk jockeys to popularize rock and roll was Alan Freed, who worked in Cleveland. The Rock and Roll Hall of Fame is located in Cleveland due in part to the role that Freed played in popularizing this type of music. Rock's origins were in African American music, often called "race music" at the time. Many African American musicians credit Freed for helping to advance race relations during a time when those relations were particularly under stress. Many white Americans found rock and roll to be offensive, in part because its name was slang for sexual activity, but were also uncomfortable that this type of music had risen from African

American culture. Several white entertainers of the 1950s, including Pat Boone, enjoyed tremendous popularity while recording and performing songs that had been composed by African American musicians.

Many of the pioneering rock and roll musicians of the 1950s found themselves overshadowed by the "British Invasion" of the mid-1960s. The Beatles' "I Want to Hold Your Hand" debuted on American radio stations in early 1964 and quickly became the #1 song in the nation. The band made its first American television appearance on "The Ed Sullivan Show" on February 9 of that year. The ensuing Beatlemania focused on not only the band's music, but also their unusually long hair for the time and their fashion sense. Other bands that characterized the British Invasion include the Rolling Stones and the Kinks.

Radio today

Radio station ownership takes two basic forms. *Owned and operated* (O&O) stations are owned by major radio networks, such as CBS. Networks produce relatively little program content compared to earlier periods, and today the term "network" indicates common ownership rather than common programming. *Affiliates* are radio stations owned by other media firms. The FCC has historically limited the number of radio stations that a network can own, in an effort to allow for a diversity of viewpoints and choices among broadcasters. However, over the years, the FCC has eased it ownership restrictions, and large corporations currently own most of the nation's most-listened-to stations. Generally, radio stations located east of the Mississippi River today start with the call letter "W," such as WNBC in New York, and with a "K" west of the Mississippi River, such as KABC in Los Angeles.

Although a handful of large firms own most of the radio stations in the nation's largest markets, numerous music formats compete for listeners today. While some stations rely on their own programming decisions, most now turn to outside program consultants. It is not uncommon to see some of the same songs on different format playlists. However, with the exception of some college radio stations and some other not-for-profit broadcasters (generally found on "the left of the dial" in the 80 and lower 90 MHz range) most stations today strictly adhere to their identified format. If they are

Active rock	Dance (Dance Top 40)
Adult album alternative (AAA)	Hot adult contemporary (Hot AC)
Adult contemporary music (AC)	Mainstream rock
Adult hits	Middle of the road (MOR)
Album rock/Album oriented rock (AOR)	Modern rock
Alternative rock	Progressive rock
Classic hits	Psychedelic rock
Classic rock	Rhythmic adult contemporary
College radio	Soft adult contemporary (Soft AC)
Contemporary hit radio (formerly Top 40)	Urban contemporary

Figure 5.2 Some of the common radio rock formats.

disappointed with listenership numbers or advertising sales, they may simply change formats until they find one that works. The list in Figure 5.2 includes just a few of the rock formats that radio stations play today. Of course, the definition of "rock" itself is subject to debate.

One of the most significant format changes in radio was the growth of talk radio. In 1987, the FCC discontinued its Fairness Doctrine, which had required broadcast licensees to provide balanced coverage on issues that are determined to be of public importance. Although the U.S. Supreme Court had decided in 1969 that the Fairness Doctrine was constitutional, the presidential administration of Ronald Reagan (1981–1988) claimed that the Doctrine violated the First Amendment rights of the owners of radio and television stations. The end of the Fairness Doctrine resulted in the rise of politically conservative talk radio personalities. These include Michael Savage, Bill O'Reilly, and Rush Limbaugh. Limbaugh has proven to be the most popular, with a salary estimated at more than $30 million a year.

Broadcast radio as we know it is now called *terrestrial radio* by those in the radio industry, to distinguish it from satellite and Internet radio. XM (2001) and Sirius (2002) began operations as the first American satellite radio firms. The business model of satellite radio differs from broadcast radio in much the same way that cable television differs from broadcast television. While broadcast radio is free, with radio stations relying on advertising revenue for profits, satellite radio programming has little or no advertising, relying on monthly or yearly subscription sales for revenue. Thus far, satellite radio has yet to generate a profit in the United States. In 2008, the FCC, which regulates satellite bandwidth, allowed Sirius to acquire XM. The FCC's approval came despite significant protests from those who pointed out that when the FCC gave the two companies satellite licenses in 1997, it was under the express condition that neither firm could acquire the other. The FCC dropped that stipulation, accepting the merging firms' argument that they were not creating a monopoly, as the Internet and other media offer listeners many competing sources for music and other radio programs. At the end of 2008, the newly merged Sirius XM reported nearly 19 million subscribers.

Sirius's management has been widely criticized for, some critics think, overpaying Howard Stern. Stern reportedly received a $500 million contract from Sirius in 2004, including $80 million in annual salary. Ironically, Stern received what was then about $200 million worth of Sirius stock, the value of which is a mere fraction of that amount today. Stern's fame came from his career as a so-called *shock jock*, a disk jockey who may or may not actually play music, but uses much of his airtime to engage in conversations that are meant to please some by offending others. Stern's discussion of sexual activity and excretory activity (sometimes discussed together) drew a series of fines from the FCC that totaled $2.5 million when Stern was broadcasting over terrestrial FM radio networks; the fines were actually paid by his employers. Some observers say that Stern lost his edge when he moved to satellite radio, which is not subject to the FCC's decency requirements. Now that Stern essentially has no rules to break, much of the tension that his listeners found attractive when Stern's program aired on FM radio is missing.

Internet radio today is a combination of terrestrial and satellite radio stations adding Internet access to their programming, as well as firms that stream music exclusively through the Internet. Because the Internet has a global reach, Internet radio is accessible throughout the world.

One of the controversies swirling around Internet and satellite radio has been the structure of the royalty rates that Internet and satellite radio providers must pay to copyright holders. Under current U.S. law, terrestrial radio stations pay copyright royalties to the publishers of a song for its composition (musical notes and lyrics) but do not have to pay performance royalties for the songs they play. Thus, an old Beatles song played on a terrestrial radio station would yield revenue for the estate of Michael Jackson, one of the owners of that song's publishing rights. However, the terrestrial radio station would not have to pay royalties to any of the living Beatles (or the estates of the deceased Beatles) for performance rights. Yet if that old Beatles song is played on satellite or Internet radio, royalties must be paid to both the holder of publishing rights and the holder of performance rights. Understandably, the owners of Internet and satellite radio providers find this to be unfair. The disparity persists, however, while all interested parties continue to debate the subject.

Although today over 90% of American teens report listening to the terrestrial radio each week, the percentage of teens who say this has dropped gradually but consistently over the past decade or so, and people older than 25 years old are actually more likely to listen to the radio than are teens.[2] This may represent a pattern, in which terrestrial radio's audience begins to skew increasingly older as young people continue to turn to alternative channels for listening to music, such as the Internet and personal music playing devices.

A brief history of the music industry

While Gutenberg's popularization of movable type in the 1400s reduced the cost of printing documents that would include sheet music, the most significant expansion of the sheet music business occurred during the Industrial Revolution. The American Industrial Revolution that began in the nineteenth century enabled manufacturers to mass-produce musical instruments, which reduced the cost of making those instruments and made them more affordable to consumers. The affordability of musical instruments fueled the sale of sheet music, which was the only recorded form of music at the time. Sheet music became such a popular item that it could be found not only in music shops, but also at general stores and other merchants. The mass distribution of musical instruments and sheet music industry meant that an increasing number of people not only learned to play music, but that even more people were able to hear music in their home. Many social critics cheered the spread of music and musicianship as a sign of an increasingly civilized population.

The trade magazine *Billboard* began publishing charts of bestselling sheet music in 1913. The center of the American music publishing industry developed along 28th Street in New York City, which became known as Tin Pan Alley. The sale of sheet music to amateur musicians continues today, although in most of the twentieth century, the music industry's revenue came chiefly from sales of musical recordings.

In 1914, music composers and publishers joined to form the American Society of Composers, Authors, and Publishers (ASCAP). ASCAP works to protect the legal right to be paid for public performances of music created and distributed by its members. ASCAP began collecting royalties from radio broadcasters in 1923, although many of ASCAP's members viewed radio as a threat, as record sales dropped dramatically during the 1920s while radio listenership increased during that period.

Other copyright royalty groups came into being. Broadcast Music, Inc. (BMI) began in 1939, focused on styles of music that were seen as less conventional than those of ASCAP composers; BMI's early roster of songwriters included a large number who wrote blues, country, and jazz. The Society of European Stage Authors and Composers (SESAC) was founded in 1930 and later expanded into the U.S. market. These groups sell licenses to radio and television broadcasters, Internet sites, as well as restaurants, clubs, and lounges—anywhere live or recorded music is played for commercial purposes. While some businesses have argued that they do not really profit from playing music, the licensing associations reply that if a business plays music, there must be a commercial purpose for doing so.

Recorded music's early history

Thomas Edison's invention of the phonograph in the late 1870s allowed consumers to obtain audio recordings of music for the first time. The initial sound quality would be considered awful by today's standards, but Edison and others brought continuous improvements to recorded music. Consumer acceptance of the 78 revolutions per minute (rpm) phonograph record in the 1920s made it the first widely available and relatively standard form of recorded music. Because these 10-inch-wide records could contain little more than three minutes of music per side, the length of the average song, which until that time had been much longer, was shortened to fit the new recording format. Jazz music, which originated among African Americans, benefited from the spread of musical recordings, as well as the advent of radio broadcasting. Although many Americans lived far away from places where jazz was played (or perhaps were afraid to visit such places at the time), the ability to listen to jazz on the radio and obtain jazz recordings locally allowed that new form of music to gain popularity across the country. As Figure 5.3 signifies, the African American influence in music continues today.

After World War II, two of the nation's largest recording companies, Columbia and RCA Victor, briefly engaged in what some called the "war of the speeds." Columbia introduced a 33 1/3-rpm record, while RCA Victor promoted a 45-rpm record. By the early 1950s, industry practice adopted the 33 1/3-rpm format for long playing records (LPs) and the 45-rpm format for singles, which would contain a "B side" song on the reverse.

One of the most important innovations in recorded music was the invention of multitrack recording in the mid 1950s. Previously, many musical recordings were done live, with all musicians performing simultaneously.

Figure 5.3 Just as jazz musicians introduced African American culture to many Americans in the early days of radio, the presence of African American culture remains important in American music today. *Source*: iStockphoto

Guitarist Les Paul (for whom the famous Gibson Les Paul guitar is named) was the first to use multitrack recording in the studio. This new technology allowed individual instruments and voices to be recorded separately, and then later mixed together.

While phonograph records were portable, playing them while moving was impractical, as they relied on the use of a stylus arm, which needed to be steady and level when used. The increasing interest among consumers to play recorded music on the go led manufacturers to develop different types of magnetic tape products. The eight-track tape was the first truly portable recorded music product to gain popularity, particularly for use in automobiles, and remained so from the mid-1960s until the 1970s, when the more durable and more practical cassette tape replaced it. In 1979, Sony introduced the Walkman; having popularized the portable personal radio twenty years earlier, Sony pioneered the first personal stereo listening device to play cassette tapes. One of the key impacts that the Walkman had on music is that people could now take their own choices of music with them almost anywhere they wanted to go. Although we may take this for granted today, this new technology posed a threat to the broadcast radio industry, as time spent listening to one's own music is time not spent listening to radio.

Recorded music today

The music recording business experienced another revolution with the advent of digital recording. This eliminated the need to record instruments through microphones, as electronic signals could be sent directly from the instrument to the recording device. The recording device itself no longer needed to use a magnetic tape. Digital recording made the process of creating recorded music much less expensive, and greatly reduced the need for large-scale professional recording studios. Many professional musicians, who previously would have had to pay hundreds of thousands, even millions, of dollars to record in a professional studio, built studios in their own homes for a fraction of the cost.

While digital technology has benefited some segments of the music industry and provided challenges to other segments, the greatest impact of digital recording was digital uploading and downloading of music recordings. From the time of Edison's invention of the phonograph in the 1870s until the 1990s, the recorded music industry had an established paradigm.

A *paradigm* is a common way of doing something or thinking about something. Under the traditional recorded music purchasing paradigm, a customer would go to a store and buy recorded music in a tangible form, whether it was the shellac 78 rpm records of the 1920s, the vinyl single and long-playing records of the 1950s and 1960s, cassette tapes of the 1970s and 1980s, or the compact disk of the 1990s. Consumers often recorded other consumer's recorded music, but the quality of that second-hand recording left much to be desired. The digitization of music destroyed the century-old paradigm for obtaining recorded music. Paradigms can last for many centuries, or they can be much more short-lived. When the common way of doing something or thinking about something changes, this is a *paradigm shift*.

Much of the recorded music industry failed to anticipate the paradigm shift away from a packaged product sold in a bricks and mortar store to a digital file available for download from the Internet. Large bricks and mortar chains such as Tower Records and Virgin MegaStores are now gone. Mike Dreese, president of Newbury Comics, the largest independent record store chain in the United States, said, "I don't see traditional music retail stores surviving past maybe seven or eight more years." Dreese made that comment in 2006.[3] However, the Recording Industry Association of America (RIAA) website still features an article entitled, "The CD: A Better Value Than Ever."[4] It does not seem that the market agrees with the RIAA, as the CD continues to lose market share to digital downloads.

The International Organization for Standardization (ISO) is an international consortium of manufacturers who try to avoid such conflicts as the "the war of the speeds" of the 1940s. The ISO created the Moving Pictures Expert Group (MPEG) in 1988, in an effort to generate standards for digital compression of audio and video recordings. In 1991, the MPEG-1 Audio Layer 3 (MP 3) standard was formally adopted. Compression of digital data allows for relatively rapid uploading and downloading of compressed files. In addition to speed, MP3's can be recorded and rerecorded repeatedly without significant loss of sound quality, unlike previous methods of recording by consumers. Although many households had dial-up Internet service that relied on phone lines in the late 1990s, it was the move to broadband Internet service in the early twenty-first century that drove the increased use of the Internet to obtain musical recordings, whether legally or illegally.

On April 3, 2008, Apple announced that its iTunes music selling service had become the nation's largest retailer of music, surpassing Wal-Mart. Apple stated that it had sold more than four billion songs in less than five years, and had over 50 million customers. Apple also boasted that iTunes maintains a catalog of more than six million songs.[5]

For the first seven years of iTunes, Apple's strategy for its pricing of songs was a simple one. The company did not make much money from sales of the songs on iTunes. The great majority of a song's price went to the holder of the rights to that song. Because of *digital rights management (DRM)* technology, iTunes could only be played on Apple's iPod, which has been a particularly profitable item for Apple. Apple essentially sold the songs as a loss leader. A loss leader is an attractive item that a seller offers at little-to-no profit, perhaps even a loss, to draw buyers toward the products that are profitable for the seller. Often, as was the case of iTunes, the buyer of the loss leader may become a captive market for the more profitable product. If a music lover owned a collection of iTunes, and wanted to put those songs on a personal listening device, one had to purchase an iPod.[6] However, in January 2009, Apple announced that it would discontinue use of the DRM. It also reconfigured its pricing strategy, so instead of all songs being uniformly priced at 99 cents each, they would vary in price, with newer songs priced at $1.29, and older songs priced at 69 cents, with other songs priced somewhere in between.

The popularity of iTunes demonstrates another significant paradigm shift in how music is sold and thought about. While many musicians have agreed to have their music sold on iTunes and similar digital download services, some musicians and listeners alike have complained about what they call "the death of the album." Many traditional albums were merely a collection of songs gathered together for sale, often including "filler" or lesser quality songs added to fill an album with the traditional minimum of 12 songs. However, some artists proudly produced *concept albums* in which the songs were written and organized around a central theme. Famous concept albums include The Beatles' "Sgt. Pepper's Lonely Hearts Club Band" (1967), Willie Nelson's "Red Headed Stranger" (1975), and Green Day's "American Idiot" (2004). While concept albums may become rare in the future, certain themes have dominated rock music over the years, and will likely continue to do so.

Sex, drugs, and rock and roll

The themes of sex, drugs, and rock and roll are popular among many young people, and young people are the most important age demographic for most recorded music companies. Responding to criticism from members of Congress, parents' groups, and others, in 1990 the RIAA adopted a policy for placing parental advisory stickers on music recordings that contain "strong language or depictions of violence, sex, or substance abuse to such an extent as to merit parental notification."[7] Wal-Mart, the world's largest retailer, leads the United States in the sale of many categories of merchandise, including clothing, groceries, and for a number of years was the nation's top seller of recorded music. Wal-Mart does not sell recordings that carry parental advisory stickers (see Figure 5.4 for a parental advisory sticker). In response, many musicians, wanting to have their recordings sold by one of the world's largest retailers, have released edited versions of their recordings.

Others, however, have resisted. In May 2009, Green Day's "21st Century Breakdown" topped the charts. Green Day declined to release an edited version of the recording, and Wal-Mart refused to carry it. Green Day's Billy Joe Armstrong said of Wal-Mart's edict, "They want artists to censor their records in order to be carried in there. We just said no. We've never done it before. You feel like you're in 1953 or something." A Wal-Mart spokesperson replied, "As with all music, it is up to the artist or label to decide if they want

Figure 5.4 Parental advisory sticker. *Source:* Recording Industry Association of America

to market different variations of an album to sell, including a version that would remove a PA rating. The label and artist in this case have decided not to do so, so we unfortunately cannot offer the CD."[8] Wal-Mart's ability to serve as a private censor may decline as Wal-Mart is challenged by new methods for distributing recorded music.

The future of recorded music

The success of Apple's iTunes has not gone unnoticed by musicians and the recorded music industry. It is likely that more digital download sites will continue to appear on the Internet, legal or illegal. Many musicians already have their own websites, or use social networking sites such as MySpace to distribute information about the musician and provide access to their music. Many question whether music really needs music labels anymore; many of those who work for music labels are wondering the same thing. In years past, many musicians would attempt to get the attention of the big labels, hoping to earn a contract. Record label contracts often provided "up front" money to help the musical act pay to record its album. Record labels would then use their marketing departments to promote the new artist, promoting the new album in stores, and if the label thought the new artist's sound was right, would use its representatives to try to get that artist's songs played on the radio. Many artists found over the years that whether or not their songs got played on the radio could either make or break them. Today, the methods for selling music and making a living as a musician are changing.

In 2004, Chris Anderson, the editor-in-chief of *Wired* magazine, popularized a term, the *long tail*. This means, Anderson says, that the future of business is selling less of more. As music lovers' tastes continue to diversify, and the channels for obtaining music continue to multiply, it is unlikely that we will see future music artists sell nearly as many recordings as did the Beatles or Elvis Presley. However, because the Internet and new media provide so many ways for musicians to deliver their music to listeners, there may be more choices of music in the future. As discussed in Chapter 10, one of the future trends across the entire range of the mass media is a process called *disaggregation*.

A record store of the 1990s stocked only a finite number of records and tapes, based on the physical limitations of the space it occupied. If the store operated at a popular mall, that space was quite expensive, and the store's managers had to make important decisions about which records to stock. Thus, it was common that the already top selling artists, who likely enjoyed significant radio play of their music, received the most attention from the record stores, while lesser-known artists had a hard time of ever becoming known. The recorded music industry was relying on its most popular artists to effectively subsidize new artists, who often ended up selling relatively few albums, losing money for their label before the label ultimately dropped them (often after the artist's first album).

Many artists today are no longer concerned about attracting record label support nor gaining broadcast radio airtime. They can release their music directly to iTunes and other Internet portals without the need for major label support. Websites that sell digital downloads only need one copy of each song or album that they offer, and each song takes up only a small amount of digital storage. They do not need to worry about physically storing large numbers of physical items, as "bricks and mortar" retailers had to. Because a digital downloading site can store literally every song ever recorded digitally, it does not have to worry about focusing on only the best-selling artists. While the royalties paid to the most popular artists may be higher than those paid to less popular artists, these royalties only have to be paid after the downloading site actually sells the song to listeners.

While in the past, there were only a limited number of channels through which musicians could get their music to the public, with a literally finite number of terrestrial radio stations, relatively few successful music labels, and comparatively few music retailers, the landscape today has changed. Several of the nation's largest music retailers have gone out of business. CDs are decreasing in sales while digital downloads are increasing, and the number of songs illegally downloaded each year is in the billions. The recorded music industry knows that it needs to reinvent itself.

In 2005, the alt-metal group Korn entered into a relatively new type of arrangement with its record label, EMI. While traditionally, a label would earn money from a band only through record sales, Korn allowed EMI to share in other revenue sources, including merchandise sales, tour income, and licensing revenue. In exchange, EMI gave Korn $15 million upfront, as well as the promise to support the band through its marketing department.[9] Korn may have been the first major American music act to enter into this type of agreement, called a *360 deal*, but it will not be the last. The 360 deal is now mandatory for all new music artists who sign with Warner Music Group, one of the world's largest recorded music labels, and established artists will likely be asked to enter into such arrangements when their recording contracts come up for renewal.

As many professional musicians know today, the key to making a living from their music is not by selling their songs; it is, increasingly, other revenue streams. While nearly anyone who wants to can illegally download musicians' entire recording catalog without paying a penny, musicians can still sell concert tickets, t-shirts, and bumper stickers to fans. Musicians can also license performance rights to their songs to those who produce television shows, movies, and advertisements. Or video games. Aerosmith, which has sold more than 66 million albums over the band's long career, reportedly generated more revenue from the Activision videogame "Guitar Hero: Aerosmith" than from any of its albums.[10] In May 2009, Aerosmith entered into an agreement with GTECH, a lottery ticket supplier, to license its song "Dream On" for a series of scratch tickets. In addition to the usual cash prizes, players can win Aerosmith concert tickets, backstage passes, and memorabilia.

Radio and music and careers

The U.S. Bureau of Labor Statistics tells us that jobs for broadcast technicians and sound engineering technicians are expected to grow 12 and 9 percent respectively between 2006 and 2016.[11] However, jobs in radio operating will decline as radio station owners continue to centralize their operations.

There is no best way to become a professional musician. Some musicians attend music school and take private lessons to learn their craft. Others learn through trial and error in their bedroom or garage. Not surprisingly, the Bureau of Labor Statistics finds that many musicians work "in cities in which entertainment and recording activities are concentrated, such as New York, Los Angeles, Las Vegas, Chicago, and Nashville."[12] The Bureau anticipates that job growth for musicians will be about the same as most occupations.

Questions for critical thinking and discussion

1. With the disaggregation of the recorded music industry, and with thousands of music portals available to consumers, does the music industry need record labels anymore?

   • Explain why or why not.

2. When Sirius asked the FCC to allow it to acquire XM in 2008, many voiced concerns that this would create a monopoly, as Sirius and XM were the only two satellite radio stations in the United States. Sirius argued that this would not be a monopoly, as satellite radio has to compete with other media that provide music to listeners.

   • Explain whether you find Sirius's argument convincing or not.

3. Certainly, the most significant trend in popular music during the past 10 years has been the rise of rap/hip-hop.

   • Why do you think that this style of music has had so much success and influence?

4. A musical artist is eligible for induction into the Rock and Roll Hall of Fame 25 years after the release of their first recording.

   • Which musical artist or group that has come onto the scene within the past five years will most likely become known as one of the true greats in the history of popular music? Why?

5. In the twentieth century, music lovers often discovered new musicians and new music by listening to the radio.

   • What is the best source for discovering new musicians and new music today?
   • For the source that you identified above, who, if anybody, is profiting?
   • Will this source continue to be important for promoting new musicians and new music in the future? Explain why or why not.

Additional resources

American Society of Composers, Authors, and Publishers, www.ascap.com

Anderson, Chris, *The Long Tail; Why the Future of Business is Selling Less of More* (New York: Hyperion, 2006).

Bordowitz, Hank, *Dirty Little Secrets of the Record Business: Why So Much Music You Hear Sucks* (Chicago, IL: Chicago Review Press, 2007).

Broadcast Music, Inc., www.bmi.com

Keith, Michael C., *The Radio Station; Broadcast, Satellite, and Internet*, 8th ed., (Burlington, MA: Elsevier, 2010).

Kot, Greg, *Ripped: How the Wired Generation Revolutionized Music* (New York: Scribner, 2009).

Knopper, Steve, *Appetite for Self-Destruction: The Spectacular Crash of the Record Industry in the Digital Age* (New York: Free Press, 2009).

Krasilovsky, M. William, Sidney Shemel, John M. Gross, and Jonathan Feinstein, *This Business of Music*, 11th ed. (New York: Nielsen Business Media, 2007).

Kusek, David, and Gerd Leonhard, *The Future of Music; Manifesto for the Digital Music Revolution* (Boston: Berklee Press, 2005).

Millard, Andre, *America on Record: A History of Recorded Sound* (Cambridge: Cambridge University Press, 2005).

National Association of Broadcasters, www.nab.org

Radio Business Report, www.rbr.com/radio/index.1.html

Recording Industry Association of America, www.riaa.org

Rock and Roll Hall of Fame, www.rockhall.com

Print Media

6

Chapter contents

Issues and trends in print media

- New media competitors are threatening the survival of many newspapers.
- Although many of the most popular consumer magazines are losing readership, trade magazines aimed at readers working in specific occupations and specialized consumer magazines aimed at smaller groups of readers with particular interests continue to do well.
- Magazines and newspapers are increasingly relying on electronic versions to maintain readership.
- The field of book publishing has consolidated, and the industry is now dominated by a relatively small group of large corporations owning most of the best-known publishing firms.
- Competition in the bookselling industry has contracted, with big box stores such as Barnes & Noble and Borders, as well as the online bookseller Amazon dominating the field.
- The interactivity of electronic media allows electronic versions of print publications to customize their editorial content and advertising based on the demographic and psychographic characteristics of each reader.

This chapter focuses on newspapers, magazines, and books. All three of these print media—comprised of ink on paper that must be physically delivered to readers—are experiencing significant changes in an increasingly electronic age. Newspapers in particular are facing an uncertain future.

Newspapers

A brief history of newspapers

Benjamin Harris of Boston published *Publick Occurrences, Both Foreign and Domestick*, in September 1690. While Harris is noted for publishing the first American newspaper, he published only a single issue, as the British colonial government forced him to cease publication immediately. The first regularly published newspaper in America was John Campbell's *Boston News-Letter*, printed from 1702 through 1776.

One of the most important events of early American newspaper journalism was the trial of John Peter Zenger, publisher of *The New York Weekly Journal*. In the early 1730s, Zenger published articles that criticized the colonial governor of New York. During the trial of Zenger for seditious libel in 1735, his attorney, future first Secretary of the U.S. Treasury, Alexander Hamilton, asked the jury to question the validity of the sedition law rather than Zenger's admitted violation of it. The jury acquitted Zenger, and the concept of freedom of the press began to develop more than 50 years before the First Amendment became law.

American newspapers throughout most of the 1700s published only several hundred copies at a time. When the American Industrial Revolution began in the 1800s, huge number of people moved to the cities from the rural United States and from abroad, creating larger markets for local newspapers. The Industrial Revolution not only created a flood of consumer goods and the need for mass marketing, but also produced tremendous advances in printing technology. The economies of scale that mass manufacturers were exploiting also benefited publishers. Some big city newspaper publishers decided to sell their papers for a penny a copy in order to generate large readerships, attractive to advertisers.

The late 1800s brought a newspaper era known as the age of *yellow journalism*. The term itself derived from "The Yellow Kid," a popular comic strip of the time (see Figure 6.1).

Figure 6.1 Yellow Kid.

The two newspapers that characterized the height of yellow journalism were Joseph Pulitzer's *New York World* and William Randolph Hearst's *New York Journal*. Often appealing to readers' baser instincts, yellow journalists exploited whatever scandals and crises were the events of the day.

If a crisis did not exist, yellow journalists were willing to create one. On February 15, 1898, the American battleship the *U.S.S. Maine* exploded while anchored in the harbor of Havana, Cuba, killing over 250 members of its crew. Although the cause of the explosion remains unclear today, American newspaper journalists quickly blamed the Spanish government for the loss of the *Maine* and its crew as an act of sabotage. (Cuba was a Spanish colony at that time.) Hearst sent the famous artist Frederick Remington to sketch the scene for his newspapers. When Remington reportedly wired, "There is no war. Request to be recalled," Hearst allegedly responded, "Please remain. You furnish the pictures, I'll furnish the war."[1] Although this exchange may be more legend than truth, the newspapers stoked enough furor among U.S. voters that Congress and President William McKinley responded by effectively declaring war against Spain.

While the Spanish-American war lasted only four months and had a relatively small death toll among American soldiers and sailors, many historians argue that it was a war that would never have begun if it had not been for the yellow journalists. According to some modern critics, yellow journalism still exists today, with sensationalism and appeals to emotion often emphasized over unbiased reporting.

The first half of the twentieth century saw a period of continued growth for newspapers, which relied heavily on local advertising for their profits. Most major American cities could support two or more daily newspapers, and even the smallest communities could support a weekly newspaper. In most communities, newspapers were the most important advertising medium for local businesses, particularly retailers.

The rise of commercial radio in the 1920s and 1930s, followed by the arrival of television after World War II brought challenges to the newspaper industry, and the percentage of American adults who read a daily newspaper has dropped gradually but steadily. In 1964, over 80 percent of American adults read a daily newspaper; today, less than half do.[2]

Newspapers today

Form and content

Newspaper writers typically employ a writing style known as the inverted pyramid, which places the most important elements of a story at the beginning, with less important information placed toward the bottom. The inverted pyramid serves several functions. First, it accommodates readers who want brief synopses of news as they quickly scan a newspaper. Second, it allows editors to shorten an article by deleting material from the end of the article without removing the most important parts of the article.

This second function is particularly useful for *wire stories*, an old expression for news and feature stories that are obtained from news services. In addition to their own reporting staff, many newspapers subscribe to these news services to provide national and international news. Among the most important news services are Reuters and the Associated Press (AP). Reuters began in London in 1851 and was acquired by the Thomson Corporation of Canada in 2008. The AP is an American cooperative owned by about 1,500 newspapers. AP writers and photographers contribute their news, feature stories, and photographs for use by AP members. Broadcasters and newspapers outside the United States can purchase subscriptions to use these materials. The AP also maintains a broadcast division for media websites and television and radio stations. Newspapers also subscribe to syndicates that provide such staple items as crossword puzzles and comics.

The two most common types of articles in a newspaper are the news story and the feature story. A news story reports a recent event, and the writer will typically adopt a neutral stance. A *feature story* may provide more in-depth information about its topic, and the writer may make his or her point of view apparent. As the timeliness of news in newspapers faces increased competition from television, the Internet, and other electronic media, many observers anticipate that newspapers will focus on non-news content in the future.

Newspaper industry structure

Congress passed the Newspaper Preservation Act in 1970. Protected from antitrust concerns by this law, approximately two dozen newspapers agreed to share the cost of certain common functions such as printing and distribution. Because the newspapers maintained separate writing and editorial staff, readers still had access to diverse viewpoints among the newspapers in their communities. Joint operating agreements remain in place today in cities such as Detroit and Salt Lake City, although many of the newspapers that entered into these agreements have failed. Fewer than 10 U.S. cities have more than one newspaper today.

Many of the nation's newspapers are owned by about a handful of publishing companies, including Rupert Murdoch's News Corporation, which owns the *New York Post* and recently purchased the *Wall Street Journal*. Gannett owns *USA Today*, as well as many local newspapers and television stations. McClatchy publishes the *Kansas City Star, Miami Herald*, and *Charlotte Observer*. Hearst Corporation owns the *San Francisco Chronicle* and *Houston Chronicle*. Hearst also publishes magazines, including *Cosmopolitan* and *Esquire*, and owns more than 20 television stations. The Tribune Company owns the *Los Angeles Times* and the *Chicago Tribune*.

The top three newspapers in the United States by circulation are *USA Today*, the *Wall Street Journal*, and the *New York Times*. Each of these has national distribution.[3] Figure 6.2 shows the circulation figures for the leading newspapers in the United States.

Newspaper Name	Daily Circulation	Sunday Circulation
USA Today	2,293,310	N/A
The Wall Street Journal	2,011,999	N/A
The New York Times	1,000,665	1,438,585
Los Angeles Times	739,147	1,055,076
Daily News - New York, NY	632,595	674,104
New York Post	625,421	386,105
Washington Post	622,714	866,057
Chicago Tribune	516,032	864,845
Houston Chronicle	448,271	584,164
The Arizona Republic (Phoenix)	413,332	463,036

Figure 6.2 Top newspapers in the United States. *Source*: Data from Newspaper Association of America

When first published in 1982, *USA Today* presented its news in a manner that was then uncommon. Compared to most other newspapers, its articles were shorter, it used more color photography and graphics, and it emphasized statistical charts to highlight contemporary trends. Most other newspapers have since adopted these practices, as they have proven popular among readers.

The future of newspapers

Newspaper readership skews toward older segments of the population. A 2009 study by Scarborough Research found newspaper readership tended to be highest in cities with older populations, including cities around the Great Lakes and Florida communities with high numbers of retirees.[4] Newspapers today struggle to draw younger readers, who tend to be more attractive to advertisers than older readers are, yet are more likely to get their information from electronic media.

Since 2000, newspapers in Seattle, Denver, Cincinnati, Albuquerque, Ann Arbor, and elsewhere have quit publishing print editions, or have ceased entirely. The newspaper boxes shown in Figure 6.3 may vanish in the future. Several major newspaper publishers, including the Tribune Company, have filed for bankruptcy reorganization in recent years, and other newspapers, including the *New York Times*, have laid off employees. In March 2009, U.S. Senator Benjamin Cardin of Maryland introduced legislation that he called The Newspaper Revitalization Act. This legislation would

Figure 6.3 A vanishing site in the twenty-first century. *Source*: iStockphoto

allow newspaper publishers to operate as not-for-profit businesses exempt from corporate income taxes. In exchange for this preferential tax treatment, newspapers would no longer be able to make political endorsements. "We are losing our newspaper industry," Cardin said. "The economy has caused an immediate problem, but the business model for newspapers, based on circulation and advertising revenue, is broken, and that is a real tragedy for communities across the nation and for our democracy."[5]

Another important change in newspaper publishing is the addition of newspaper websites. To generate traffic, many newspapers have contracted with Internet portals to allow users to link content from local newspapers to their homepages. Clicking on content links takes these Internet users to those newspaper websites, where newspapers sell advertising space, often splitting the advertising revenue with the portal provider. As Leon Levitt, Cox Newspapers' Vice President of Digital Media states, "This has changed the way we sell. We're no longer selling the *Atlanta Journal Constitution* or AJC.com. We're selling audience to advertisers and we're agnostic as to the product we sell to get advertisers that audience. That's much more of an internal change. If we're going to survive, and I believe we will, we have got to be able to do that."⁶ In late 2007, the Audit Bureau of Circulations released newspaper circulation figures that combined print and online readers for the first time.

Magazines

A brief history of magazines

The move toward compulsory education in the mid 1800s led to rising literacy rates in the United States. Large-scale expansion of rural free delivery of the mail, first begun in 1897, greatly aided magazine subscription sales. The expansion of the railroad network also facilitated broader distribution of magazines.

Advances in printing technology facilitated the use of photography in publications and encouraged advertisers to illustrate their advertisements. This new interest in illustrated advertising helped boost the size of advertisements from the small, words-only *classified* style typical in the nineteenth century to the large *display* advertisements with graphics and photography that are common today. In the process, the physical size of many magazines grew larger. Larger magazines full of illustrations spurred an already growing readership. Improved papermaking and printing technology lowered production costs, allowing publishers to sell popular magazines for as little as a dime a copy in the 1890s, less than a third of the price of most magazines only a few years before.

Between 1890 and 1905, monthly magazine circulation rose from 18 million to 64 million copies. The circulation figures for weekly publications grew from 28 million to 36 million during this period. According to one estimate, over 7,000 magazines were started in the United States between 1885 and 1905, although many of them quickly failed.⁷

The first U.S. magazine to report a circulation over 1 million was *Ladies Home Journal* in 1903.⁸ Its editor, Edward Bok, attributed the magazine's success to its ability to serve as an important source of information for its female readers about marriage, motherhood, and family life. As Bok said of himself in his autobiography, "He had divined the fact that in thousands of cases the American mother was not the confidante of her daughter, and reasoned if an inviting human personality could be created on the printed page that would supply this lamentable lack of American family life, girls would flock to such a figure."[9] One of the key reasons for the lack of connections between young women and their mothers was the urbanization of America in the late 1800s and early 1900s. Many young people left rural farms and small towns (and their families) to seek work in factories and offices in the cities. The trend of young people relying on the media as a source of information about gender roles and social customs rather than relying on one's parents continues today. Magazines such as *Cosmopolitan* and *Esquire* sell more than the clothing, cosmetics, and personal care items that their advertisers produce; they also try to sell certain attitudes and beliefs to their readers.

While the *Ladies Home Journal* claimed to be the first magazine to have a circulation over 1 million, it was almost impossible for advertisers of the time to verify that circulation figure, or the circulation figure of any other magazine or newspaper. Because it was in publishers' interest to inflate circulation figures in order to overcharge advertisers, many advertisers suspected that some publishers were lying. In 1914, a group of advertisers, advertising agencies, and publishers joined to form the Audit Bureau of Circulations (ABC). The ABC's logo appears in Figure 6.4.

The ABC's purpose then and today is to conduct independent audits of publishers' circulation figures, and report those figures to advertisers and advertising agencies.

Second class mail

As magazines enjoyed a steep rise in popularity in the late nineteenth century, their publishers placed pressure on Congress and the Postmaster General (then a cabinet-level position) to give large-scale mailers a discounted postage rate. The Post Office Act of 1879 created four classes of mail, which provided magazine publishers with a discounted postage rate, called second class. Many small town merchants opposed these new rates, as they considered the advertisements in magazines to be their economic enemy. Opponents of the new rate system argued that it was a type of

Figure 6.4 The Audit Bureau of Circulations (ABC) verifies magazine circulation figures.

corporate welfare, as it took revenue away from the government to benefit large-scale advertisers.

Many national advertisers sold directly to the public through the mail, frequently at prices lower than those charged by local merchants for similar products. Because most local merchants at the time were small business owners rather than corporate chains, they often lacked the ability to buy enough products at wholesale to receive significant quantity discounts from manufacturers. In addition, manufacturers often advertised the suggested retail price for their products that were available at local merchants' stores, undercutting those merchants' ability to price products at a more profitable price point.

Magazines today

Between 1999 and 2008, the Magazine Publishers of America (MPA) tell us that the number of regularly published magazine titles increased from under 18,000 to over 20,500. However, the number of consumer magazines decreased from 9,300 to 7,400 during this period.[10] The increase in trade magazines (aimed at readers who are in specific types of businesses) and concurrent decrease in consumer publications reflects the growing specialization of the magazine industry. Figure 6.5 displays some magazines.

In particular, single copy sales have dropped significantly among many magazines while subscription sales have been relatively flat. Consumer

Figure 6.5 Magazines. *Source:* iStockphoto

magazines rely more heavily on single copy sales than do trade publications. In 1999, the MPA reported a total magazine circulation of 372 million, not much less than the 368 million magazines reported in 2008. During this same period, however, single copy sales dropped from 62 million to 43 million.[11] Magazine publishers emphasize that many magazines have a *readership* that is much larger than *circulation* figures indicate. For example, a magazine may be read not only by its purchaser, but also by other family members or office workers. Because readership estimates are larger than verified circulation figures, it is in the best economic interest of the magazines to emphasize readership claims.

As is the case of many other media types, magazines are demonstrating a process of *disaggregation*; while there are more magazine titles in circulation today, the total circulation of magazines is declining. In other words, there are more magazines, but they have a smaller number of readers per magazine. The top three magazines have a relatively older readership, with two AARP publications, the *AARP Bulletin* and *AARP the Magazine* the leading magazines by total circulation in the United States and *Reader's Digest*, with a median reader age of 52 years, in third place.[12] Figure 6.6 shows the data from the Magazine Publishers of America on the circulation figures of the top magazines in the United States. Notice that among the 10 magazines with the highest circulation in the United States, few are read by relatively younger readers.[13]

In terms of advertising revenue, *People* is the top magazine in the United States, with sales of $899 million in 2008, a drop from advertising sales of

Magazine Name	Average Circulation (First Half 2009)
AARP the Magazine*	24,554,819
AARP Bulletin*	24,305,715
Reader's Digest	8,158,652
Better Homes And Gardens	7,634,197
National Geographic	4,708,307
Good Housekeeping	4,630,397
Woman's Day	3,933,990
Family Circle	3,932,510
Ladies' Home Journal	3,842,791
AAA Westways*	3,831,215

Figure 6.6 Circulation figures of top magazines in the United States. *Source:* Data from Magazine Publishers of America

$979 million the year before.[14] Some of this drop in advertising revenue is attributable to the economic recession that began in 2008; among the 254 titles recorded by the Magazine Publishers of America, advertising revenues dropped from $25.6 billion in 2007 to $23.6 billion in 2008, a decrease of 7.8%. Even in better economic times, the increasing number of media choices for both consumers and advertisers makes it likely that the top publications will continue to experience decreasing advertising sales in the future.

The so-called general interest magazines, once among the most widely circulated in the United States, have either gone out of print or have reinvented themselves as niche magazines. Successful magazines today must identify a very sharply defined reader profile. New magazines must distinguish themselves from existing publications. For example, when Disney decided to introduce *ESPN the Magazine* in 1998, it did not make sense to produce another sports magazine just like Time Warner's long-established *Sports Illustrated*. Instead, it targeted a younger reader than the typical *Sports Illustrated* reader, offering edgier writing and popular culture references that younger readers were more likely to embrace.

Magazines and advertising

As is true of newspapers, most magazines rely more on advertising revenue than they do on subscription and single copy sales to generate income. A common standard for measuring a magazine's success is the number of advertising pages it contains in each issue. On average, a little over 46% of magazines' content is advertising.[15]

Approximately 17 percent of the money that advertisers spend on advertising goes to national magazines.[16] National magazine advertising revenue trails television, but leads all other advertising media, including newspapers, radio, and the Internet. The top three product categories in terms of advertising spending in magazines are toiletries and cosmetics, drugs and remedies, and food and food products.[17]

Because advertisers and advertising agencies are so important to magazines, publishers strive to provide magazines that will be a comfortable fit for advertisements. This is known in the trade as *complementary copy*. For example, an advertisement for frozen cookie dough may appear across from an article about quick and easy entertaining tips. Similarly, an advertisement for men's shaving products may appear next to an article about how men can make themselves more attractive.

But this comfort level also means that magazine publishers often avoid topics that may annoy or offend advertisers. The article "Sex, Lies, and Advertising," Gloria Steinem's account of the early history of *Ms.* magazine, explains the problem:

> [The editors of *Ms.*] hear in 1980 that women in the Soviet Union have been producing feminist samizdat (underground, self-published books) and circulating them throughout the country. As punishment, four of the leaders have been exiled. Though we are operating on our usual shoestring, we solicit individual contributions to send Robin Morgan to interview these women in Vienna. The result is an exclusive cover story that includes the first news of a populist peace movement against the Afghanistan occupation, a prediction of glasnost to come, and a grass roots, intimate view of Soviet women's lives. From the popular press to women's studies courses, the response is great. The story wins a Front Page award. Nonetheless, this journalistic coup undoes years of efforts to get an ad schedule from Revlon. Why? Because the Soviet women on our cover are not wearing makeup.[18]

The management of *Ms.* decided to stop running advertising and later sold the magazine to a not-for-profit organization. For most magazines, this is not a feasible option. For most magazines to succeed, it is important that they provide an advertiser-friendly environment.

Books

A brief history of book publishing in America

Large-scale book publishing in the United States began under a cloud. Many of the most popular authors in the United States in the nineteenth century were British writers. However, until 1891, U.S. copyright law protected only American authors and considered the works of foreign authors to be in the public domain. As a result, U.S. printers could print copies of British books and sell them without paying royalties. Because British authors had no legal recourse in U.S. courts, British authors capitalized on their popularity in the United States by engaging in speaking tours. (Note that this is similar to the music industry today. Many musicians, who are losing money to illegal downloading, now rely on concert tours as their primary source of income.)

Although American authors enjoyed copyright protection within the United States in the 1800s, many had to have agents sell subscriptions to prospective readers of their books before publishers would agree to publish those books. To help sell subscriptions, authors would have sections of their books published in magazines to generate interest among readers.

The power of the book is evidenced by Harriet Beecher Stowe's *Uncle Tom's Cabin*, first published in 1852. This novel, which told the sad and compelling story of the plight of slaves, is often credited with generating critical public sentiment against slavery, leading to the Civil War and the abolition of slavery by the 13th Amendment to the U.S. Constitution. *Uncle Tom's Cabin* also may have been the best-selling American novel of the 1800s.[19]

One particularly successful type of book in the mid to late 1800s was the *dime novel*. These were targeted to younger members of the working class, and their relatively low price and themes of adventure and escape made them popular with their readership. "Wild West" themes were also prevalent, as they tapped into the allure of the frontier during the U.S.'s rapid expansion across the continent during this period.

The book industry today

As are the newspaper and magazine industries, book publishing is experiencing tremendous changes. The industry has undergone a steady process of consolidation over the past several decades. A few large corporations now own most of the better-known *imprints*, or publishing brands. For example, the German firm Bertelsmann owns Random House, one of the largest and best-known book publishing firms. Among the dozens of Random House's imprints are Bantam, Crown, Alfred A. Knopf, Doubleday, Pantheon, and Vintage.

Large corporate publishers typically produce both fiction and nonfiction titles, as well as children's titles, textbooks, and technical publications. *Forbes* magazine estimates that the book publishing industry generates about $32 billion in the United States annually, with the rest of world's book publishing industry generating another $36 billion.[20] *Forbes* estimates that booksellers receive about half of this revenue.

The bookselling industry has also changed. Many smaller bookselling chains and independent stores have gone out of business over the last few decades, and the two largest chains—Barnes & Noble (which also owns B. Dalton) and Borders (which owns Waldenbooks)—dominate the "bricks and mortar" segment of the bookselling industry. In addition, Amazon. com, which began selling books online in 1995, is now among the nation's top three booksellers, outselling Borders for the first time in 2006, and perhaps outselling Barnes & Noble in 2008.[21] Large retailers such as Wal-Mart and Target also sell significant numbers of books, but tend to stock only the best-selling titles.

Just as digital downloading of music has caused many to wonder if the music industry still needs record labels today, many are unsure if the book industry needs publishing companies. By making their work available online, either as web-based reading or as downloadable material, authors today may be able to cut out the middleman altogether. Although this also means losing the marketing support of publishers, authors may be satisfied to sell fewer copies of their books while receiving higher payments per copy sold, as authors typically receive less than $2 a copy through traditional book distribution methods. To generate interest in their work, authors may be able to offer some free content online to encourage readers to purchase other work by those authors.

While some people complain that Americans are reading less, the real issue may be that Americans are consuming books through a variety of media today. Many books are available as audio books, playable in handheld devices and automobile audio systems. The Audio Publishers Association reported U.S. sales of $331 million in 2008, with CDs accounting for 72% of the market and downloads comprising 21%.[22]

Visual versions of books in electronic forms can be read on a computer or downloaded into various mobile electronic devices. Amazon introduced its electronic book reader (or e-reader) Kindle in November 2007, and began selling the Kindle 2 in February 2009. While Amazon does not release sales figures, the Kindle has proven so popular that Amazon has had trouble meeting consumer demand. Sony also offers an e-reader, the Reader, and has partnered with Google to provide over 500,000 public domain titles available. (*Public domain* books are older works that are no longer covered

Figure 6.7 The e-reader: is this the future of books? *Source*: iStockphoto

by copyright protection.) For its part, Barnes & Noble introduced its e-reader, the Nook, in October 2009. Figure 6.7 displays one type of e-reader.

Just as downloading of music has meant that consumers can download either individual songs or entire albums, some publishers such as Harlequin are selling electronic versions of short stories in addition to books. Magazines are also available on e-readers. Manufacturers of e-reading devices have begun joining the Audit Bureau of Circulations, the organization that audits the circulation of print publications to verify readership claims for advertisers.

The future of print media

> *"The last paper edition of* The New York Times *will appear in 2018."*
> *Dick Brass, vice-president of Technology Development*
> *at Microsoft Research, 2001*[23]

Many thought that Brass overstated the future of print media at the time he made the comment. Did he? It is too early to tell. However, technology has brought significant change to the print media and their competitors over the past decade. What would it mean to the print media industry and to consumers if the future of print media was electronic?

Electronic versions of print media are less expensive to produce than printed materials. There is no need for paper or ink; there is not the expense of distributing printed materials throughout a community or the world. While there is the expense of having an electronic device to download and present electronic texts for viewing, this is an expense typically borne by the reader, not the publisher. In addition, electronic media can target their advertisements to individual readers, with advertisements targeted based on the reader's demographics or psychographics. The 19-year-old male reader of the *New York Times* will see different advertisements on his screen than will the 47-year-old female reader of the same page. The same reader may see different advertisements based on where he or she is at a particular time. The advertisements that one sees when reading an online publication while waiting at the doctor's office could be very different from the advertisements seen while flying on an overseas flight to Europe. The advertisements can also vary by time of day—a Dunkin' Donuts advertisement that appears in the morning may be replaced by a Budweiser advertisement in the evening.

Electronics firms are currently developing thin, flexible monitors that replicate the feel of a traditional print publication. These monitors, attached to a wireless Internet connection, will allow readers to hold the reading device in much the same way they hold magazines and newspapers. LG-Philips introduced one of the first versions of the flexible monitor in 2005, and others have followed. Arizona State University's Flexible Display Center, established in 2004, is researching affordable versions of flexible monitors. Many of these new generation monitors rely on organic light emitting diodes (OLEDs) which work in monitors that were once too thin to be feasible.

Print media and careers

Newspapers employ reporters, feature writers, and photographers. These employees may be full-time, or they may be part-time "stringers" who are paid by the article. Magazines also employ writers, photographers, and graphic artists. Full-time employees hold some of these positions, but many of the contributors to magazines are paid for individual projects. Editors at newspapers and magazines supervise the work of others and get their publications produced.

Graphic designers and photographers are increasingly in demand among print publications, due to consumers' increased interest in graphic presentations of information. As most magazines and newspapers now feature websites, web designers often work with print specialists to generate online content.

Circulation jobs include generating both subscription and single copy sales. Magazines that rely heavily on single copy sales are very aware that what or who is on the cover of their magazines can help sell copies. *People* relies heavily on single copy sales, and knows which celebrities help sell copies of its magazine and which are less helpful.

Printing and distribution responsibilities may be handled in-house, or contracted out to printing and distribution specialists. The move toward electronic media poses a significant threat to those in printing and distribution, while also creating demand for those with skills and training in web design and information technology.

Advertising salespeople are vital to the financial wellbeing of most magazines and newspapers. The advertising representative for newspapers tends to focus on local advertisers, while most magazines focus on national or regional advertisers. During the recession that began in 2008, many advertisers cut their advertising budget, which made the job of those in advertising sales even more challenging.

Traditionally, authors contract with literary agents to help get their books published. Literary agents' knowledge of the business allows them to assess whether an author's work is likely to be published, and if so, by whom. Agents then negotiate with publishers on behalf of their clients to obtain the best contractual terms possible. Literary agents typically charge a commission of a percentage of the book sales, usually starting at 15%. Book editors help writers produce books that are likely to be commercially successful. Many book editors also seek new writers, often through relationships with literary agents.

The U.S. Bureau of Labor Statistics estimates that there will be little job growth in the newspaper industry over the next few years. As the

Bureau tells us:

> Many factors will contribute to the limited job growth in this occupation. Consolidation and convergence should continue in the publishing and broadcasting industries. As a result, companies will be better able to allocate their news analysts, reporters, and correspondents to cover news stories. Constantly improving technology also is allowing workers to do their jobs more efficiently, another factor that will limit the number of workers needed to cover a story or certain type of news. However, the continued demand for news will create some job opportunities.[24]

The employment forecast looks better for writers and editors working in the magazine and book publishing fields. The Bureau of Labor Statistics emphasizes a theme that runs throughout the book before you: the future of mass media is carefully identified niches in the marketplace and expanded use of electronic media. As the Bureau tells us, "Print magazines and other periodicals increasingly are developing market niches, appealing to readers with special interests, and making Internet-only content available on their websites . . . Online publications and services are growing in number and sophistication, spurring the demand for writers and editors, especially those with Web experience."[25]

Journalism and publishing are not disappearing. However, electronic media will challenge some forms of print media, and print media will continue to seek out small yet profitable market niches, which other media are also seeking.

Critical Thinking: Questions about Advertising

1. If the Newspaper Revitalization Act is passed into law by the federal government, newspapers will enjoy not-for-profit tax status. However, a condition of this status would be that these newspapers would not be able to make political endorsements, as they commonly do today, for candidates for public office.

   • Would the inability of newspapers to make political endorsements be fair to the owners of those newspapers? Explain why or why not.
   • Even without political endorsements, would newspapers still be able to maintain a political agenda and make that political agenda known to its readers? Explain your answer.

(Continued)

Critical Thinking: Questions about Advertising—Cont'd

2. As mentioned in Chapter 5, radio station owners were forced to change their programming in order to survive after the introduction of commercial television. Sixty years later, newspaper owners are trying to reinvent their publications due to the challenges that the Internet and other electronic media pose. While newspapers' websites allow their owners to maintain a presence in the business of distributing news, print versions of newspapers lack the timeliness of electronic media.

   • If you were a newspaper editor, what types of content would you add or expand in your print edition in order to get readers to keep reading your paper? Explain.

3. Every fall, the American Library Association (ALA) celebrates "Banned Books Week." The banning of books is a critical issue for librarians. Some taxpayers believe that their tax dollars should not be used to purchase books that contain offensive language and extreme sexual or violent situations. The ALA replies, "Librarians and governing bodies should maintain that parents—and only parents—have the right and the responsibility to restrict the access of their children—and only their children—to library resources."[26] As it turns out, parents are the group mostly likely to challenge the books that are available in school libraries and public libraries.

   • Should parents have a say in which books are available to their children in libraries? Explain why or why not.

4. Section 215 of the USA Patriot Act gives the FBI the authority to seize the borrowing records of library patrons and sales records of bookstore customers.[27] Some have criticized this as a violation of the First Amendment's protection of free speech and press as well as the Fourth Amendment's prohibition against unreasonable searches and seizures. Others have said that this provision helps government authorities fight terrorism, as terrorists often use written material to identify targets, obtain weapons, and travel, and that law-abiding citizens should have nothing to hide.

   • Which side of the debate do you agree with—does Section 215 create an unreasonable intrusion into our rights, or is it necessary to help fight the war against terrorism?

5. Imagine that someone who lives outside of the United States is preparing to visit the United States for the first time. To prepare for the trip, they pick up some American news and fashion magazines that are available at their local newsstand.

   • Look through some news and fashion magazines. After you have done so, discuss whether they provide an accurate view of what life in the United States is really like.

Additional resources

American Booksellers Association, http://www.bookweb.org/index.html

American Booksellers Foundation for Free Expression, http://www.abffe.org/

American Society of Journalists and Authors, http://www.asja.org

Association of American Publishers, http://www.publishers.org

Audio Publishers Association, http://www.audiopub.org/

Audit Bureau of Circulations, http://www.accessabc.com

Clark, Giles, and Angus Phillips, *Inside Book Publishing*, 4th ed. (New York: Routledge, 2008).

Franklin, Bob, *The Future of Newspapers* (New York: Routledge, 2009).

Johnson, Sammye, and Patricia Prijatel, *The Magazine from Cover to Cover* (New York: Oxford University Press, 2006).

Magazine Publishers of America, http://www.magazine.org

Meyer, Philip, *Vanishing Newspaper; Saving Journalism in the Information Age* (Columbia: University of Missouri Press, 2006).

Newspaper Association of America, http://www.naa.org

Publishers Weekly, http://www.publishersweekly.com

Sumner, David E., and Shirrel Rhoades, *Magazines: A Complete Guide to the Industry* (New York : Peter Lang, 2006).

Suzanne, Claudia, *This Business of Books; A Complete Overview of the Industry from Concept Through Sales*, 4th ed. (Winston-Salem: WC Publishing, 2004).

The late John Tebbel was the leading historian of print media in America in the last century. His works include *Between Covers; The Rise and Transformation of American Book Publishing* (New York: Oxford, 1987), *The Compact History of the American Newspaper* (New York: Hawthorn, 1969), and Tebbel and Mary Ellen Zuckerman, *The Magazine in America, 1741–1990* (New York: Oxford, 1991).

7 Movies and Video

Chapter contents

Issues and trends in movies and video

- The in-home movie viewing industry is changing, as bricks and mortar video stores close, while online distribution of movies expands.
- Movie theater owners are concerned about competition generated by new in-home and mobile media technologies.
- Due to the high cost of producing major theatrical releases, most moviemakers try to stick with proven movie genres.
- The age group most likely to see a movie in a theater is those between the ages of 12 to 24; more than two-thirds of movie tickets are purchased by those under the age of 40.
- Because of the age demographics of American movie audiences, many older actors, especially older females, find it difficult to get starring roles.
- While the movie and video industries continue to grow, finding employment in them is difficult because of the large number of those seeking jobs in these industries.

Although the United States was in the midst of a significant economic recession in 2008 and 2009, the American movie industry prospered. When times get tough, people go to the movies, seeking escape.

A brief history of movies

The word photograph came into public usage in the 1830s. Moving photographs or movies became popular toward the end of the 1800s. Movies soon moved past the experimental or novelty stage and became a regular form of artistic expression and public entertainment in the early twentieth century. The first attempt to tell a story in a movie was *The Great Train Robbery* of 1903. In 1915, D. W. Griffiths' *The Birth of a Nation* appeared, and is often credited as the first American movie to attain artistic excellence, despite its racist theme.

The area of Los Angeles known as Hollywood has long been associated with the movie industry. Southern California's attraction to the new movie industry drew from its wide-open spaces (which allowed for large studios and outdoor sets) and its temperate weather, which meant that movies could be made year-round. The first permanent studio, opened in 1911, was Nestor Studio. Major studios with names that are still familiar today, including Paramount, Warner Bros., and Columbia, soon followed. By the 1920s, movie making was the dominant industry in the area. Television studios would follow in the late 1940s and 1950s.

Until the mid-to-late 1920s, all movies were silent. Instead of a soundtrack, captions explained what the actors' gestures could not.[1] Movie theaters, numbering in the thousands, relied on either recordings or live musicians to provide background music. The 1927 movie *The Jazz Singer* is often cited as the first successful talkie, or movie that included recorded dialogue. Audio technology changed the movie industry in several ways. Warner Bros., the studio that most enthusiastically embraced sound on film, grew from a mid-level studio to one of the nation's largest within a few years. However, some smaller studios lacked the capital to acquire sound technology and failed. Another negative consequence was that some actors who had weak voices or heavy accents found it difficult to continue to get acting roles. Also affected were the musicians who had played in theaters during silent movies.

Although the 1930s were the age of the Great Depression, the movie industry did well. The tough economic times led people to seek means of escape. Many movie historians see the 1930s and early 1940s as the peak of Hollywood's Golden Age. The movie industry did not yet have to compete with television, and Americans spent 20–25 percent of their recreational expenditures on movies.[2] The technical and artistic aspects of filmmaking had also grown highly proficient. Thus, the movie industry enjoyed both financial and creative success during its Golden Age.

This was also the age of the *studio system*. Actors were referred to as contract players, as they were under contract, normally for seven years, with a particular studio. If a director wanted a particular star that was not under contract to the studio the director was working for, the director's studio would negotiate with the studio holding the actor's contract to loan out that actor. Because studios had a financial interest in their contract players, studio executives attempted to control aspects of actors' personal lives. For example, gay actors such as Rock Hudson were encouraged to enter into sham marriages at a time when homosexuality was considered taboo.

During World War II, some famous actors fulfilled their military duty in studio work. Hollywood studios produced movies that glorified the nation's efforts in the war and also produced various types of propaganda. Such propaganda included Bugs Bunny cartoons that insulted Hitler. Many Americans went to movie theaters to escape the dreariness of war. Paradoxically, many also went to the theater to see the war. Short documentary movies called *newsreels* provided an important part of the movie-going experience between the late 1920s and the early 1960s. Newsreels were the only contemporary visual accounts of the news of the day. Of course, the advent of television changed that.

The perceived threat of communism, the real threat of television

In response to propaganda from Nazi Germany, Congress created the House Committee on Un-American Activities (HUAC) in 1938, before World War II. When the war ended in 1945, the committee switched its focus to communism, since many Americans saw the Soviet Union as the biggest threat to America's domestic and international interests. In 1947, HUAC began to hold hearings about the presence of Communists in the movie industry and other entertainment industries. As many of those who were called to testify before HUAC found, it was a no-win situation. If one refused to testify, he or she could be jailed for contempt of Congress. If some were brave enough to testify and admit to have been involved in activities seen as pro-communist, they were shunned socially or professionally. If those who testified "named names"—discussed the political activities of others—they were also shunned.

Fearing negative public opinion, movie executives blacklisted (refused to employ) more than 200 people, including actors, directors, and about 150 screenwriters. These people were believed to have been involved in pro-communist activities or to be protecting others who were. The fact that supporting communism was protected by the First Amendment did not matter, as the First Amendment only protects against actions by the government, not by private firms, including the movie studios. Some blacklisted figures were able to find work using pseudonyms (false names). Other used fronts or stand-ins; for example, a blacklisted screenwriter's friend would represent the screenwriter's work as his own. The effects of the blacklist slowly faded during the 1950s, although for some, especially actors who could not conceal their identity, careers were damaged or ruined.

A bigger postwar threat to the movie industry was commercial television, which became accessible to many American homes soon after World War II ended. For the first time, people could watch moving images in their homes, and often, those images were live rather than recorded. A housing shortage after the war and the introduction of the federal highway system led many Americans to move to new suburbs, relatively far from the grand old theaters downtown. The movie industry responded with changes in content and format in its efforts to compete against television. Movie themes had increasing amounts of sexual content and violence, which television at the time avoided. These themes were also popular with younger audiences, who still wanted to go out on weekends, regardless of the presence of a new television at home.

Westerns were also popular during this period. The vastness of the American west provided a large-scale spectacle that was best appreciated at a theater rather than on television. In addition, the Wild West reflected the American ideal of rugged individualism, in which the hero had to struggle against nature, his enemies, and often, himself, in order to survive.

Another effort to draw viewers away from their new televisions and into theaters was the big-budget epic movie. These included *The Ten Commandments* (1956) directed by Cecil B. DeMille, and William Wyler's *Ben-Hur* (1959). Musicals, which often included lavish dance numbers, also were common.

The movie industry also relied on color cinematography, as most Americans had only black and white television until the 1960s. Some movies relied on gimmicks such as 3-D and a variety of wide-screen formats to draw audiences. These techniques made movies more expensive to create and to exhibit, and they proved to be merely a fad.

The movie industry today

Although the world was in a severe economic recession in 2008 and 2009, industry analysts were not surprised that the movie industry did quite well. During difficult times, people seek entertainment and escape, which is what the movie industry sells. According to the Motion Picture Association of America (MPAA), U.S. movie theaters took in $9.8 billion in box office sales in 2008, while the rest of the world's movie theaters took in another $18.3 billion.[3] This represented a domestic box office record, with 1.4 billion tickets sold at an average price of $7.18 per ticket. The fact that the recession occurred worldwide also helped foreign ticket sales of exported American movies. For example, *Ice Age: Dawn of the Dinosaurs* broke box office records in Russia, Mexico, and Brazil during the summer of 2009.[4]

In 2008, 610 American movies were released, but only 162 of them were released by distributors that were MPAA members; the rest were released by independent movie distributors. Although independent releases are less likely to be shown by most major movie theater chains, some moviemakers continue to make movies that are experimental or that emphasize artistic achievement rather than commercial success. Many independent filmmakers do not seek large financial rewards. However, movies released by the major studios typically represent multi-million dollar investments, and those involved in the production and distribution of these movies are hoping for a significant financial success.

Product placement

One of the ways movie producers increase revenue is through product placement. Manufacturers of any number of consumer items pay to have their products featured in movies. Interbrand's Brand Cameo tracks movie product placement. It found that some of the most active brands placed in movies in 2009 included Apple, Budweiser, Dell, Ford, Cadillac, and Coca-Cola.[5]

Perhaps the largest controversy regarding product placement concerns tobacco. As part of the 1998 Master Settlement Agreement between American tobacco companies and 46 states, tobacco companies vowed to discontinue product placement in movies. However, many observers point to the prevalence of smoking in movies, and are concerned that even though tobacco companies claim not to be paying for product placement, that they are indeed providing some sort of financial incentive to film-makers to feature smoking. One study found that smoking is particularly prevalent in youth-oriented movies that are rated PG-13, with smoking taking place in more than 80 percent of these movies since 1998.[6] Several organizations track cigarette usage in movies, and argue that the tobacco industry is using the movie industry to coerce young moviegoers into thinking that smoking is cool.

Synergies

Some would argue that much of what a child sees in a Disney movie (especially an animated Disney movie) is essentially product placement for Disney merchandise. Before a Disney movie is released, toys, clothing, and other items based on the movie are put on sale in Disney's stores at malls, resort parks, and online. Disney has also entered into strategic partnerships with major fast food chains, with kid's meals toys based on Disney characters and advertising that ties the food chain and the Disney movie together. Here, Disney is pursuing a *synergy*—a coordinated interaction between two or more of its divisions (television, movies, merchandise, and resorts) or two or more companies (for example, Disney and McDonalds). A synergy generates a combined effect that is greater than the results those divisions or companies could have each had on their own. Of course, such arrangements are not exclusive to Disney, as other motion picture producers regularly enter into similar arrangements with fast food chains and other retailers. For example, the Subway sandwich chain promoted *Land of the Lost* and Burger King promoted *Star Trek* during the summer of 2009.

Common movie genres

When discussing types of movies, critics use the term *genre*, which is also a literary term. The most common genres in movies are comedies, action adventures, and dramas. Within each genre, there are numerous subgenres. For example, some comedies are romantic comedies; some action movies are buddy movies. Because of the substantial investment required to create movies intended for mass distribution, their producers tend to seek plots and themes with which viewers are familiar. Although there may be some unexpected events within a movie, to be "popular" a movie must be easy for a potential customer to be able to understand and describe.

Romantic comedies are often referred to as date movies because they typically lack violence and explicit sexual situations, and are unlikely to cause discomfort among a couple on a date. Romantic comedies are also often referred to as chick flicks, as they are popular with females. The romantic comedy usually introduces two people who are from very different socio-economic situations or backgrounds. For example, a female character is rich and becomes involved with a male character who is poor. A complication arises when another male character who is more socio-economically appropriate enters into the storyline. Often, the audience knows about some significant personality flaw with this third person, yet the female lead character is unaware of this flaw. In the end, love conquers all, and the seemingly unfit couple is together again.

Action adventure movies are fast moving and can often be very violent. A subgenre is the vengeance movie. In the first half-hour of the movie, bad things happen to good people. The hero or heroes, known as the *protagonist*(s), then spend the rest of the movie pursuing the bad guy (*antagonist*), who is typically killed in spectacular fashion near the end of the movie.

The buddy movie is a subgenre of action adventure movies in which two protagonists work together to resolve conflicts, often while dealing with conflicts between themselves. The conflicts between the characters frequently arise because the two characters are very different people. As movie scholar Robert B. Ray points out, one of the characters is often what is known as the "outlaw hero." This character is an adventurer, explorer, gunfighter, wanderer, and loner. He stands for self-determination and free-dom from entanglements; he is the "natural man." He may see women as the object of lust, but views any significant relationship with a woman as an impediment to his freedom. The other character is the "official hero," who may be a teacher, lawyer, politician, farmer, or family man. This character stands for collective action and objective legal process that supersedes private notions of right and wrong; he is the "civilized man." If he is involved in a romantic relationship, he sees it as desirable and fulfilling.[7]

Dramas take many forms. One of the common dramas is the disaster movie, in which a group of ordinary people is forced to deal with the aftermath of a disaster. Legal dramas typically contain situations in which a group of ordinary people find themselves at the mercy of big business or big government, and rely on the courts (or themselves) to achieve justice.

The movie industry has also given us *auteur* movies (from the French for "author") in which the directors become known for bringing their personal style to the movies they make. Examples of auteur movies include the work of Alfred Hitchcock, Quentin Tarantino, and Spike Lee.

More common today than auteur movies that feature directors are "star delivery vehicles" that feature actors. Certain top actors can draw audiences regardless of the particular movie that they appear in, and thus these movies are written to feature these stars in the types of role for which they are most famous. Major stars such as Reese Witherspoon, Will Smith, Angelina Jolie, and Johnny Depp typically command salaries of $20 million or more for a movie, plus *participation*, or a percentage of profits. Of course, predicting a movie's success is not a perfect science. Even the biggest names have been in movies that did not draw large audiences. If this happens too many times, those big names are no longer viewed by the movie industry with the same esteem.

One career challenge that no actor can avoid is growing older. According to the MPAA, the age group most likely to attend a movie is 12–24 years. Those under the age of 40 purchase more than two-thirds of movie tickets.[8] Partly because of the fact that moviegoers trend toward the younger portion of the population, older actors, especially older female actors, find it difficult to get leading roles in movies. While 45% of American women are age 40 and over, one could not tell that from watching movies and television, in which only about a quarter of female leading roles feature actors 40 and over, according to the Screen Actors Guild (SAG). Male actors age 40 and over fare better than female actors, appearing in about 40 percent of male leading roles, a couple of percentage points below the actual percentage of men age 40 or over in the United States.[9] Perhaps, then, it is no surprise that female actors often submit to cosmetic surgery, in an effort to keep themselves marketable.

The blockbuster and its progeny

The term *blockbuster* typically refers to a movie that generates box office receipts of over $100 million. However, even a blockbuster may not be particularly profitable, as some of the movies that are predicted to achieve blockbuster status may cost over $100 million to produce, and several, including *Pirates of the Caribbean: Dead Man's Chest* and *Spider-Man 2* reportedly cost over $200 million. The highest grossing movie of all time is *Avatar*, released in 2009, which had American box office sales of over $700 million, and nearly $2.7 billion worldwide.[10] Adjusted for inflation, a handful of older movies, including *Gone with the Wind*, *Star Wars*, and *The Sound of Music* would have out-grossed *Avatar*.[11] (In other words, had these older movies been released with twenty-first century ticket prices, their box office sales would have been more than those of *Avatar*.)

Of course, many successful movies are followed by sequels based on the same characters. These include the *Spider-Man 2* and *Shrek 2*. Occasionally there are "prequels," which are sequels that are set in a time before the original movie. Perhaps the best-known prequels are those in the *Star Wars* series; *Star Wars: Episode I* was released more than 20 years after the original *Star Wars*. In many cases, sequels are parts of *franchise movies*; the original movie is made with the intention of producing later movies based on the same theme or characters. Recent franchise movie series include the *Harry Potter* movies and *The Lord of the Rings* series. While some would argue that this is Hollywood giving fans what they want, others say that Hollywood does not have enough ideas for good new movies and relies on remaking different versions of the same movie. Whatever the case, almost all of the top grossing movies thus far this century are either sequels or franchise movies.

Another way to tap into the success of previous movies is to remake them. A recent example is the 2007 movie *I Am Legend* that starred Will

Smith. The storyline of this movie is essentially the same as *The Omega Man* (1971) and *The Last Man on Earth* (1964), all based on Richard Matheson's 1954 novel *I Am Legend*.

The movie rating system

Between 1930 and 1968, the major studios relied on the guidance of the Motion Picture Production Code, commonly known as the Hays Code (named after its creator, Will H. Hays) to determine appropriate content in movies. This method of self-regulation within the movie industry was devised to avoid regulation and restrictions by outside agencies or organizations, including local censorship boards. Without a certificate of approval from the Production Code Administration, a movie could not be released to the public. As a result, some movies had to be edited before being released.

The 1960s was a period of tremendous social upheaval. The MPAA knew that it needed to revamp its content rating system to reflect changing social morality, while still avoiding any efforts by the government to regulate movie content. In 1968, the MPAA, together with the National Association of Theatre Owners (NATO) and International Film Importers and Distributors of America (IFIDA), released the content rating system that is in use today, with some modifications. Figure 7.1 shows the rating system followed by the MPAA.

MPAA members voluntarily submit their movies to the MPAA for review by the rating board, which is comprised of about a dozen individuals. According to the MPAA's database, only 48 movies have been released with an NC-17 rating since 1990. Most filmmakers view an NC-17 rating as commercial suicide. This is because some theater owners will not show NC-17 rated movies, and many teenagers, the prime demographic group for most movies, could be denied admission to theaters that do exhibit NC-17 movies. Thus, on those occasions when the MPAA gives a movie an NC-17 rating for sexual content or violence, filmmakers will usually edit the movie and resubmit it to the rating board.

Eleven of the top 20 movies in box office sales for 2008 were rated PG-13, with the rest divided among G, PG, and R ratings.[12] The MPAA reports that this distribution of ratings among the 20 most successful movies has been relatively constant over the past five years.

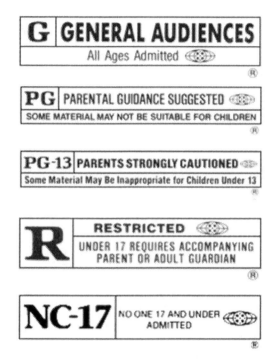

Figure 7.1 MPAA ratings. *Source:* Motion Picture Association of America

The documentary *This Film is Not Yet Rated* provides interesting insights into the MPAA's rating process: http://www.chaincamera.com/thisfilmisnotyetrated

The movie theater industry today

The trend for more than a decade is toward fewer theaters with more screens. There were 5,786 theaters operating in the United States in 2008.[13] Multiplex theaters with between two and seven screens are the most common type of theater in the United States today, with over 2,200 theaters of this size. However, this size of theater is declining in favor of multiplex theaters with at least 8 and perhaps more than 16 screens.[14] Overall, there are nearly 39,000 commercial movie screens in the United States, according to the National Association of Theatre Owners.[15] Approximately a dozen companies operate the great majority of the commercial movie screens in the

United States and Canada. The largest is Regal Entertainment, with over 6,300 screens at 527 locations.[16] There remain over 600 independent theater operators, with about 8,000 screens, in North America today.[17]

The movie theater industry has long been wary of in-home movie viewing since the introduction of home video players in the 1970s. Many theater owners worried that the home video player would effectively kill their industry. These fears proved to be unsupported, however. In hindsight, many observers believe that home video players essentially "primed the pump," as they got people into the habit of watching movies. In addition, young people still want to go out on the weekends, and theaters know that their top audience demographic is people in their teens and twenties. Consequently, each decade since 1971 has seen a steady growth in movie theater box office sales.[18]

Just as the theater industry had to differentiate itself from television viewing in the 1950s, it has made efforts recently to compete against increasingly sophisticated home entertainment systems and portable media devices. One of the most noticeable changes is the improvement of audio systems in movie theaters, which provide much cleaner sound than before, and allow for the use of multidirectional sound effects. Stadium-style seating, as seen in Figure 7.2, and improved food and

Figure 7.2 Despite home and mobile movie viewing, many still prefer the movie theater experience. *Source*: iStockphoto

beverage options are other efforts to enhance the theater experience. Recent developments in digital technology and 3-D technology may further help the theater industry compete against home viewing. NATO reports that nearly 5,700 screens in the United States now exhibit digital cinema and almost 2,100 are equipped for 3-D.[19]

Movie viewing at home today

One potential benefit for both the movie industry and movie viewers is that even if a movie is not as successful in theaters as its creators hoped, that movie can still generate revenue in the home viewing market. Indeed, some movies that are determined to be unlikely to make a profit in the theaters are released directly to video formats. For some major filmmakers, this represents disappointment tempered by an effort to recover at least some of a movie's production costs through video release.

Direct to video releases are also common as sequels to popular theatrical releases. The decision to release a sequel direct to video is based on the prominence of the earlier release, while also recognizing that the sequel will generate diminishing returns: the more enthusiastic fans of the original release will likely embrace the sequel, but few other viewers will. Examples of sequels released directly to video including several *American Pie* movies. Disney had regularly released direct to video sequels of some of its animated theatrical releases, such as *Lion King II* and *Cinderella III*, but reportedly will cease to do so, as there is a belief that lower quality sequels hurt the marketability of the original releases. On a brighter note, the ability to make money through direct-to-video releases enables small independent moviemakers to create less mainstream movies that are enjoyed by a more select audience.

As is the case with many other types of media, movie platforms are going through a paradigm shift. In the mid-1990s, various computer and electronics firms conferred with each other and agreed on the current international DVD standard. The recent rivalry between Blu-ray and HD-DVD technology to replace older DVD technology (in which Blu-ray prevailed) reminded some observers of the videotape format conflict of the early 1980s, when Sony's Betamax technology failed to gain the industry acceptance that the VHS format attained.

Piracy

All involved in the creation, distribution, and exhibition of movies are concerned about movie piracy. A basic type of piracy is simply making copies of a DVD or other optical disc and distributing them. Although the original disc usually incorporates anti-piracy technology, this technology can be hacked.

The MPAA reports that 90 percent of pirated movies are still showing in theaters and have yet to be released on disc.[20] In these cases, the pirate secretly brings a camcorder into theaters and records the movie as it is being shown. Although the quality of these pirated movies is inferior, there is still a substantial market for movies that are at the peak of their popularity. Just as legitimate commerce is increasingly global, so is movie piracy. The MPAA estimates that movie piracy costs the world's movie industry over $18 billion annually.[21]

The future of movies

Part of the explanation for the popularity of expensive home entertainment systems with large viewing screens, high-definition images, and high-fidelity audio is the aging of baby boomers (Americans born between 1946 and 1964). As this large demographic group begins to enter into senior citizenship, a process occurs that trend analyst Faith Popcorn has labeled *cocooning*. Many older consumers prefer to stay at home in the evenings and on weekends, yet they still want to enjoy the theater experience. Of course, many younger consumers also find home entertainment systems provide a good reason to stay home. Theater owners are responding to cocooning by equipping their screens with advanced visual and audio technology to provide an attractive experience for those (of all ages) who do choose to go out at night.

The future of movie viewing at home likely lies with on-demand streaming of movies as Internet service providers continue to increase their connectivity speeds. Many movie rental stores have closed due to competition from Netflix, which has been successful with its very efficient movie rental by mail system, and through streaming movies over the Internet. Netflix claimed to have 10.3 million subscribers in 2009. On-demand movies, available through cable television systems, also have hurt movie rental retailers. While Netflix has generated profits over the past few years, the nation's largest movie rental retailer, Blockbuster, suffered a net loss of $374 million in 2008. Blockbuster has closed hundreds of stores and has placed increased emphasis on direct streaming of movies to viewers' homes. In March 2009, it announced a partnership with TiVo that will deliver Blockbuster's movie library to homes through TiVo DVRs. As of late 2009, the second largest movie rental retailer, Hollywood Video and its parent company Movie Gallery, had yet to join Netflix and Blockbuster's move to online movie streaming. Movie Gallery went through bankruptcy reorganization in 2007 and has closed hundreds of stores.

Movies and video and careers

Careers in the movie industry fall into three general categories: creative, technical, and administrative. Creative careers are the most apparent, as they include acting, directing, and writing. Technical careers include pre-production, production, and post-production work. Pre-production work includes set design and construction, casting, and costumes. Production work includes not only the acting and directing, but also the efforts of the camera crew, sound crew, stage crew, and electrical crew. Post-production work includes editing, music, and adding the movie's titles. Administrative careers focus on the business end of filmmaking such as accounting, law, and human resources. Altogether, some movies use the talents and services of hundreds of people, most of whom are never seen on the screen.

The movie industry has the well-deserved reputation of being a tough business to get into. The issue is one of supply and demand; there are a far greater number of those who want jobs in the industry than there are available positions. The U.S. Bureau of Labor Statistics predicts job growth in the movie and video industry to be around 11 to 12 percent from 2006 through 2016. However, the Bureau goes on to say:

> The number of individuals interested in positions as videographers and movie camera operators usually is much greater than the number of openings. Those who succeed in landing a salaried job or attracting enough work to earn a living by freelancing are likely to be the most creative and highly motivated people, able to adapt to rapidly changing technologies and adept at operating a business. The change to digital cameras has increased the importance of

strong computer skills. Those with the most experience and the most advanced computer skills will have the best job opportunities.[22]

The situation is even tougher for those who want to appear on screen. Los Angeles is famous for the large number of aspiring actors who are waiting tables and parking cars, hoping to get their big break. For many, that big break never comes. The Bureau of Labor Statistics warns, "The large number of highly trained and talented actors auditioning for roles generally exceeds the number of parts that become available. Only performers with the most stamina and talent will find regular employment."[23] Unfortunately, many in the industry will tell you that luck usually counts more than stamina and talent. Nevertheless, a basic tenet of finance is that return is based on risk. While few aspiring actors will receive top billing in a major Hollywood production, those who do can find themselves quite wealthy. Ending on an optimistic note, the Internet, discussed in the next chapter, may provide a number of new opportunities for those who want to create and appear in entertainment media.

Questions for critical thinking and discussion

1. Violence is an element of many movies. However, there are two types of violence presented: gratuitous violence and purposeful violence. Gratuitous violence serves no purpose for the story's plot—it is simply included in movie for the sake of violence itself. Purposeful violence serves a role in the story's plot, such as when the protagonist kills the antagonist in order to protect innocent people.

    -   Is gratuitous violence "bad?" Explain why or why not.
    -   Is purposeful violence "good?" Explain why or why not.

2. Movies often reflect the common beliefs and ideals of their time. For example, movies with a distinctly anti-communist message were released during the Red Scare of the late 1940s and 1950s. Movies that cast government in a critical light were released following the Watergate scandal of the 1970s.

    -   Think about some of the movies that you have seen in the last year or two. Explain how some of those movies reflect the public opinion and sentiments of today.

3. There is no science to creating a blockbuster. Sometimes, a movie that seems to have the right script and the right stars still does poorly at the box office.

    -   List and describe three common elements that are necessary to make a movie that will be financially successful. Be more specific than the "right script" or the "right stars."

(Continued)

Questions for critical thinking and discussion—Cont'd

4. Product placement, by which advertisers pay to have their products displayed in movies, is discussed in this chapter.

   • Is product placement ethical? Explain your answer.

5. In his book, *Reel Bad Arabs*, Jack G. Shaheen tells us that the U.S. movie industry depicts Arabs as "brute murderers, sleazy rapists, religious fanatics, oil-rich dimwits, and abusers of women."[24] Shaheen points out that this depiction has been historically consistent—that American movies have always made Arabs look bad, and they continue to do so today.

   • Have you ever seen a positive depiction of Arabs in the movies? If so, describe that depiction.
   • Have you ever seen a negative depiction of Arabs in the movies? If so, describe that depiction.
   • Does a negative depiction of an ethnic stereotype in the movies cause (or at least nurture) biases and prejudices among moviegoers? Explain why or why not.

Additional resources

American Film Institute, www.afi.com

Ascher, Steven, and Edward Pincus, *The Filmmaker's Handbook; A Comprehensive Guide for the Digital Age* (New York: Plume, 2007).

Bill, Tony, *Movie Speak; How to Talk Like You Belong on a Film Set* (New York: Workman Publishing, 2008).

Finler, Joel W., *The Hollywood Story* (New York: Crown Publishers, 1988).

Levy, Frederick, *Hollywood 101: The Film Industry* (New York: St. Martin's Press, 2000).

Lumet, Sidney, *Making Movies* (New York: Vintage Books, 1996).

Motion Picture Association of America, www.mpaa.org

National Association of Theatre Owners, www.natoonline.org

Salamoff, Paul J., *Movie Sets 101: The Definitive Survivor's Guide* (Burbank: Tavin Press, 2005).

Screen Actors Guild, www.sag.org

Shaheen, Jack G., *Reel Bad Arabs; How Hollywood Vilifies a People* (Brooklyn: Olive Branch Press, 2001).

The Internet 8

Chapter contents

Issues and trends on the Internet

- The Internet has created a new way for businesses to deliver goods and services to their customers.
- The Internet facilitates mass customization of products and services.
- The Internet provides tremendous amount of information as well as misinformation.
- The power and the reach of the Internet provide challenges that governmental institutions are struggling to address.
- Although U.S.-based websites currently dominate the Internet, rapidly increasing Internet usage in Asia and Africa will likely lead to the end of U.S. dominance in the near future.
- The growth of Internet usage and Internet sites means that those seeking Internet-related careers have a wide variety of employment possibilities.

We begin this chapter with a note on capitalization. When referring to the worldwide publicly accessible system of interconnected computer networks, the word "Internet" is capitalized. However, the Internet is an example of many types of computer networks also known as internets (without capitalization).

A brief history of the Internet

The creation of the Internet began in the United States in the 1960s. The United States Defense Department's Advanced Research Project Agency (ARPA) built a small network called ARPANET. The agency's goal seems modest today; it wanted to create a medium that allowed researchers to communicate about the work they were doing on behalf of the government. The network began when UCLA, UC Santa Barbara, Stanford, and the University of Utah networked their supercomputers in 1969. By 1971, more than 20 universities and government research centers were online. Two years later, the network expanded to research centers in Europe. The most popular early use of the network was e-mail.

By the late 1970s, ARPANET developers began to look beyond military applications for the network. The term "Internet" was used for the first time in 1982. The following year, the Domain Name System came into effect. Instead of trying to remember a web site address by a long number, as had been the practice, a user only had to remember an address such as www.continuumbooks.com. In 1990, the ARPANET network went out of existence in favor of the broader Internet. Two important changes occurred in 1991. First, commercial use of the Internet was allowed, and was no longer restricted to educational and governmental institutions. Second, the World Wide Web was introduced, which made getting information on the Internet much easier, as one could then connect to a website via a hyperlink. The hyperlink, developed by Tim-Berners Lee, links an electronic file to other electronic files, which we access by simply clicking on the link.

Mosaic, a computer program that allowed users to see photographs and other graphic items on the Internet, was developed by the National Center for Supercomputing Applications and was made available to the public in 1993. Of course, with graphics came banner ads. The first banner ads appear on hotwired.com in October 1994. They were for the alcoholic beverage Zima and AT&T.

The need for a uniform system of assigning domain addresses led to the creation of the not-for-profit Internet Corporation for Assigned Names and Numbers (ICANN) in 1998. After being spun off by the U.S. Commerce Department, ICANN has pursued a process of internationalization that reflects the global nature of the Internet. In other words, neither the Internet nor ICANN belongs to a particular nation.

The 1990s: dot coms to dot bombs

The 1990s was the decade of the so-called dot coms: new firms that saw the Internet as an important opportunity in the commercial world. Many of these firms were quite popular with investors who wanted to invest in firms when they were still young and small. However, while these firms seemed to multiply overnight, many of them failed just as quickly. For some firms, the business model simply did not make sense. For example, pets.com tried to sell dog food and cat litter online.[1] The problem was that a 40-pound bag of dog food or a 40-pound bucket of cat litter is expensive to ship, and neither the company nor the consumer wanted to bear the cost of shipping. Many companies that tried to sell furniture online failed for the same reason.

By the middle of 2000, it was clear that the so-called Internet bubble had burst, and many of the best-known dot coms became equally famous "dot bombs" and failed. The Internet remains an important commercial conduit, but many companies that earn a profit from selling on the Internet have had to refine their business models.

The Internet today

Internet service providers

In the 1990s, the most convenient and inexpensive way to access the Internet was through one's telephone line. Most Americans relied on dial-up service for a decade or more, paying an Internet Service Provider (ISP) for access to software. Millions of Americans received unsolicited CDs from

American Online (AOL) and other companies, offering many hours of free Internet time in order to encourage new subscriptions for dial-up service. The popularity of the Internet led other companies, particularly cable television providers and telephone companies, to equip homes and businesses with coaxial or fiber optic wires that bypassed traditional telephone lines. Because this new technology allowed for faster downloading and uploading than a dial-up Internet connection, dial-up services quickly faded. AOL, which controlled a significant part of the ISP market during the 1990s, has had to reinvent itself as a firm that generates most of its revenue from selling advertising space on the Internet.

Business models for Internet sites

Today, we expect most government agencies, businesses, and organizations to maintain a presence on the Internet. Government sites allow us to purchase stamps, find out the name of our local politicians and contact them, find tax forms and instructions, learn about flu clinics, and view school lunch menus. Organizations' websites allow us to pay our dues, contact other members of the organization, and keep abreast of organizational activities. The presence of public and not-for-profit websites is substantial, but perhaps not as substantial as the presence of for-profit websites. Figure 8.1 displays internet terminology.

Figure 8.1 The Internet presents numerous opportunities for businesses and consumers. *Source*: iStockphoto

Virtual retailers

Businesses use the Internet for a variety of reasons. Some businesses are virtual—they have no bricks and mortar locations, and conduct all of their selling activities online. Consumers love the convenience that the Internet provides—we can shop at any hour and on any day. Most virtual businesses are never closed. However, consumers also love instant gratification—we want it now, or as soon as possible. Many consumers are willing to pay more for speedy delivery of their orders. Virtual businesses rely heavily on information and transportation technology to get their goods and services to consumers as quickly and efficiently as possible. The process of delivering items to consumers is called fulfillment.

Amazon.com is one of the earliest and largest examples of *virtual retailers*. People seek out these sites in order to buy things. Amazon sells downloads of music and books at its site for use in various electronic devices. Amazon also sells a wide variety of physical objects for delivery to consumers' homes. It also acts as a fulfillment service for many other businesses. These businesses have decided to contract for Amazon's services rather than bear the cost of these capacities on their own. Similarly, small-scale sellers can tap into the resources that eBay provides so that those who sell only occasionally can reach a national or global market.

Other businesses rely primarily on physical locations for their sales. They may use their websites to advertise new products and specials to generate traffic for their stores. Their websites provide locations, directions, and hours for those stores. If the business is a restaurant, its website will offer menus and perhaps a means of reserving a table.

Bricks and clicks retailers

Many businesses today are a hybrid or combination of physical locations and online selling. This is bricks and clicks retailing. Retailers such as Target, Wal-Mart, and Best Buy sell merchandise directly through their websites and also provide information about their physical locations at their websites. Apple's customers can buy music, movies, and mobile device applications through direct download at its iTunes website. Visitors at Apple's websites can order computers and iPods online, or find the location and business hours of the nearest Apple store. Retailers can also allow web users to shop for products online and pick them up later at a physical location.

Subscription or pay-per-view content providers

Many websites are in the business of selling information, or content. This content may be available by subscription for a certain period, typically monthly or annually. Content may also be available through pay-per-view access. For example, imagine that you want to open a chain of restaurants in a state. You have not done business in the state, and know nothing about its employment laws, its health regulations, nor the requirement for getting liquor licenses. Because the restaurants will be in different communities, you need to learn about state and local laws. You might be able to find all the information you need about the laws for operating restaurants in that state by checking government agencies' websites or calling those agencies or by visiting a library in that state. Imagine how much more convenient it would be if a single website offered all the information that you needed: every applicable state law and every applicable local law in each community in the state.

Of course, this information may not be free. Remember, people love convenience and are willing to pay for it. Presume that you operate a website that provides detailed and localized information about restaurant regulations. You could charge for the information you sell. Now think about some of the businesses and services that would want to advertise on your website. They might include lawyers, commercial real estate brokers, food service suppliers, and janitorial supply companies. Businesses that maintain websites strive to "monetize" those websites—to make as much money as possible from each person who visits the site. Many websites try to upsell customers to increase the revenue per customer. Thus, when you purchase a book at Amazon.com, the website suggests other books that you might be interested in, it tries to sell you an Amazon credit card, and it offers you faster shipping for a higher price.

Websites may provide free content supported by advertising, paid content for which users must subscribe, or offer a combination of both free and paid content (with free content often offered as a teaser for the paid content). Many trade and professional organizations provide information at their websites for their members; one of the main reasons that many members join these organizations is to access this information. There are also an ever-increasing number of online publications with news or feature stories. These sites cater to visitors' personal interests rather than their professional interests.

Of course, there is also pornography, which has boomed with the advent of the Internet. Instead of visiting seedy bookstores in sketchy neighborhoods, Americans can now access seemingly unlimited pornography from the privacy of their home. Obviously, this causes problems. In particular, parents who were once able to shield their children from most types of pornography find it increasingly difficult to do so with the presence of the Internet in their homes. Others worry that Internet addiction in general, combined with addiction to pornography in particular, is a problem to which a growing number of people are susceptible. These addictions fuel an online pornography industry that earned an estimated $2.8 billion in 2006.[2]

Advertiser-supported content providers

Many websites rely primarily on revenue from the firms that advertise at those sites. This model replicates older media models such as broadcast television or radio, which provide free content to listeners, relying on advertisers for revenue. As discussed in Chapter 3, traditional advertising is based on the *cost per thousand* people who view or listen to a particular program. This model, known as CPM (M is the Roman numeral for thousand), is offered by some Internet sites. A newer pricing model facilitated by the interactivity of the Internet is *cost per click* (CPC) which charges advertisers based on the number of site visitors who click on their advertisements. Typically, cost per click will cost an advertiser more than cost per thousand, but for many advertisers, it is worth the additional expense, as a web user who clicks on an advertisement is more likely to become a customer. Internet search sites such as Google and Yahoo rely heavily on CPM or CPC advertising for much of their revenue.

Online education

One of the Internet's most significant contributions to contemporary lifestyles is online education. Hundreds of colleges and universities now offer courses online. Because of the global reach of the Internet, neither students nor instructors need to live in the same state or country as the degree-granting institution. In addition, most online courses are *asynchronous*—students and instructors do not have to be online together at the same time. As a result, students with work and family responsibilities can pursue their education even if their schedules do not allow them to attend face-to-face

Figure 8.2 Any place that has Internet access has access to education. *Source*: iStockphoto

classes. Online education also allows American military personnel in Iraq and Afghanistan and elsewhere to continue their educations while serving their country. As Figure 8.2 symbolizes, electronic schools have a global reach.

Online education assists grade school and high school students as well. Students in rural communities with school enrollments too small to offer some specialized courses in the classroom, such as foreign languages or advanced placement courses, can make these courses available to their students by contracting with other schools to provide them online. During tough economic times, larger school districts can economize by exchanging online courses: one school may provide advanced science courses online, while a partner school offers advanced math courses online, etc.

Unfortunately, some unscrupulous people have created fraudulent online universities and schools offering bogus degrees that are often expensive. Some of the customers of these "diploma mills" are dishonest themselves, seeking a fake credential to advance their careers. Other customers, however, are sincere yet gullible. Because of the global nature of the Internet and the anonymity it provides, it has been difficult to regulate disreputable online education sites. Nevertheless, government regulators and educational organizations are developing practices to do so.[3]

Social networking

You already know that the Internet is changing the way people communicate. For centuries, humans could communicate only in person. Later came postal systems to distribute written communications over great distances and later still came the telegraph, then the telephone. Today, Internet users can communicate individually through e-mail or instant messaging, or with large groups of people through blogs, social networking sites, or other websites. We can also post much more than printed words, as current technology allows us to upload our photographs, artwork, videos, and music. Unlike previous forms of mass communication in which the communication came only from those who controlled the media, we are no longer merely consuming communications. We are creating and participating. In addition, because of the global nature of the Internet, we are communicating without regard to distance or time. Social networking is discussed further in the next chapter.

Interactivity

One of the most attractive aspects of the Internet to advertisers is its interactivity. In the case of older media, the consumer is exposed to advertising, but it is difficult for the advertiser to determine whether the consumer noticed the advertisement and how the consumer reacted. An online advertisement can provide instant feedback if a viewer clicks on it. Advertisers can easily measure the *click-through rate* of their online advertisements. Many advertisers find the click-through rate to be disappointing, with less than 2 percent of those exposed to an advertisement clicking on it.

However, because many Internet sites cater to the particular interests of each user and can use interactive data that users voluntarily or involuntarily provide site operators, advertisers are able to focus their advertising expenditures on the types of sites that their target market is most likely to frequent. For example, suppose that a 19-year-old college student in Missouri has a Yahoo start page, as does a 50-year-old college professor in Massachusetts. Each of these users will customize their start page to suit their particular interests and lifestyles. Yahoo is able to deliver different advertisements to those two Internet users, based on age and geography (basic demographic data). In addition, Yahoo is also able to deliver different advertisements based on Internet surfing habits. For example, the college professor may be more interested in political news than the college student, who is more interested in sports news. Using algorithms, Yahoo can further determine whether the college professor is more likely to click on stories that concern Republican or Democratic politicians. Yahoo also offers a search engine. It is quite easy for search engines to correlate advertisements with the types of searches that users make. For example, if a college student is shopping for a used car, and enters the search term "reliable used car," the advertisements that appear on Yahoo will likely feature for automobile dealers, and also advertisements for automobile rating services, automobile insurance, and automobile financing. A Google search for "baby" yields advertisements for baby formula, baby food, photography services, and life insurance.

Let us compare Internet advertising and television advertising. As discussed in Chapter 4, there are three basic types of television advertisements: national advertisements (national advertisers advertising on national television networks), national spot advertisements (national advertisers advertising on local television stations), and local spot advertisements (local advertisers advertising on local television stations).

You have never seen a national television advertisement for funeral services, although you may have seen a local spot advertisement for a funeral home in your community. It makes little sense for a funeral home to pay for advertising on national television. For one thing, relatively few funeral service providers have a national network of funeral homes. More importantly, most television viewers will not need funeral services in the near future. Even though a local spot advertisement for a local funeral home would only be shown where that funeral home is located, once again, the average television viewer is not seeking funeral services. This is why most funeral homes have traditionally focused their advertising on yellow page advertising.

Now consider Internet advertising. The second-most common use of the Internet (after e-mail) is using a search engine to find information; 88 percent of Internet users do so, and about half of users report that they do so every day.[4] If you visit some of the popular search engines and enter the term "funeral services," you will find thousands of links to websites that contain that term. You will also see sponsored links, which are advertisements paid for by advertisers who want to communicate with Internet users who are seeking funeral services. These advertisers are able to target their advertisements to those Internet users who have identified themselves as interested in funeral services. Of course, not all of the sponsored links will be for funeral homes—they may also be for related services, such as florists, life insurance companies, and firms that produce grave markers.

The advertising auction

Google earned over $23 billion in 2009. Google's main business is selling advertising at its various domestic and foreign search sites. Google does not set the prices for advertisements at its sites; its advertisers do. Every advertisement you see at a Google site is the result of a computer-operated auction. Advertisers establish their budget with Google, and then indicate how much they would be willing to pay to associate their advertisement with a particular search term or keyword. Moreover, advertisers do not pay for *impressions*—the number of times that Internet users see their advertisement; they only pay for the number of times that Internet users click on their advertisements. Google uses mathematical formulas to determine which advertisements are most likely to generate clicks by determining which types of advertisements are the most relevant to the keywords. This benefits Internet users, who do not want to click on sponsored links that are irrelevant to their search. Yahoo's and Bing's advertising pricing is similar, using a bidding approach and charging for clicks, not impressions.

Cybersquatting

Suppose that your last name is MacDonald. That last name is similar to, but not the same as McDonalds, the hamburger chain. It is likely that McDonalds would have its lawyers contact you if you tried to use your last name in a business that sold hamburgers. Those lawyers would also be concerned about you using your name in a website that promoted your hamburgers. For this reason, when a company decides to change its name or create a new subsidiary, one of the considerations is whether the name is available as an Internet domain name. That company may also want to purchase domain names that could be critical of the company. Imagine there is a company named Xylxqqr. It may want to purchase xylxqqr.com, xylxqqr.net, and xylxqqr.biz, and also xylxqqrsucks.com and ihatexylxqqr.com. What if somebody heard that a new company called Xylxqqr was going to be created, and bought the domain name xylxqqr.com before the company did? This is "cybersquatting," and it has been against the law in the United States since 1999. The Anticybersquatting Consumer Protection Act would allow Xylxqqr to sue anybody who registered a similar domain name for the sole purpose of selling it to somebody else who holds a trademark for that name.

Another issue is "typosquatting." For example, if one mistypes google. com as goole.com in the address box, a search engine appears—and it is not Google. Merely coincidental? What do you think? Companies often purchase domain names that are similar to their own to avoid this problem.

How reliable is information on the Internet?

For those seeking information from the Internet, Wikipedia is often one of the first sites consulted. The popularity of Wikipedia underscores how the Internet seems to be changing people's concept of what is factual. Does one have to be an expert to state a fact? If so, what makes somebody an expert? Wikipedia and similar sites seem to present a more democratic version of what constitutes a fact. If information is posted on these sites and the consensus of those who read it, whether they are experts or otherwise, treat the information as accurate, is that sufficient? After all, if others find the information misleading or wrong, they can challenge it or correct it. A 2005 study by the British scientific journal *Nature* found that information posted at Wikipedia on science topics was about as accurate as were entries in the *Encyclopedia Britannica*, although both sources contained some factual errors.[5] Perhaps facts produced by numerous contributors are as accurate as the facts provided by experts are. (Experts surely disagree.)

Many commercial sites that sell goods or services on the Internet allow customers to post reviews of those products. Most of these reviews are skewed toward the very positive ("Best product ever!") or very negative ("Worst product ever!"). Consumers who have had particularly good or particularly bad experiences are more likely to post a review than are those whose experience with a product is relatively mixed or neutral. However, it is not always possible to tell if the review is that of an actual consumer. Some reviews are a form of *stealth marketing*. The manufacturer of a product may use its employees to post bogus positive reviews of its own products and bogus negative reviews of its competitors' products. The temptation for the manufacturer to do so is clear. These fake reviews tap into the power of social networking, while at the same time allowing the manufacturer to tout its products without paying for advertising. In 2009, the Federal Trade Commission revised its rules on endorsements and testimonials. As of December 1, 2009, if someone posts a review of a product online, that person must disclose if there are "material connections" (such as payments or free products) between the product's manufacturer and the reviewer.[6]

Some people believe that the Internet has practically eliminated the need for libraries. It is true that many of the services that libraries offer can be obtained online, either through libraries' online services or through other information sites on the Internet. However, when seeking reliable information, the Internet may not always be as helpful as many people think. Before information can be presented as fact (rather than opinion or speculation) in a library, those trained in library science have screened the information for veracity. On the other hand, anyone can post information on the Internet and claim it to be accurate. Fortunately, many Americans maintain a healthy skepticism about information on the Internet; in a study by the World Internet Project, only 48 percent of Americans polled said that they thought that most or all information available online is reliable.[7]

A person who posts incorrect information may be simply be mistaken. For example, urban legends have proliferated on the Internet, often posted or forwarded by those who believe them to be true. Many of us have been warned about being slipped a drug in one's drink by someone who wants to steal one of our kidneys. Such tales are interesting and perhaps scary, but also not true.

Others who misrepresent opinions or speculation as truth on the Internet have an ideological agenda, and intentionally misrepresent the truthfulness of their information. Racist hate sites attacked Barack Obama before the 2008 presidential election, and have been attacking him since. Some of the misinformation they have presented has gone viral, and ends up presented as fact at websites that are not racist. One example that returned over 10 million hits on Google in November 2009 is that "Obama is not a U.S. citizen." (He is.) This misinformation also extends to John McCain, Obama's Republican opponent in the 2008 election. "McCain is not a U.S. citizen" returned over 2.4 million hits on Google. (He is.)[8]

Cybercrime

Technological lag refers to humans' ability to invent technology before we learn to control it. Although the Internet provides many benefits to society, it also generates problems. Some of these problems seem to be beyond our current ability to control them. Chapter 5 discusses the challenges the music industry faces from illegal downloading of songs. Chapter 7 looks at how the film industry is confronting illegal uploading and downloading of movies. Despite industry efforts, you are probably not surprised to know that every day, thousands of people around the world illegally upload or download copyright-protected files, easily and with little fear of being caught.

Another prevalent form of cybercrime is "phishing," a process by which a criminal generates e-mails fraudulently seeking financial information from others. The criminal typically links the e-mail to a bogus website for a financial institution that looks authentic. Financial fraud is also the goal of those who send out the so-called "419 letter" (named for a criminal law in Nigeria, where some of these e-mail messages have originated). The sender claims to be a bank official or government official trying to distribute the financial accounts of a dead foreigner, and is seeking the assistance of the recipient of the message in exchange for a share of the proceeds. The duped recipient, expecting to earn a windfall, provides personal financial information, allowing the sender of the message to exploit that information and perhaps clean out the recipient's bank account. Figure 8.3 shows another example of a phishing scam.

The ability to misrepresent one's identity also helps pedophiles. Pedophiles enter into conversations with young Internet users, typically through chat rooms. The pedophile may initially misrepresent his or her own age as that of a teenager or preteen in order to meet teenagers or preteens more easily. Many pedophiles will attempt to make physical contact with their intended victims. This information may hardly be news to you, but thousands of online sexual predators are arrested each year, which tells us that the Internet remains a hazardous place for children.[9] Pedophiles also use the Internet to exchange files that contain child pornography. Of course, the Internet can help protect society from sex offenders. Many states now post information about sex offenders online, allowing citizens to learn where convicted sex offenders live or work.

Dear valued customer of TrustedBank,

We have recieved notice that you have recently attempted to withdraw the following amount from your checking account while in another country: $135.25.

If this information is not correct, someone unknown may have access to your account. As a safety measure, please visit our website via the link below to verify your personal information:

http://www.trustedbank.com/general/custverifyinfo.asp

Once you have done this, our fraud department will work to resolve this discrepency. We are happy you have chosen us to do business with.

Thank you,
TrustedBank

Member FDIC © 2005 TrustedBank, Inc.

Figure 8.3 An example of a phishing scam—this message is fraudulent, and bears telltale misspellings.

Viruses

Computer viruses have existed since the beginning of electronic computing in the late 1940s. Most of these viruses were created accidentally rather than maliciously. More significantly, most of these viruses had limited effect, as few computers were networked. The term "virus" was popularized by computer security specialist expert Fred Cohen in the early 1980s. One of the earliest viruses to spread from one computer to others affected Apple computers in 1981. The first virus to spread through a Microsoft operating system was the Brain virus in 1986. Two Pakistani brothers created the Brain virus as a means of protecting their software from piracy. Today there are hundreds of thousands of identified viruses, with more created daily.

Why do some people create viruses? There are too many viruses, and too many people who create viruses, to identify a single cause. Some of the more common reasons seem to be the desire to demonstrate technical skills, anti-social feelings, or to profit through extortion of potential victims. It is believed that some of those who create viruses are neo-Luddites. Neo-Luddites are the contemporary version of the Luddites, a movement that opposed the mechanization of factories during the British Industrial Revolution of the early 1800s. Naming themselves after the perhaps mythical Ned Ludd, some Luddites vandalized factories and damaged machinery, as they viewed mechanized labor as dehumanizing. Neo-Luddites share this fear of technology, but focus on computers and information technology rather than industrial machinery. You probably know people who complain that society has become too reliant on technology. They may complain that we allow computers to make too many decisions that humans should be making instead. Ironically, some neo-Luddites are skilled with computers, yet create viruses in an effort to persuade people to become less reliant on computers.

The Internet in the future

Cloud computing

Imagine how much you could save on the cost of a new computer if you did not have to pay for the software that most of us need installed on a computer. You would not have to pay for productivity suites (which include word processing, spreadsheet, e-mail, and presentation software, such as Microsoft's Office), graphic design programs, and accounting software. Many students already use web services and applications rather than computer-based software to communicate, relying on web-based e-mail services such as Hot Mail or G-mail. But if these services are available free online, how will the companies that provide these services generate a profit? One of the most obvious ways is through advertising. As Google's Chairman and Chief Executive Officer Eric Schmidt has stated, "cloud computing and advertising go hand-in-hand."[10] Cloud computing's capacity to bring computer applications to disadvantaged people is discussed in Chapter 12.

Voting

Many politicians and others have advocated for Internet voting. They argue that it should be as convenient as possible for citizens to cast their vote, and that Internet voting is particularly beneficial to those who are elderly, are mobility impaired, or lack personal transportation. Others oppose Internet voting, saying that it is too prone to fraud. Those who support Internet voting point out that there is available technology to assure that online voters are who they claim to be. However, this ability to identify voters raises privacy concerns. Some people fear that online voting would make it too easy for government officials to identify how voters cast their ballots.

The virtual economy

You probably know some people who are afraid of shopping on the Internet. The most common fear is that online shopping typically requires releasing one's credit card information. However, credit card issuers benefit considerably from the Internet, since most Internet shoppers use credit cards, allowing card issuers to earn fees and interest charges. In order to assure those who fear Internet-related credit card fraud, most credit card issuers offer fraud protection. Clearly, this creates a cost for card issuers, who must absorb the cost of fraud, but card issuers view this as a necessary overhead expense.

Online merchants point out that even in face-to-face credit card transactions, a cardholder's information typically is sent over a communication network for approval prior to a purchase—each time we swipe our card at the mall or the gas station, our credit information is distributed electronically, often by wireless devices. Many believe that the increasing ease and mobility of electronic transactions may lead the United States and other nations to move from a cash-based currency to an electronic currency.

The digital divide and the demographics of Internet usage

Guess what? You probably use the Internet much more than your grandparents do. Okay, you already knew that. You can also probably explain why—your generation grew up with computers and the Internet, your grandparents' generation did not. According to the Pew Internet & American Life Project, a little over 30 percent of Americans aged 73 and older use the Internet, while 87 percent of those between the ages of 18 and 32 do so.[11] While 72 percent of those between the ages of 18 and 32 who use the Internet watch videos on the Internet, only 14 percent of those aged 73 and older do. However, an almost equal percentage of Internet users in each age group use the Internet to research health issues (a little over two-thirds of each group).

The Pew Project's analysis of who uses the Internet and who does not tells us that Internet usage is also based on household income—the higher the income, the more likely it is that members of that household use the Internet. Additionally, the more educated a person is, the more likely she or he is to use the Internet—while 95 percent of college graduates use the Internet, only 67 percent of those whose highest educational attainment is a high-school diploma do. Race is also a factor; non-Hispanic white people are more likely to use the Internet than Hispanic or Black people are. One of the socio-economic concerns here is that information is power. If people with below average education who are living in poverty are less likely to use the Internet, whether by choice or by lack of access, it is much more difficult for those people to obtain the information about resources that can assist them, or more importantly, help them move out of poverty. (Think about how much students rely on the Internet to help them with their schoolwork. Then imagine not having easy Internet access.)

There is also a gap in Internet usage globally—for the moment. As of November 2009, there were 68.9 million domains in the United States.[12] More than half of the world's web sites originate in the United States, and nearly three-quarters of the world's web sites are in English. There are many who believe that the Internet facilitates the spread of English speaking globally. As you read this, there are more people speaking English as a second language than there are people speaking English as their native language.

According to Internet World Stats, around 25 percent of the world's population uses the Internet.[13]

Note that while about 74 percent of North Americans use the Internet, less than 7 percent of Africans currently do. However, although only about 18.5 percent of Asians use the Internet, Asia's population is so large that Asians constitute the largest number of Internet users—over 700 million, compared to about 250 million North Americans. The chart in Figure 8.4

WORLD INTERNET USAGE AND POPULATION STATISTICS						
World Regions	Population (2009 Est.)	Internet Users Dec. 31, 2000	Internet Users June 30, 2009	Penetration (Percentage of Population)	Growth 2000-2009	Users (Percentage of Table)
Africa	991,002,342	4,514,400	65,903,900	6.7 %	1,359.9 %	3.9 %
Asia	3,808,070,503	114,304,000	704,213,930	18.5 %	516.1 %	42.2 %
Europe	803,850,858	105,096,093	402,380,474	50.1 %	282.9 %	24.2 %
Middle East	202,687,005	3,284,800	47,964,146	23.7 %	1,360.2 %	2.9 %
North America	340,831,831	108,096,800	251,735,500	73.9 %	132.9 %	15.1 %
Latin America/ Caribbean	586,662,468	18,068,919	175,834,439	30.0 %	873.1 %	10.5 %
Oceania / Australia	34,700,201	7,620,480	20,838,019	60.1 %	173.4 %	1.2 %
WORLD TOTAL	6,767,805,208	360,985,492	1,668,870,408	24.7 %	362.3 %	100.0%

Information in this site may be cited, giving the due credit to www.internetworldstats.com.
Copyright © 2001 - 2009, Miniwatts Marketing Group. All rights reserved worldwide.

Figure 8.4 World internet usage and population statistics. *Source:* www.internetworldstats. com

shows that Asia and Africa have experienced growth rates of Internet usage of about 1,360 percent so far this century. The North American growth rate during this period has been 133 percent, only a tenth of that of Asia and Africa.

Currently, many of the Internet's most popular websites originate in the United States. With the rapid increase in Internet usage in more populous parts of the world, this American dominance is unlikely to last much longer.

Currently, Baidu, a Chinese search engine, and Yahoo Japan are among the world's ten most popular Internet sites; Asian sites comprise five of the Internet's 20 most popular sites.[14] See Figure 8.5 for a list of the top 20 internet sites, according to www.internetworldstats.com. Chapter 12 examines the relationship between globalization and mass media.

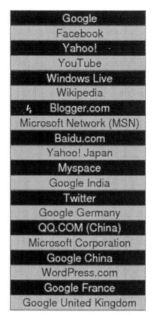

Figure 8.5 Top 20 Internet sites. *Source:* www.internetworldstats.com

The Internet and careers

Internet firms require many diverse skill sets among their employees. The Internet obviously employs many people with computer and other technical skills. The Bureau of Labor Statistics estimates that demand for computer scientists and database administrators will remain strong from 2006 to 2016, outpacing many other types of careers.[15] The Bureau's outlook for those seeking careers as computer and information systems managers is also encouraging.[16]

Internet content providers need content; the Bureau tells us that, "Online publications and services are growing in number and sophistication, spurring the demand for writers and editors, especially those with Web experience."[17] Other creative careers include web graphics and design, which are highly competitive because of the large number of those seeking jobs in these fields. However, the Bureau's estimate is encouraging for artists interested in Internet careers, stating that, "Individuals with a bachelor's degree and knowledge of computer design software, particularly those with

Web site design and animation experience will have the best opportunities."[18] Because Internet firms are businesses, they also need those trained in fields such as management, marketing, human resources, and accounting.

Questions for critical thinking and discussion

1. The technology needed for online education is too complicated for most schools to develop themselves. As a result, most schools contract with companies that provide course management systems. Because of their sophisticated nature, these course management systems are quite expensive. Suppose that the course management system provider that your school uses offers a significant discount if your school is willing to allow advertisements to appear online. (In other words, while taking a history course online, you may see advertisements for Pepsi or iTunes.)

   • Would this be acceptable to you? Explain your answer.

2. Many people now rely on Internet dating services to find suitable partners. Some claim that it is too easy to be dishonest about one's self on the Internet. Others point out that there is little motivation to be dishonest, as eventually, people who meet on the Internet will meet in person.

   • Do you think that Internet dating services are useful for people to find romantic partners? Explain why or why not.

3. In 2003, the U.S. Supreme Court ruled in *Smith v. Doe* that sex offender registries that post convicted sex offenders' name and address on the Internet was constitutional. The challenge to the registry laws came from ex-offenders who argued that they were being punished twice for the same crime, first by imprisonment, and later by having their personal information posted online. The U.S. Supreme Court said that posting this information online was "nonpunitive."

   • Explain whether you think having embarrassing information posted about someone on the Internet is a form of punishment or not.

4. Many argue that the Internet facilitates the spread of the English language globally, sometimes at the expense of local languages.

   • Is that a good thing, a bad thing, or a mixed blessing? Explain your answer.

5. The Internet is obviously a powerful medium—it may turn out to be the most powerful in human history. It also is not perfect.

   • What is the best thing about the Internet today? Explain.
   • What is the worst thing about the Internet today? Explain.
   • Are you generally optimistic about the Internet's future role in our lives or pessimistic about the Internet's future role? Explain.

Additional resources

Anderson, Janna Quitney, *Imagining the Internet* (Lanham, MD: Rowman & Littlefield, 2005).

Dictionary of Internet Terms, whatis.techtarget.com

Electronic Privacy Information Center, www.epic.org

Evaluating Information Found on the Internet (Johns Hopkins University), http://www.library.jhu.edu/researchhelp/general/evaluating/

Head, Tom, ed., *The Future of the Internet* (Farmington Hills, MI: Gale, 2005).

Hoaxbusters, www.hoaxbusters.org

Internet Corporation for Assigned Names and Numbers, www.icann.org

Internet Society, www.isoc.org

Internet Usage and Population Statistics, www.internetworldstats.com

Pew Internet & American Life Project, www.pewinternet.org

USC Center for the Digital Future, www.digitalcenter.org

World Internet Project, www.worldinternetproject.net

New Media

9

Chapter contents

Issues and trends in new media

- New media provide users with a mix of interpersonal and mass communication capabilities that have not existed before, with an emphasis on interactivity and mobility.
- New media allow advertisers to create new methods of communicating with their target markets, including highly personalized and interactive advertisements.
- Video games have proven to be highly popular, and advertisers recognize the opportunities that video games offer them to reach consumers.
- Social networking continues to be one of the fastest rising forms of media, but social networking's popularity does not necessarily translate to profitability for social networking sites.
- New media have proven to be risky enterprises, with firms quickly rising and falling.
- Jobs in new media are expected to be plentiful as new media industries continue to grow.

Suppose that you are a huge fan of a professional football team. Dozens of firms will send you scores and other team news as text messages to your cell phone. Planning outdoor activities and worried about the weather? Other companies provide free weather updates. You can also receive free celebrity gossip alerts. (Maybe one of your favorite actors just got divorced. Again.) Why are these updates free? Because these updates come with advertising. Texting is also interactive. You can text your vote on who you think is going to win a particular basketball game, who should win "American Idol," or whether your favorite actor should get divorced. Again.

Consumers in their teens and twenties are one of the most attractive demographic groups for advertisers and one of the most confounding. Advertisers often refer to college-age consumers as moving targets. People in their teens and twenties tend to do more things, but spend less time doing any one thing. They watch less television than most other age groups, they spend less time at home, and their opinions change frequently. As advertisers pursue this elusive target market, many are moving away from traditional forms of advertising media and turning to what are commonly described as new media. These new media include Internet websites such as MySpace, Facebook, Twitter, Flickr, and other social networking and sharing sites, as well as blogs, video games and virtual worlds, and mobile telephones, text messaging devices and GPS devices. See Figure 9.1 for the addresses of various social networking websites.

In the near future, we are expected to embrace electronic forms of newspapers and magazines, which, using lightweight, flexible computer monitors and wireless technology, will not merely replace the delivery of content of existing newspapers and magazines, but will replicate the look and feel of these traditional media as well. Many media firms that have relied on traditional media forms in the past are incorporating new media in their effort to compete with the many new ways people share information. Thus, many television and newspaper reporters maintain blogs, which are discussed later in this chapter. Many television outlets post the comments of viewers during telecasts to depict an interactive environment to viewers.

The interactive nature of many new forms of information and entertainment media, as well as the ability to mass-customize these media, allow advertisers to pinpoint their target markets more effectively. Advertisers are better able to gauge the efficacy of their advertisements, based on whether

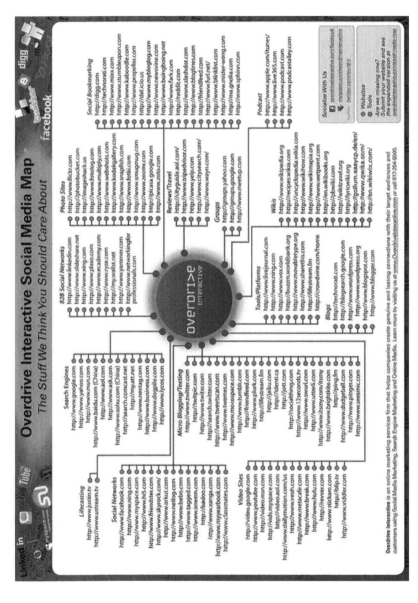

Figure 9.1 Social networking websites. *Source:* www.OverdriveInteractive.com

users click on electronic advertisements, or engage in dialogue or interaction with advertisers' computerized avatars, or how much time users spend engaged in media in which advertising is present. In situations where information or entertainment content is popular among a variety of demographic and psychographic groups, advertisers incorporate a range of electronic user databases to deliver varying advertising messages to each group.

User-generated content: blogs and social networking sites

Blogs (slang for "web logs") allow users to maintain their own websites, often at no cost. Most blog hosts earn revenue by selling advertising on individual blogs. Blogs may contain the blogger's (blog owner's) ideas and observations, may be a journal of the blogger's activities, or may be devoted to a subject of personal or professional interest. Blogs are typically posted in chronological order, like a diary or journal, with the most recent posting appearing at the top of the blog.

Technorati, a blog search engine and marketing firm, tracks over 100 million blogs, and identifies the most popular blogs and the most common topics discussed on blogs. While some bloggers attempt to generate income through their blogs, Technorati estimates that 72 percent of blogs belong to hobbyists who do not seek income from their blogs.[1] However, many businesses maintain blogs to communicate with their stakeholders—customers, suppliers, partners, and employees.

For many Internet users, blogging has given way to social networking sites. Nielsen Online described social networking as "the global consumer phenomenon of 2008," stating that two-thirds of Internet users visit a social network or blogging site, and that 10 percent of total Internet usage is devoted to social networking.[2] The largest social networking sites include Facebook and MySpace, which are among the top 10 websites by number of weekly visits.[3] Facebook, started in 2004, is privately held, and does not release financial data. However, in May 2009, Facebook sold a two percent interest in the company to a Russian firm for $200 million, which would make Facebook worth $10 billion.[4] MySpace, started in 2003, was purchased in 2005 for $580 million by the News Corporation (which also owns the Fox Broadcasting).

Social networking provides people with a way to stay in touch with friends, family members, customers, and suppliers. It also helps users accumulate and maintain social capital. Social capital can mean the number of friends one has and the degree of respect those friends have for someone. (You may know someone who has attempted to amass as many Facebook friends as possible.) It can also mean the ability to influence the opinions and actions of others.

The fastest growing social networking site of 2009 was Twitter. Twitter allows users to upload posts ("tweets") of no more than 140 characters; this abbreviated form of blogging is aptly referred to as microblogging. The concept behind this is that users will frequently create new tweets to provide updates to their followers, which will generate a steady stream of traffic to the site. Eleven percent of American adults who go online use Twitter or a similar service to provide updates of their activities or to check on the activities of others.[5] About 20 percent of those between the ages of 18 and 24 use these services. You probably recognize the Twitter logo in Figure 9.2.

Many of those who use social networking media do so for financial reasons. While we may be Facebook friends with people we know, we can also "friend" celebrities like Shaquille O'Neal. Similarly, we can follow our pals on Twitter, or find out what Martha Stewart is serving at her next cocktail party. Shaq and Martha Stewart are more than just celebrities that we see on television; they are brands that enjoy significant social capital. Advertisers are striving to associate their goods and services with people who possess social capital. At the same time, social networking sites offer users a platform for sharing one's creative work, whether literature, music, graphic art, or photography.

It is too early to tell if social media are a fad that will pass or if they will prove to be a long-term, significant method of communicating. If the lifecycle of traditional media is instructive, there will be some consolidation in the industry, with only a few firms dominating the marketplace. Moreover, as we are seeing with several types of social media, it is one thing to be popular with users and quite another to be profitable for the medium's owners.

Figure 9.2 Twitter logo.

Social networking and audience

According to comScore, social networking sites had nearly 140 million visitors in April 2009, or nearly three-quarters of the U.S. online population.[6] MySpace had 71 million visitors, followed by Facebook with 67.5 million visitors, an increase of 10 percent from the previous month. *Fortune* magazine reported that Facebook has 15 million users who update their status daily, and that visitors to Facebook spend more than 3 billion minutes on the site each day.[7] Twitter, the third ranked social networking site, jumped 83 percent in a single month, to 17 million visitors. As the result of the significant increase of social networking sites' popularity, Nielsen Online reported that in February 2009 the amount of time spent by Americans at social media sites had surpassed time spent reading and sending e-mail for the first time.[8]

Popularity and profitability are not the same things, however. As Twitter tells visitors, "Twitter has many appealing opportunities for generating revenue but we are holding off on implementation for now . . . While our business model is in a research phase, we spend more money than we make."[9] MySpace cut 30 percent of its U.S. staff and two-thirds of its international staff in the summer of 2009 due to weak advertising sales in a poor economy. Facebook, despite its impressive viewer traffic, has demonstrated poor click-through rates for its advertisements—too few Facebook users click on the advertisements that appear there. MySpace's click-through performance, though better than Facebook's, is also disappointing to advertisers.

In the beginning of social networking sites, there was a correlation between age and social networking usage—the younger an Internet user was, the more likely that user was to use a social networking site. This trend is shifting, however. For example, Facebook started as a site for college students, but the fast growing group of Facebook users is those over the age of 55.[10] In some ways, the presence of older users "kills the cool" of a website. As a result, younger users typically move on to the next, newer social network.

Social networking and content

In many ways, social networking is a website owner's dream. Consider first the costs relative to the overhead of traditional media. Traditional media spend millions of dollars for content. Television programming involves paying for the rights to broadcast sports events; paying for the dramas and comedies that involve writers, actors, directors, and technical staff; maintaining a news organization, etc. Print media involves writers, reporters, editors, graphic artists, printers, paper costs, and distribution costs. Movies cost millions of dollars to make.

Contrast traditional media's overhead with that of social networking sites, or rather, the lack of overhead. At social networking sites, users create the content, for which the sites pay nothing. This is *crowdsourcing*—those who use the content generate the content. Users may also be able to upload and download content without paying for that content. How, then, do these sites make money? The answer is simple: advertising. Some new media sites are wildly popular, while some attract only a few visitors. Because those sites that collect relatively few visitors also have relatively few costs (other than server costs) they can still generate a profit for their owners.

Social networking and the changing concept of privacy

The amount of information about us that others can access continues to expand. It only takes a minute or two for someone to find out where we live, how much we paid for our home, what organizations we belong to, and where we work or go to school. We generate much of this information ourselves when we participate in social networking. Our willingness to share this information obviously has a direct effect on our privacy.

What people consider to be private or personal information and what they consider to be public information is in transition. Older generations tend to be much less willing to share information about themselves than younger generations are. A complicated issue surrounding social networking sites is the ability of one's employer (or prospective employer) to monitor employees or job applicants' personal lives. The National Association of Colleges and Employers reports that many companies review the social networking sites of job applicants before making hiring decisions.[11] Comments or discussions posted online about alcohol or drug usage, promiscuity, or other issues that may seem appropriate in a social setting may reflect poorly on job candidates. And if a picture is indeed worth a thousand words, some of the photographs that people choose to post online tell an employer or prospective employer more than we want them to know.

Social networking and advertising

Advertisers are attracted to both popular sites and not-so-popular social network sites, as the cost of advertising is proportionate. In many cases, the less popular sites may have appeal to a particular type of visitor who is attractive to a particular type of advertiser. For example, there is a website called the Daily Hamster, which provides visitors, as the site tells us, with "Your Daily Dose of Cute Hamsters."[12] Users generate content, which costs the site owner nothing. Of course, the typical visitor is a hamster enthusiast, and likely the owner of a hamster or two. Sellers of hamster care products—food, wood shavings, hamster habitats—are more likely to advertise on this site than on a general interest site like CNN.com, or even a site devoted to pet enthusiasts in general.

Because many people tend to disclose a lot of personal information about themselves on social networking sites, advertisers have access to lots of data. In addition, advertisers try to capitalize on the social environment. Which would you rather try: a new product that you know nothing about or a new product recommended to you by a friend? Not surprisingly, Facebook refers to these advertisements as "Social Ads." As its Privacy Page tells us, "Facebook occasionally pairs advertisements with relevant social actions from a user's friends to create Social Ads. Social Ads make advertisements more interesting and more tailored to you and your friends."[13] Later, a Facebook user may see a message about a friend becoming a fan of a page related to an advertisement the user sees. In addition to Social Ads, Facebook offers advertisements that are more traditional. In either case, advertisers can target their ads based on users' location, age, sex, education (including schools attended), workplace, relationship status, language, etc. MySpace offers advertisers the chance to target viewers based on over 1,100 interests, which MySpace calls "Hyper Targets."[14]

Targeting provides advertisers with a means of reaching their intended audience. *Contextual targeting* matches advertising to the content of the page. The focus here is on the content rather than the profile of a particular user. A website may know what you are looking for, but will not know who you are. For example, visitors to Merriam-Webster's online dictionary who entered the search term "Democrat" during the 2008 presidential campaign saw advertisements for Democratic candidate Barack Obama. Visitors who entered the search term "Republican" saw advertisements for John McCain, the Republican candidate. As discussed in Chapter 8, advertisements appearing on search engines such as Google and Bing are always based on contextual targeting.

Behavioral targeting matches advertising to the demonstrated interests (via cookies or consumer-generated content) of individual users. In this case, the website knows something about you, perhaps your name, gender, age, and place of residence. For example, MySpace offers advertisers access to a program that scans users' profiles, makes note of their interests, and then delivers thematically appropriate ads. Google's G-Mail posts advertisements based on keywords that appear in the content of users' e-mail messages. When the author of this book visits his Facebook page, the advertisements that appear are based on the fact that the author is male, middle-aged, married, and teaches for a living, information that appears in the author's Facebook profile.

Social networking sites often include individuals' reviews of concerts, movies, television shows, and new products. These reviews are quite common at other sites as well. But are they really posted by consumers? Apple had to change its system of allowing people to review iPhone and iTouch applications at the iTunes site. Apple found that many "reviews" were either hype generated by the creator of the application, or slams against competing applications. To post a review today, one has to buy the application first. In another case, a representative for a computer peripherals firm was caught offering to pay people for positive reviews of the firm's network router at Amazon.com.[15] As discussed in Chapter 8, the Federal Trade Commission (FTC) has modified its regulations in an effort to assure consumers that consumer reviews actually come from fellow consumers and not from marketing representatives. Nevertheless, advertisers continue to spend a significant amount of money trying to generate "buzz" for their products and services through "word of mouth marketing."

Understandably, the Word of Mouth Marketing Association (WOMMA) defends its members' activities, stating that they are simply engaged in, "Giving people a reason to talk about your products and services, and making it easier for that conversation to take place. It is the art and science of building active, mutually beneficial consumer-to-consumer and con-sumer-to-marketer communications."[16] Commercial Alert, an organization that says it wants to keep "commercial culture within its proper sphere," questions the mutual benefit of word of mouth marketing. Commercial Alert and other groups have asked the FTC to regulate "buzz marketing" more stringently. Others believe that government regulations are not necessary, due largely to the interactive nature of the Internet, where many people have a voice. As WOMMA says in its Code of Ethics, "Sleazy behavior will be exposed by the public and backfire horribly on anyone who attempts it."[17]

Mobile phones

Mobile phones, initially introduced by Motorola in the 1980s as a means of allowing people to communicate with each other while traveling, have evolved into a type of mass media. Advertisers gain contact information about the owners of each phone through a variety of data sources. The advertisers can then custom-tailor audio, text, or graphic advertisements based on the demographics of each owner.

In the early days of the mobile telephone industry, many consumers received their telephone either at no cost or at a price greatly below the actual value of the phone. The device served as a loss leader for mobile phone companies, who relied on the standard two-year service contract with users for their profit. With the recent addition of features such as cameras, music playing capacity, and Internet access, consumers typically pay a price closer to the device's actual value. Some devices such as the iPhone and Blackberry are so popular that wireless phone firms seek exclusive contracts with manufacturers in order to create a competitive advantage over other phone companies.

Some wireless providers, such as MyScreen Mobile and Virgin Mobile, provide advertisements at the end of phone calls, with a series of incentives (gift cards, extra user minutes, etc.) offered to those who agree to participate. In 2009, Google purchased AdMob, another firm that specializes in mobile advertising, for $750 million. Some of the applications available as free downloads for various smart phones also include advertising.

Texting

Texting is possible on any device that accommodates the Short Message Service (SMS). Phone manufacturers introduced the first mobile devices with SMS capability in the early 1990s. Advertisers are attracted to SMS because of how precisely they can target their market. The person using a mobile device with SMS capability can be monitored by Global Positioning System (GPS) technology. So, drive by a pizza restaurant, and it might send you a text offering a special offer. Many SMS users request content from providers for sports scores, weather, traffic reports, celebrity gossip, jokes, music videos, and other information. Using another pizza example, presume that Domino's is advertising during a basketball tournament. The television network broadcasting the tournament runs advertisements during the tournament asking viewers to vote for their favorite team in the tournament. A few minutes before halftime of a game, Domino's texts viewers with a half-time pizza offer. For those who are unable to watch the game but are still interested in following the tournament, Domino advertisements may appear in texted score updates.

Old advertising agency folks talk about an advertisement's "call to action." In other words, an advertisement tries to get consumers to do something. Asking a consumer to send a text message in response to an advertisement may seem like a relatively low-involvement decision by the consumer. For example, it is much easier for a consumer to ask a carmaker for more information about a car than it is to go out and buy that car. But by asking for more information through a text message, that consumer has now become a sales lead. Information about that consumer's request will be sent to the closest car dealer, which can then pursue this lead.

Text messages also help advertisers measure the effectiveness of their advertisements. Suppose that an advertisement on television or radio encourages consumers to text the name of their favorite television program or song to a telephone number maintained by the advertiser. The response rate for that advertisement can be easily measured, by how many people texted a reply. Because most who respond will do so shortly after hearing the advertisement, the advertiser can also determine which day segments yield the most response to the advertisement.

Sexting

According to a 2009 study on behalf of The Associated Press and MTV, 30 percent of Americans between the ages of 14 to 24 have electronically sent or posted sexual graphic text or nude photographs of themselves.[18] Another study found that more than a third of young adults, described by this study as people between the ages of 20 and 26, have engaged in this behavior.[19] Furthermore, this second study found that 39 percent of teens, and 59 percent of young adults say that they have sent sexually suggestive messages through IM, e-mail, or text messaging. Not surprisingly, the great majority of people who say that have engaged in sexting did so with a boyfriend, girlfriend, or somebody that they wanted to date or hook up with. "So what?" you may ask. The concern here is that none of this information is truly anonymous, and anything posted in cyberspace is essentially permanently out there. Couples break up, sometimes angrily. Thus, inappropriate images or messages can come back to haunt us.

There is another concern here. Under the laws of most states, sending a nude picture or image of somebody who is under the age of 18 can constitute the crime of distributing child pornography. The fact that the person sending the image is also under the age of 18 is no defense. Prosecutors have brought charges against teens in several states. Many law enforcement agencies exercise broad discretion in this area, depending on the circumstances.

Video games

As was the case for the Internet, video games were originally invented for military use. The military still uses video games today to simulate combat activities without anybody or anything actually getting hurt. The earliest consumer video games were coin-operated arcade games that appeared in the early 1970s. The first home console games followed shortly thereafter.

Today, there are three main platforms for video games. Computer-based games can be played on personal computers, either as software-based games or played on the Internet. Console games are played on machines made specifically for video games. Console games are connected to televisions or computer monitors, or can be self-contained units. Arcade games use machines specifically designed for one particular game and are often coin-operated. Arcade games' popularity is in decline with the widespread availability of console and PC games today.

Not only are console and PC games widely available; they are also wildly popular. Released in April 2008, "Grand Theft Auto IV" was named by *Guinness World Records* as the most profitable entertainment release of all time.[20] First-day sales of the game were estimated at $310 million, and first week sales were estimated at over $500 million. The previous one-day entertainment sales record was set by the book *Harry Potter and the Deathly Hallows*, which sold $220 million in the first 24 hours of its release in July 2007.

The Entertainment Software Association (ESA) reported that total video game software sales approached $11.7 billion in 2008, more than quadrupling sales since 1996. Sixty-eight percent of American households play computer or video games. In addition, many video games are played online, and their vast popularity is not reflected in software sales figures. Although gamers tend to be relatively young, the ESA tells us that the average age of game players is now 35, and the over 50 market for games is growing. The number of female players is also growing.[21]

Video games provide various types of revenue streams. Console producers earn money from the hardware they sell. Video game creators earn money from selling software, either as packaged games or as online subscriptions. Musicians earn royalties from licensing their music and images to video game creators. As discussed in Chapter 5, Aerosmith has earned more money from licensing itself to Activision for "Guitar Hero: Aerosmith" than from any of its albums. A year after the release of the Aerosmith game, "Guitar Hero: Metallica" was released, and "The Beatles: Rock Band" appeared several months later. (There is likely a correlation between the popularity of older bands' music in video games and the increasing age of the average gamer.) Musicians have enjoyed royalties from more than just the games themselves; there is also a strong correlation between songs appearing on "Guitar Hero" and "Rock Band" and sales of downloads of songs by the musicians who perform them.

In-game advertising

Another revenue stream of video games is advertising. Advertisers are particularly attracted to games played online, as advertisements can be customized based on the demographics of a particular player (gender, age, location) and the time of day (for example, a Pizza Hut advertisement will be more effective in the evening than it will be first thing in the morning). Because many games' popularity relies on creating realistic environments, the presence of advertising and other commercial images actually boosts many players' appreciation of these games. If the game is a racing game (one of the most common genres), billboards and other advertisements may appear. The types of cars seen may be the result of paid product placement—automakers pay to have their cars featured in games. Sports games played in virtual arenas or stadiums may contain advertisements, just as would be seen in real sports venues. Interactivity between the consumer/player and the advertisement can also be measured online. The video game controller shown in Figure 9.3 is a resource for both the gamer and the advertiser.

Figure 9.3 Video games are popular among both players and advertisers. *Source:* iStockphoto

Video games that are not played online may also contain advertising. Unlike online in-game advertising that changes over time, games that are not played online contain static advertising placed during the game's development. However, just as with online games, advertising creates a realistic game environment. One technology-consulting firm estimates that in-game advertising revenue may total more than $970 million by 2011.[22]

One major in-game advertising service is Massive, a subsidiary of Microsoft. Massive places advertisements in Microsoft's Xbox 360 games. Other major in-game advertising services include IGA Worldwide and Engage. In-game advertisers include carmakers, fast food companies, movie studios, mobile phone providers, and the military. Many in-game advertisers also create entire games that are themselves advertisements, called *advergames*. Examples include the U.S. Army's "America's Army" and games distributed by Burger King that feature His Highness himself.

Video game ratings

A common complaint about video games concerns violence. Just as the Motion Picture Association of America created a voluntary rating system to avoid governmental efforts to regulate movie content, the video game industry's Entertainment Software Rating Board (ESRB) provides game ratings and attempts to restrict young people's access to some games. Figure 9.4 displays the ESRB's video game ratings.

ESRB Rating Symbols for Video Games

EARLY CHILDHOOD
Titles rated **EC (Early Childhood)** have content that may be suitable for ages 3 and older. Contains no material that parents would find inappropriate.

EVERYONE
Titles rated **E (Everyone)** have content that may be suitable for ages 6 and older. Titles in this category may contain minimal cartoon, fantasy or mild violence and/or infrequent use of mild language.

EVERYONE 10+
Titles rated **E10+ (Everyone 10 and older)** have content that may be suitable for ages 10 and older. Titles in this category may contain more cartoon, fantasy or mild violence, mild language and/or minimal suggestive themes.

TEEN
Titles rated **T (Teen)** have content that may be suitable for ages 13 and older. Titles in this category may contain violence, suggestive themes, crude humor, minimal blood, simulated gambling, and/or infrequent use of strong language.

MATURE
Titles rated **M (Mature)** have content that may be suitable for persons ages 17 and older. Titles in this category may contain intense violence, blood and gore, sexual content and/or strong language.

ADULTS ONLY
Titles rated **AO (Adults Only)** have content that should only be played by persons 18 years and older. Titles in this category may include prolonged scenes of intense violence and/or graphic sexual content and nudity.

RATING PENDING
Titles listed as **RP (Rating Pending)** have been submitted to the ESRB and are awaiting final rating. (This symbol appears only in advertising prior to a game's release.)

Figure 9.4 Video game ratings. *Source*: Entertainment Software Rating Board

The ESRB lacks legal authority to enforce these restrictions among the various retailers who sell or rent ESRB rated games. However, using secret shoppers, the ESRB's Retail Council reports that about 80 percent of member retailers enforce sales restrictions of games rated M (Mature) or AO (Adults Only).[23]

Virtual worlds

Technically, virtual worlds are a type of video game known as a Massively Multiplayer Online Role Playing Game (*MMORPG*). In many ways, they are the ultimate *sandbox game*, as there are very few rules, players can come and go as they wish, and there is no clear "end" of the game. Perhaps the biggest difference between virtual worlds and video games is that many participants in virtual worlds are not trying to "win" or reach a higher status. However, just as in real life, some participants in virtual worlds are more successful than others are. This success is another form of social capital. Some people are also earning a good deal of money selling virtual items for real money.

Some of the best-known virtual worlds include Active Worlds, There. com, and Club Penguin. The most popular virtual world is Second Life. In September 2009, Second Life's owner reported that its members were logged on a total of 126 million hours in the second quarter of 2009. Members spent an average of 100 minutes per visit.[24]

Participants in virtual worlds (or "residents") create *avatars*, which are the participant's graphic representation of himself or herself on the screen. The real-world participant can often create an avatar that is realistic, completely fantastic, or somewhere in between. This ability to change one's identity in a variety of ways is one of virtual worlds' primary attractions to participants. A male participant can create a female identity, and vice versa. A teenager can assume the identity of a much older person, although more likely, this process works in the opposite direction. Participants can vary race, hair color, and other physical characteristics. In addition, the participants can create names for their avatars. This ability to reinvent one's self is so compelling that many virtual world participants actually expect others to have altered themselves in some way.

As is true of most media, advertisers have a presence in virtual worlds as well. These include Sony, IBM, Adidas, and Nissan. The interactivity of virtual worlds makes them particularly attractive to advertisers. As There. com tells prospective advertisers, "Imagine a world where you can demonstrate a new product, test a prototype, or spin out a new brand and get instant real-time reaction from your customers."[25] Businesses also use virtual worlds for employee training and collaboration, as virtual worlds allow people to share a common space no matter where they are. This sense of building a virtual community led Bryant & Stratton College, a real world college, to hold the first virtual graduation for its online students in June 2009.[26]

GPS devices

In addition to the GPS technology available in many mobile phones, many consumers use GPS devices in their vehicles. A key source of revenue for the firms that market these GPS devices is selling advertising to the types of businesses that people seek when they are on the road. Restaurants, hotels, gas stations, and tourist attractions pay for listings on GPS software.

The future will bring more interactive GPS devices. When driving past a restaurant, one may receive a message through the GPS device from that restaurant to come in and try its food. Similarly, work is being done to customize radio advertising based on the location of an automobile. Google entered into the geographically targeted radio advertising business in 2006. However, this technology may have been before its time, and Google discontinued the venture in 2009.

Podcasting

Podcasts are recorded audio or video presentations that are made available to users through Apple's iTunes site. There, iTunes users can listen or watch podcasts on their computer or iPod. Apple states that over 30 million people subscribe to podcasts.[27] While large corporations create many podcasts, just about anyone can create one. The only limitations that Apple places on podcasts are that they cannot contain unauthorized copyrighted material, erotica, illegal solicitations, or hate speech. Many college professors use them to supplement their teaching.

RSS feeds

RSS (Really Simple Syndication) feeds allow for the easy distribution of content updates from content providers to users. An RSS feed may come from a major media firm or from an individual blogger. Users subscribe to RSS feeds, which are automatically downloaded to users' computers or mobile devices. The convenience for users is that they do not have to check a website for updates, as updates will be delivered to users as they occur. In addition, just as newspapers use stories from other newspapers to provide content, RSS allows websites to share headlines and stories from other sites.

The future of new media

By their very nature, new media are innovative and quite attractive to younger consumers who are searching for new communication technologies and new social opportunities. Because many new media firms are unproven, they are attractive to venture capitalists. These investors seek young firms with new ideas that may provide tremendous returns on investment—if they provide any return at all. A basic adage in business is that return is based on risk. New media ideas come and go, but some of them have found a profitable place in the market. Others have grown to be extremely popular with consumers, yet their owners are still identifying ways to profit from this popularity.

To what degree new media pose a threat to more traditional forms of media has yet to be completely determined. Certainly, print media (especially newspapers) are challenged by new technology that provides mobility and allows for frequently updated content. Television and radio also recognize the threat that new media pose. How successfully these older media adapt will largely determine their futures.

New media and careers

New media careers include web design, game design, online marketing, and numerous management and support positions. New media require animators, audio and video technicians, and computer programmers. In a report titled "Tomorrow's Jobs," the U.S. Department of Labor's Bureau of Labor Statistics tells us:

> Employment in the information supersector is expected to increase by 6.9 percent, adding 212,000 jobs by 2016. Information contains some of the fast-growing computer-related industries such as software publishing, Internet publishing and broadcasting, and wireless telecommunication carriers. Employment in these industries is expected to grow by 32 percent, 44.1 percent, and 40.9 percent, respectively . . . Increased demand for telecommunications services, cable service, high-speed Internet connections, and software will fuel job growth among these industries.[28]

The Entertainment Software Association notes that California, Washington, Texas, New York, and Massachusetts currently have the highest concentration of video game jobs, employing more than 16,000 employees in those five states. With its well-deserved reputation as the nation's (if not the world's) entertainment capital, California is home to about 40 percent of video game jobs.[29] Many of those who are pursuing careers in new media are self-employed content providers who sell advertising space to support their sites and themselves.

Questions for critical thinking and discussion

1. One of the major concerns about social networking sites is that of establishing boundaries.

   - Would you let your parent "friend" you on a social networking site? Explain your answer.
   - Would you let your boss "friend" you on a social networking site? Explain your answer.
   - If you are in school, would you let your teacher "friend" you on a social networking site? Explain your answer.

2. Social networking allows people to stay connected with friends, reconnect with old friends, and meet new friends.

   - Is there a difference between "online friends" and "offline friends?" Explain why or why not.

(Continued)

Questions for critical thinking and discussion—Cont'd

3. This chapter discusses fake product reviews posted by advertisers on social networking sites and other websites.

   • As a consumer shopping for a particular product, what methods would you use to determine if a product review was legitimate or not? Explain.

4. As this chapter discusses, being a popular medium does not necessarily equate with being a profitable one.

   • Which of the new media discussed in this chapter do you think is likely to be the most profitable for its owners in the future? Why?
   • Which of the new media discussed in this chapter do you think is likely to be the least profitable for its owners in the future? Why?

5. Many of the new media discussed in this chapter are particularly popular among young people.

   • Will people lose interest in new media as they grow older? Explain why or why not.

Additional resources

Castronova, Edward, *Exodus to the Virtual World; How Online Fun is Changing Reality* (New York: Palgrave Macmillan, 2007).

Commercial Alert, www.commercialalert.org

Entertainment Software Association, www.theesa.com

Entertainment Software Ratings Board, www.esrb.org

Gee, James Paul, *What Video Games Have to Teach Us About Learning and Literacy* (New York: Palgrave Macmillan, 2003).

Mobile Marketing Association, www.mmaglobal.com

Palfrey, John, and Urs Gasser, *Born Digital; Understanding the First Generation of Digital Natives* (New York: Basic Books, 2008).

Pew Internet & American Life Project, www.pewinternet.org

Sex and Tech: What's *Really* Going On, www.thenationalcampaign.org/sextech

Taylor, Allan, and James Robert Parish, *Career Opportunities in the Internet, Video Games, and Multimedia* (New York: Ferguson, 2007).

Tremayne, Mark, ed., *Blogging, Citizenship, and the Future of Media* (New York: Routledge, 2007).

Virtual World News, www.virtualworldsnews.com

Wolf, Mark J. P., ed., *The Video Game Explosion; A History from Pong to Playstation and Beyond* (Westport, CT: Greenwood Press, 2008).

Disaggregation and Convergence

Chapter contents

Issues and trends with disaggregation and convergence

- Disaggregation occurs as our choice of media channels expands, yielding increasing competition for audiences among those media channels.
- Disaggregation also arises from advertisers identifying relatively small, highly-defined consumer segments for specialized products and services.
- Convergence results as increasingly sophisticated communication technology allows us to communicate in different ways; our mobile phone can also be our music player, our Internet browser, and our text-messaging device.
- Convergent communication technology enables millions of individuals to create and distribute media content.
- Convergence also comes from communication providers offering a variety of communication services; our cable television provider can also be our landline and mobile telephone provider, as well as our Internet service provider.
- Media firms rely on convergence to leverage personalities or programs through many different media channels in order to attain a higher return on their investment.

A *paradigm* is a common way of doing something or thinking about something. When the way of doing something or think about something changes, there is a *paradigm shift*. A couple of examples may help you understand paradigm shifts. For many years, a telephone number identified a place more than it did a person. A landline phone was fixed at a particular location—a house or a business. Today, a telephone number represents a person, not a place. With mobile phones, we no longer have to be at a particular location to send or receive communications over a telephone. Another example of a paradigm shift is how we obtain recorded music today. For decades, consumers would go to a store and buy a physical item—first a vinyl record, then a cassette tape, and later a CD. Now, the largest music retailer in the United States is Apple's iTunes. The music package is a digital file rather than a physical item, and is more likely to be a single song than an entire album. This chapter discusses two significant paradigm shifts that are affecting the way we communicate and the way we think about communication: *disaggregation* and *convergence*.

Disaggregation

For decades, many Americans had only three choices on television. The three television networks—CBS, NBC, and ABC—attempted to attract as broad an audience as possible. The spread of cable, and later, satellite, television changed that, and broadcasting gave way to *narrowcasting* to smaller, more select audiences through a hundred channels or more. The total audience continues to grow as the nation's population increases, but that total audience divides itself among an increasing number of television channels. We have an increasing number of media choices, and the media are targeting increasingly smaller *niches*, or segments of the market.

Today we have television networks aimed at specific groups, including women, men, African Americans, Spanish speakers, gays and lesbians, and children. There are also networks devoted exclusively to particular subjects, such as news, sports, weather, politics, music, and religion. Because of this disaggregation, major television networks are struggling to attract the most attractive demographic group to advertisers: viewers between the ages of 18–49. In June 2009, the networks posted their lowest combined ratings ever among viewers in this age group.[1]

Disaggregation: media content

For years, television networks have undertaken expensive risks, spending large sums of money for new television programming. In addition to the financial cost of programming, there is an opportunity cost. Because there are a limited number of hours available in prime-time broadcasting, and because programs usually occupy a time slot of at least half an hour, the decision to add one program requires the cancelation of the program already airing in that time spot. Thus, some viewers who liked the older program but dislike the new program will change channels. In addition, if a television network has many choices of programs to fill a particular time spot, it risks choosing the wrong one, while what could have been a more successful program is lost, perhaps forever.

Contrast the old method of programming with what is available today. Every minute, 10 hours of video is being uploaded to YouTube.[2] Google, the owner of YouTube, does not pay a dime for content. It is provided without cost by the individuals and media firms who upload it. There is a problem, though, and it is a big one. Google paid $1.65 billion for YouTube in 2006. Although nearly 100 million viewers watch almost 6 million videos on YouTube each month, YouTube is not profitable.[3]

Google, which generates huge revenue connecting advertisements to search terms, has yet to figure out how to connect advertisements to videos profitably. For example, suppose your cousin uploads a video clip of her wedding to YouTube. Who would want to watch it? Yes, your cousin will watch her video repeatedly, especially when she and the groom do that cute thing with the cake. You, other relatives, and some friends may watch the video a few times. Perhaps people who are curious about the weddings of complete strangers may watch.

Which advertisers would want to pay to have their advertisement linked to her video? Your first response may be companies that provide wedding services. (A cynical reader may say, "divorce lawyers.") However, connecting advertisements for wedding services to a wedding video will likely produce few click-throughs. After all, your cousin just got married, so she is not in the market. Friends and family may be planning another wedding, but there is no guarantee that any of them are. Ironically, the viewer most likely to be interested in wedding services may be the complete stranger who searches for "weddings" in general on YouTube—anybody's wedding, because they are planning their own. However, the search term "weddings" returned 614,000 hits at YouTube on November 19, 2009—perhaps too disaggregated for most advertisers.

Disaggregation: mass customization

New media allow us to customize our media experiences based on our likes and dislikes. We will use the Internet as an example. Chances are that you have set up a homepage on the Internet. This page appears when you start your Internet browser. There are many choices of homepages available. Search engines such as Yahoo, Google, and Bing encourage users to create homepages through them in order to generate traffic for their search engines and their advertising. Social networking sites such as Facebook and Twitter also encourage users to begin their Internet sessions there.

The ability for each user to customize their homepage is particularly attractive to many of us. This attractiveness may be aesthetic, as each user gets to create the "look" of their homepage. Even more important to most users are customized modules that contain the user's local news, weather, sports and entertainment listings, as well as modules that focus on the user's personal and professional interests. Of course, each user's choices of customized features also provide data to the homepage provider about that user. As Figure 10.1 indicates, customization also includes where and when we decide to access the media.

Many other firms provide opportunities for mass customization via the Internet. We can order M&M candy, Nike shoes, or Dell computers in our choice of colors, and we willingly pay extra for that choice. NetFlix, iTunes, and Amazon are only a few of the many Internet sales portals that make suggestions for future orders based on our past orders.

Disaggregation: movies

Consider the film industry before the age of television. If one wanted to see a movie, he or she had relatively few choices: select one of the local theaters and hope that what was showing was to that person's liking. In the early years of the movies, theaters had only one screen, and so the moviegoer's choices were far fewer than in today's era of the multiscreen cineplex. When

Figure 10.1 Disaggregation means that we choose which media we use and when we use them. *Source*: iStockphoto

television began arriving in homes in the late 1940s, movie fans had more choices about what they could watch, as television also broadcast movies. Remember though, for the first few decades of commercial television, most Americans received only three television networks. The arrival of cable television in the 1960s and home video players in the 1970s offered movie fans many more choices.

The concept of the *long tail* was first discussed in Chapter 5. The term describes a business phenomenon made possible by the Internet and other communication technology. Because the Internet is global in its reach, the markets for many products and services today are also global (this is one of the subjects of Chapter 12). It is possible for a business to generate a profit even though most people are not interested in its products or services. This is because that business can now reach nearly everybody in the world, rather than focus on a single local or national market.

For example, let us look at a video store. Video stores are a dying industry, due in part to the long tail effect. A video store in a mall, paying high rent for each square foot of space, carries a limited number of video titles. Because those who live within driving distance will be the only customers who visit that store, it will focus on the language(s) those who live in the area speak.

Compare that suburban store to a website that allows users to stream videos. This website does not have to absorb the overhead that a chain of video stores must pay for: hundreds or thousands of locations, each with inventory, rent, utilities, taxes, insurance, and personnel costs. True, the website will have to pay licensing fees in order to distribute copyrighted material. However, because the material is not distributed until a user downloads it, there is little or no overhead upfront. The video store has to pay to stock its shelves with thousands of titles before the first customer walks in the door.

Theoretically, the video website can offer every movie ever made. This is because each movie can be digitally loaded on a series of servers, taking up relatively little physical space. The website may be accessible throughout the world, so it can offer videos in every language.

This changes the economics of movie making. There will still be movies that cost many millions of dollars to produce, which will require exhibition in theaters to return a profit for their producers. However, there are now alternative platforms for filmmakers, especially filmmakers who create movies on a relatively low budget. The direct to DVD or direct to Internet avenues allow these filmmakers to distribute their creations without theater exhibition.

Another aspect of disaggregation of movie watching is that it encourages experimentation in movies. Experimental films online do not have to fill theaters to generate a profit. If only a few people in every community in the United States view the film, it can make money for the people who made the film and for the online video services that offer it.

Disaggregation: music

The first significant disaggregation in the music industry was the result of both technological changes and the post–World War II baby boom and youth movement. With the introduction of television into homes in the late 1940s, the radio industry focused on music rather than the drama and comedy programs that they had relied upon in the past, as those programs moved to television. A variety of radio formats were developed. Some songs and artists appear on more than one format, but the typical commercial radio station today will base its programming on the format that its management has embraced. If that station's ratings or advertising sales are unsatisfactory, the station will simply change its format.

The old business model of commercial music emphasized a musical artist being signed to a record firm, or "label." The label's promotional staff would then attempt to get radio stations to play that artist's music. The contract between the artist and its label typically required the artist to undertake a concert tour to promote its records. While some musicians achieved commercial success without significant radio play, this required a patient record label and lots of touring.

Today, many wonder if a significant role remains for record labels. It is becoming common for musicians, whether widely popular or relatively unknown, to release their music directly to Internet sites without labels' involvement. This process removes two obstacles that musicians formerly encountered: the need to attract a record label and to receive radio airplay. The future may mean that fewer musicians will become millionaires, but consumers will have more choices of music.

Disaggregation: magazines

Today, there are thousands more magazine titles than there were 10 years ago. The largest growth in magazine titles is among trade publications—magazines aimed at specific industries and occupations. The magazines with the highest circulation figures tend to be consumer magazines, aimed at the general public rather than particular occupations. However, many of the most popular magazines have been experiencing steady declines in circulation. These two phenomena—more titles, but with declining circulation among the most popular titles—epitomize disaggregation.

An increasing number of magazines offer online versions of their publications. Today's magazine sites on the Internet and the electronic magazines of the future have the ability to target articles and advertising to each individual reader. For example, suppose that a college student in California and a college professor in Massachusetts both enjoy reading *Sports Illustrated*. The college student is more interested in following the professional and college teams in California, while the professor follows the teams in New England. A certain amount of what each reader sees at the *Sports Illustrated* website will be the same—this is *push content*, as it is delivered to the reader without the reader specifically asking for that content. In this example, the push content may relate to some sporting events that Time Warner, the owner of *Sports Illustrated*, is broadcasting on one of its television networks, such as TBS. This would be an example of Time Warner using its media holdings to generate synergies. The *pull content* at the *Sports Illustrated* website would be information about the teams or events for which the individual subscriber has identified his or her interest.

Suppose that the student and the professor are interested in the same teams. Although the pull content will be the same for these two readers, the advertising will likely be different. The advertisements that appear on the student's screen will be based on the fact that this reader is 19 years old and lives in California. The advertisements for the college professor will be based on his age, his location, and perhaps his educational attainment.

Disaggregation: marketing and advertising

The automaker Henry Ford supposedly made the remark that consumers could have his Model T "in any color, so long as it's black." Ford gave little thought to how consumers would perceive his vehicles or how consumers would perceive themselves when seen in his vehicles. Ford was selling transportation, little more.

General Motors' approach was markedly different: it sold a variety of cars for different types of people. GM engaged in *market segmentation*. The key factor was income. As GM originally saw it, a motorist would begin with a Chevrolet, the company's least expensive brand. As that motorist's career advanced, future purchases would include the pricier Buick and perhaps ultimately, a Cadillac. GM also realized that other factors affected consumer's choices. The consumer who bought a red Chevrolet was different from the consumer who preferred a gray Chevy. GM offered both colors and many more. (Many observers have blamed GM's current financial woes partly on its recent management's inattention to product differentiation among its brands and models, which had made the company successful in the past.)

Product segmentation looks for different niches in the marketplace. The most common identifiers for market niches fall within two categories: *demographics* and *psychographics*. (These terms were first introduced in Chapter 1.) Demographics are measurable statistics of people based on such factors as age, gender, income, education, and geographic location (usually identified by zip code). Psychographics examine consumers' attitudes, beliefs, and habits (including buying habits). Consumers shopping for a car today, or other products, usually make their selections based on demographic and psychographic factors.

For many firms, the consumer niche the company serves defines that company. We will use Hollister as an example. The average college student can identify a Hollister store, even though the store (intentionally) has little or no signage. Instead of having merchandise on display in store windows as traditional retailers do, Hollister conceals its windows with shutters—the feeling is one of exclusivity, of some shoppers being kept out. The message Hollister is trying to convey is, "you either 'get' us or you don't." Teens and twenty-somethings are much more likely to get it than older consumers are. Similarly, Hollister and its parent company Abercrombie & Fitch do not advertise on television, which is "everybody's medium."

Dog whistle marketing describes how certain consumers will attend to advertising and marketing campaigns in different ways. For example, Subaru is happy to sell its automobiles to any motorist. Yet Subaru hardly promotes its products as transportation for everyone. This message would be too broad in a highly competitive industry that spends billions of dollars on advertising. Since the 1990s, Subaru has made a concerted effort to attract gay and lesbian drivers. For example, the tagline for Subaru's advertising campaign in 2000 stated, "It's not a choice. It's the way we're built." Subaru's wish is that gay consumers would interpret this message as demonstrating sympathy with their sexuality. Subaru also aired advertisements with former tennis star Martina Navratilova, who is a lesbian. Subaru's efforts over the past decade have proved successful. A survey of gay and lesbian car owners in March 2009 found that 45 percent of those polled believed Subaru to be a gay-friendly brand with second place Volkswagen far behind at 9 percent.[4] The survey was reported by gaywheels.com, which calls itself "the gay-friendly automotive resource." Of course, not everyone who buys a Subaru is gay, and in fact, Subaru is not the brand that most gay and lesbian drivers buy. Being gay friendly is only one factor among many for these consumers. Subaru competes with other car companies that also seek to appeal to the particular demographic and psychographic characteristics of drivers.

Convergence

At the same time that we are witnessing disaggregation, we are also experiencing convergence. The iPhone or Blackberry that we carry in our pocket is our telephone, camera, texting device, e-mail portal, planner, music playing device, video playing device, and Internet connection. At some airports, our cell phone can also function as our boarding pass.

For at least a decade, media observers have discussed the process of media converging from traditional types (television, newspaper, radio, etc.) to a single electronic online platform. This means more than using the same device to access all media content. One of the best-known scholars of media convergence, Henry Jenkins of the University of Southern California, argues that media convergence is actually five different processes:[5]

- Technological convergence through digitization of media content. Photographs, videos, films, music, and words can all be captured and transmitted in digital form.
- Economic convergence through corporations seeking synergies. Less than a dozen corporations control the bulk of our entertainment media.
- Social convergence through consumers' use of multiple types of media simultaneously. Many of those reading this sentence are listening to music, and have their wireless phone/texting device powered on and close by.
- Cultural convergence through multiple platforms that allow consumers to create, mash-up, critique, and share media content. Media companies provide these forums in order to generate content that costs those companies little or nothing.
- Global convergence through the ability for consumers to interact with those in nearly every other society. In the process, cultures blend, as do ideas and beliefs.

We examine global convergence in Chapter 12. Below we look at the first four of the processes that Jenkins identifies.

Technological convergence

In your lifetime, the United States, perhaps the world, will become one large WiFi (wireless fidelity) hotspot. Electronic books and newspapers are already available through devices such as the iPhone, Blackberry, and Kindle. Technology firms are developing devices that resemble magazines in feel. These devices are the size of an ordinary magazine, with a flexible monitor that can bend and fold just as a magazine does, with WiFi capability. But this device is more than just an electronic magazine or newspaper. It will also provide Internet access, texting capabilities, and audio and video streaming.

Technological convergence: the digital home

Imagine that you are at the grocery store and cannot remember which food items that you are running short of at home. Fortunately, you can turn on your mobile communication device, which will connect to your refrigerator. As you have placed items in and removed them from the fridge, a Radio Frequency Identification Device (RFID) tag on each item has recorded food usage. The device in your hand tells you that you need more orange juice. You may not even need to ask. Presume that your mobile device is powered on as you drive by the grocery store. Your smart refrigerator may text you to remind you about that orange juice problem. "Smart" refrigerators are among the types of home appliances that technology companies are designing with integrated communication systems. We may want to conserve energy, but have a comfortable house when we arrive home. We will be able to turn on the heating or cooling system as we get ready to head home from wherever we are. If we forget to adjust the thermostat before we leave for the day, the thermostat may text message us later to ask for permission to make that adjustment.

The discussion of digital homes equipped with smart appliances began many years ago. Thus far, it seems to be an idea ahead of the consumer demand curve. LG's Internet Refrigerator, introduced several years ago for about $8,000, turned out to be a flop. However, recent events have seen both industry and consumers seeking "green" devices that are more energy efficient. If the ability to communicate distantly with one's furnace, oven, or refrigerator begins to be seen as desirable by an increasing number of consumers, this technology will soon be available to many of us.

Economic convergence

Many of us now have the same company providing our telephone, Internet, and television service. Although we may have over one hundred choices of television programming in our homes, most of the channels we have are controlled by less than a dozen companies. Many of these companies own a variety of different media. Companies strive to use their various assets in a complementary way. You have heard the expression, "one hand washes the other." In business, the discussion is about leveraging assets to create a *synergy*.

A synergy uses two or more assets of a business to generate more revenue (money) than each single asset can generate individually. Perhaps one of the most remarkable examples of using multiple media platforms to create a set of synergies was Viacom's marketing of Howard Stern. Stern's radio program aired on Viacom-owned Infinity's stations throughout the United States. His program was also recorded on video and shown late on Saturday nights on television stations owned by or affiliated with CBS (owned by Viacom). Stern wrote a book, *Private Parts*, published by Simon and Schuster (owned by Viacom). The book was made into a movie for Paramount Pictures (owned by Viacom). The movie was shown in National Amusement theaters (owned by Viacom). Clips from the movie were shown on MTV (owned by Viacom) and Stern pitched the book and the movie on his radio program. When the movie was released on home video, it was available for rent or purchase at Blockbuster (you guessed it—owned by Viacom). Viacom has since spun-off some of these companies and Stern has moved to Sirius Radio. Yet at the time when Stern immodestly claimed to be "The King of All Media," he may have been right. Viacom's leveraging of Stern to generate synergies is only one example of how the world's largest media firms use their corporate holdings to help each other.

Economic convergence: non-media industries

Media convergence affects many non-media industries. We will use the travel and tourism industry as an example. Imagine that you are going to take a trip to South America. Not sure when to go? You can check destinations' weather and events online. You can then visit any number of travel websites to find the best airfares and hotel rates. If the airline prices are similar, various websites rate seats, cabin service, and airline food. Once you decide on an airline, you can select your seat online and order a special meal, such as kosher or vegetarian. Likewise, you can select the type of bed you want at the hotel and specify smoking or nonsmoking. Other sites provide restaurant reviews, shopping tips, and information about various attractions.

As you prepare for your trip, you can visit the airline's website to see whether you will have a power port for your laptop or portable media device. You can also check the airline's website for which movies will be playing on your flight; some airline websites offer links to movie reviews. Lousy movie or one you have already seen? Then it is time to load up your portable media device with music, videos, e-texts, and game applications to keep you busy on your long flight. However, you may not need to, as many airlines are now offering personal entertainment devices with choices of movies and television programs, multiple music channels, and various games to keep you occupied. Airlines are highly competitive, and know that passengers often choose a flight based on what types of amenities are available. As you leave for the airport, you can use your personal data device to check whether your flight is on time, and whether there are anticipated delays at any of the airports through which you will be traveling.

The travel and tourism industry provide only one example of how media convergence affects an industry. Convergence will continue to bring changes to many other industries as well. Yet convergence is not exclusive to business, as we see next.

Social convergence

The death of Michael Jackson in June 2009 demonstrated the social power of media convergence. For many Americans, news of Jackson's death came from television or radio announcements. Those who wanted more information surfed online for newsfeeds from Los Angeles news outlet, music outlets, and Jackson fan sites. The memorial tribute to Jackson on July 7, 2009 was broadcast live on television and streamed live on the Internet. Prior to the tribute, some of those who were able to obtain tickets sold them on eBay and Craigslist. Television stations and websites asked fans to text or e-mail their thoughts about Jackson and his career. These same television stations and websites offered to send updates by text message, e-mail, or Twitter to interested fans.

Fans of Jackson created tribute websites that received heavy traffic. Fans viewed videos of Jackson's performances, stories about his death, fans' comments, and related videos on YouTube. Sales of Jackson's music soared. Billboard.com reported that Jackson occupied all 10 spots in the Catalog Album category's top 10, the first time a single artist had done so. Over

5.6 million digital music tracks were sold in the two weeks following Jackson's death and millions of additional tracks were downloaded illegally. Nearly 100,000 music videos were sold during the same two-week period, as were over 300,000 ringtones.[6]

The reaction to Jackson's death demonstrated how the media have changed from the old model, with a limited number of media firms creating content and directing their material at passive spectators, to a new model that is highly interactive and participatory, allowing multiple content creators to share their material. Fans were able to provide feedback to the media firms through text messages, tweets (Twitter messages), and e-mails, and were also able to connect with each other directly, without those media firms serving as intermediaries. Here, fans created their own *passion communities*, connecting with other fans all over the world.

The same month that Michael Jackson died, presidential elections were held in Iran. According to most observers, those working for incumbent president Mahmoud Ahmadinejad rigged the election. Many thousands of Iranians protested in the streets for weeks afterward. The Iranian government attempted to prevent any news of the election protests and the military's violent reaction to those protests from being shown to Iranians and foreigners. The Iranian government found it relatively easy to block information about the protests distributed by accredited journalists representing traditional media firms. However, the Iranian government was virtually powerless against the average citizen. Too many Iranians held the ability to upload photographs, videos, and written and oral commentaries in their own hands.

Those following Michael Jackson's death and the election in Iran did not use "a single black box," as Henry Jenkins would point out. Instead, they used multiple platforms to experience these events together, such as some of the devices shown in Figure 10.2. Again, although the major media outlets participated in this convergence, they were only a few among millions of participants. This relative subordination of the major media represents a significant paradigm shift, as the media now must share information *with* us, rather than direct information *at* us.

Cultural convergence

For many news outlets, the need to provide up-to-date content 24 hours a day, seven days a week makes it increasingly likely that these outlets are

Figure 10.2 Media convergence uses multiple forms of communications technology.
Source: iStockphoto

willing to rely on viewers themselves to provide some of that content. Chances are that your local television stations offer viewers a chance to upload their photographs and videos to those television stations' websites. This is *crowdsourcing—we* create media content.

Media news crews cannot be everywhere that news happens. Many of us have the ability to record events as they happen with our personal media devices. Media news outlets find it challenging to balance timeliness with appropriateness: images of a bloody car accident or homicide scene may be accurate, but displaying those images may be beyond the boundaries of responsible journalism. One of the benefits of "citizen journalism" is that it allows us to witness events that may otherwise be suppressed by traditional media. Numerous examples of embarrassing or illegal behavior by public officials and the elite have been captured by passersby. These images, when communicated to others, often go viral, with an increasing number of people rapidly forwarding those images to others, and the parties involved are unable to suppress or distort our knowledge of those events.

An event does not have to be scandalous to go viral. Just as we see the long tail effect altering traditional media formats, it is changing content as well. We are constantly searching for "breaking news" and "developing stories," which come and go quickly. Today, there are more news stories generated by more news sources than ever before, but each individual news story tends to hold our attention for a shorter length of time.

Another issue driving the citizen journalism trend is news outlets' effort to embrace the interactivity that consumers increasingly expect. Thus, traditional news media such as television and newspapers provide various methods for members of the public to provide feedback. We are increasingly being asked, "What do you think?" and what we think is being reported as news.

Cultural convergence: the democratization of expertise

It is safe to guess that many who are reading this have relied on Wikipedia more than once. Contributors who submit to Wikipedia do not need to hold advanced college degrees. For most subjects, anybody who cares to may submit; over 85,000 people have done so. If there is a question about the authenticity or accurateness of the information posted, the crowd of Wikipedia users decides. As is typical of crowdsourcing, this *knowledge community* creates content and evaluates content posted by others. Substandard or disputed information is subject to removal.[7]

Because of crowdsourced knowledge, many of those individuals whom we once considered experts (and who understandably enjoyed that status) are finding their influence diminishing. We can read restaurant reviews written by food critics with trained palates in magazines and newspapers, or we can go online and see what other ordinary diners like ourselves have to say. Of course, the restaurants' owners may have deviously placed some of those online reviews, but what is more important is that other reviews have just as much authority as those "placed" reviews have. Similarly, while we once relied on movie reviews in newspapers and magazines written by film critics who attended film school and have graduate degrees in journalism, today we may turn instead to what other moviegoers like ourselves have to say.

This reliance on the opinions of those we see as more like ourselves than the supposed experts leads to *information cascades*. We supplement the information we already have with what other people are saying. At their best, information cascades represent collective wisdom, with the different viewpoints of many individuals helping us choose wisely. At their worst, information cascades can produce a herd mentality in which we do or think things primarily because other people are.

The future of disaggregation and convergence

Media disaggregation and convergence, although relatively recent phenomena, will likely continue significantly in the future. Two groups with very different agendas are driving these phenomena. Consumers want to access and share information in a variety of ways, with a variety of different collections of other people. We will communicate with increasingly versatile communication technology. Advertisers seek highly defined niches of consumers that allow them to distribute their advertising by the most efficient and economic means possible. Advertisers realize that communicating with these disaggregated niches requires the use of many different media channels.

Disaggregation and convergence and careers

Technological unemployment occurs when technology changes, lessening demand for some occupations or eliminating those occupations altogether. Because of the invention of the automobile, we need fewer blacksmiths today than we did in the 1800s. There is little available research on how media disaggregation and convergence by themselves will affect employment in the future. Previous chapters of this book have highlighted how paradigm shifts in the media affect careers. Among the most volatile careers today are those in print media, with many large newspapers and magazines experiencing significant losses in readership and advertising revenue. However, new media technology will certainly create new employment opportunities, as consumer demand for new media technology remains strong.

Questions for critical thinking and discussion

1. In 1970, musician Gil Scott-Heron released a song, "The Revolution Will Not Be Televised." Most media observers today would say that Scott-Heron's prediction would not hold true.

   - Explain what has changed since 1970 to prove Scott-Heron's prediction wrong.

     (Continued)

Questions for critical thinking and discussion—Cont'd

2. Although there are over 304 million people in the United States, there are only two major political parties. Third party candidates for president have done relatively poorly since Theodore Roosevelt and the Bull Moose Party finished a distant second in 1912.

   A successful presidential candidate needs name recognition among voters, which comes through media access. In the past, with relatively few media channels, name recognition has been difficult to attain. The disaggregation discussed in this chapter means that there are now numerous media channels available to political candidates.

   • Will the disaggregation of media audiences benefit third party candidates? Will disaggregation hurt third party candidates instead? Or will it have no significant effect either way? Explain your answer.

3. This chapter discusses crowdsourcing, the process by which individuals can upload content in various media channels, typically providing that content for free.

   • Will crowdsourcing reduce or eliminate our willingness to pay for media content? Explain why or why not.

4. One of the most significant outcomes of audience disaggregation is the loss of audience size among the major television networks, as viewers have more choices of television programming on cable or satellite systems.

   • If you were an executive at one of the major television networks—CBS, NBC, or ABC—explain what you would do in response to the disaggregation of television audiences.

5. Media convergence allows people to develop and maintain passion communities, as we saw following the death of Michael Jackson. Passion communities use electronic media to share information and exchange ideas and feelings about a particular interest.

   • Would you currently identify yourself as a member of a passion community?
   • If you answered yes to the question above, discuss how you use media technology to participate in that community.
   • If you answered no to the question above, discuss how you could use media technology to participate in a passion community in the future.

Additional resources

Bruns, Alex, *Blogs, Wikipedia, Second Life, and Beyond: From Production to Produsage* (New York: Peter Lang, 2008).

Center for Social Media, www.centerforsocialmedia.org

Generation Engage, www.generationengage.org/index.php

Hawk, Byron, David M. Rieder, and Ollie Oviedo, eds., *Small Talk: The Culture of Digital Tools* (Minneapolis: University of Minnesota Press, 2008).

Jenkins, Henry, *Convergence Culture; Where Old and New Media Collide* (New York: NYU Press, 2006).

The Long Tail (Chris Anderson's Blog), www.longtail.typepad.com

MIT Convergence Culture Consortium, www.convergenceculture.org

Project New Media Literacies, www.newmedialiteracies.org

Sunstein, Cass, *Infotopia; How Many Minds Produce Knowledge* (New York: Oxford University Press, 2008).

Wasik, Bill, *And Then There's This; How Stories Live and Die in Viral Culture* (New York: Viking, 2009).

Weinberger, David, Everything is Miscellaneous; The Power of the New Digital Disorder (New York: Holt, 2008).

Mass Communications and the Legal Environment

Chapter contents

Issues and trends in mass communications and the legal environment

- Legal issues arise from the ability of everyone with online access to communicate their thoughts and feelings with millions of others.
- Online access to digital music, video, and business software files has proven to be both a benefit to consumers and a challenge for media producers.
- Heavy lobbying by the media industry has led to new copyright legislation that many believe is excessive in its scope and duration.
- New media allow us to create and share fan fiction and fan films based on the original works of others.
- The interactivity of new media technology allows media companies and their advertisers to obtain significant personal data from consumers—much of which is voluntarily provided.
- Criminals are using recent advances in communication technology to commit a variety of crimes.

Just as mass communications are in a state of significant change, so are the laws that govern the mass media and those who use media. In this chapter, we will discuss defamation, privacy issues, electronic stalking, and government regulation of media ownership. A discussion of media law usually begins with a look at the First Amendment.

The First Amendment: protection of free speech and free press

The First Amendment says in part that "Congress shall make no law . . . abridging the freedom of speech, or of the press." The First Amendment was originally intended to protect against interference with free speech by the federal government. The U.S. Supreme Court extended this protection against state interference in 1925, saying that, "freedom of speech and of the press—which are protected by the 1st Amendment from abridgment by Congress—are among the fundamental personal rights and 'liberties' protected . . . from impairment by the states."[1]

The First Amendment not only protects what we say; it also protects our right not to say something. A media outlet cannot be forced to run advertisements or other types of content without the consent of the owners of that media outlet. For example, if a theater owner wanted to run a newspaper advertisement for a movie that was rated NC-17, the editor of the newspaper has a First Amendment right to refuse to publish the advertisement. Likewise, Google's Terms of Service tells visitors that, "Google reserves the right (but shall have no obligation) to pre-screen, review, flag, filter, modify, refuse or remove any or all Content from any Service."[2]

Although freedom of speech and the press seems to be absolute when reading the First Amendment, this protection has been limited in several situations. One situation is Oliver Wendell Holmes Jr.'s example of "falsely shouting fire in a theater and causing a panic."[3] Words that needlessly endanger others have no First Amendment protection. Other examples of unprotected speech include defamation and obscenity.

Unprotected speech: defamation

There is often uncertainty about the difference between "libel" and "slander." Traditionally, libel was communicated in writing and slander was communicated orally. Both involved intentionally making false statements about someone that damaged that person's reputation. The distinction between libel and slander can be confusing today, and thus many legal scholars simply refer to either as "defamation."

Well-known people receive more press coverage than the average citizen does, and thus are more likely to be the victim of defamation. The U.S. Supreme Court has distinguished between ordinary people and those who have intentionally made themselves "public officials or public figures."[4] Public officials include government officials and politicians; public figures include celebrities. If a person is found to be either a public official or public figure, he or she must prove that the defendant acted with "actual malice." This means that it is not enough for the plaintiff (the person who files a lawsuit) to prove that the published statement is false. Instead, the plaintiff must prove that the defendant published a statement that the defendant knew was false or acted with reckless disregard for whether the statement was false or not.

Unprotected speech: obscenity

Many people confuse the term obscenity with pornography. Pornography includes material that is sexual or erotic in nature. For example, *Playboy* magazine, which contains nude photography and sexual content, is pornographic. Most pornographic material has First Amendment protection.

As the diagram in Figure 11.1 demonstrates, obscenity is a subset of pornography—it is pornography that "goes too far." The courts have

Figure 11.1 Obscenity is a subset of pornography.

determined that those who create and distribute obscenity do not enjoy First Amendment protection and can be prosecuted.

In *Miller v. California* (1973) the U.S. Supreme Court provided its definition of obscenity. In order to punish someone for creating or distributing obscene material, all of the following criteria must be met:

- An average person, applying contemporary community standards, must find that the material, as a whole, appeals to the prurient interest;
- The material must depict or describe, in a patently offensive way, sexual conduct specifically defined by applicable law; and
- The material, taken as a whole, must lack serious literary, artistic, political, or scientific value.[5]

Notice that the court stresses community standards rather than a uniform national standard. The Supreme Court recognized that different parts of the country have different attitudes about sex and sexuality. The court also uses a word with which even most legal scholars were unfamiliar. "Prurient" means a shameful interest in sex, as distinguished from a biological or emotional interest.

Note that the first two parts of the *Miller* test can be met but the defendant can still prevail if the work is found to have serious value. Thus, a 1989 exhibit of Robert Mapplethorpe's photography in Cincinnati, which contained homoerotic images, was found to be protected by the First Amendment due to the artistic value of the exhibit. Similarly, in 1992, the Eleventh U.S. Circuit Court of Appeals reversed a trial judge's determination that the rap group 2 Live Crew's *As Nasty as They Wanna Be* was obscene, in light of the defense that the album had artistic value.[6] Predictably, the publicity generated by these two cases promoted the popularity of the respective work.

We see relatively few prosecutions for obscenity today. An important exception to this trend is obscenity that involves minors. One of Congress's first efforts to control sexual content on the Internet, the Communications Decency Act of 1996, was overturned the following year by a unanimous U.S. Supreme Court.[7] The specific provisions that the court objected to concerned the knowing transmission of "obscene or indecent" messages to any recipient less than 18 years of age. "Obscene" messages could be defined, using the criteria provided in the *Miller* case. However, the statute failed to define "indecent," and failed to make allowances for material that may have redeeming social value. Thus, the court found the Communications Decency Act to be unenforceable, as it was unconstitutionally vague.

Another law passed by Congress in 1996, the Child Pornography Prevention Act (CPPA), punished "any visual depiction, including any photograph, film, video, picture or computer or computer-generated image or picture" that "is, *or appears to be*, of a minor engaging in sexually explicit conduct."[8] (emphasis added) The CPPA targeted three different types of child pornography: visual material that showed actual children, visual material that showed youthful adults who appeared to be children, and "virtual" (computer generated) child pornography. In 2002, a divided U.S. Supreme Court struck down the law as unconstitutional. The majority's decision pointed out that not all sexual images of those under the age of 18 can automatically be assumed obscene under the *Miller* standard. The Court also said that the CPPA was overbroad in its prohibition of visual images of youthful looking adults and "virtual" child pornography.

One should not regard the U.S. Supreme Court's decisions to overturn both the Communications Decency Act and the Child Pornography Prevention Act as a refusal by the court to fight sexual exploitation of children. Rather, the Court has made it clear that legislation must clearly follow the standards the Court created in *Miller* when defining criminal activity and setting punishment for those who seek to sexually exploit children.

Obscenity versus indecency

Perhaps the greatest source of governmental restrictions and requirements for the media industry is the Federal Communications Commission (FCC). The FCC's authority to regulate television and radio broadcasting was discussed in Chapters 4 and 5. In addition to regulating broadcast technology, the FCC also regulates content. The FCC prohibits obscenity on radio and television broadcasts at all times, and prohibits indecency between 6 a.m. and 10 p.m. The Commission defines indecency as "language or material that, in context, depicts or describes, in terms patently offensive as measured by contemporary community standards for the broadcast medium, sexual or excretory organs or activities."[9]

Considering context, after Bono of U2 accepted a Golden Globe award in 2003, and exclaimed, "This is really, really f . . . ing brilliant," the FCC's enforcement staff decided not to fine NBC, which broadcast the program, determining that Bono did not use the word in a sexual context. Responding to the outcry from some groups, the FCC commissioners reversed the decision of its enforcement staff. Broadcasters challenged the FCC's ruling in the courts. In April 2009, the U.S. Supreme Court held that the FCC could fine broadcasters even for occasional or isolated uses of crude language. The context of that language was unimportant, said the majority of the members of the Court. Justice John Paul Stevens disagreed, writing in his dissenting opinion, "As any golfer who has watched his partner shank a short approach knows, it would be absurd to accept the suggestion that the resultant four-letter word uttered on the golf course describes sex or excrement and is therefore indecent. But that is the absurdity the FCC has embraced in its new approach to indecency."[10] Absurd as it may seem to Stevens, the Court's majority opinion allows the FCC to fine broadcasters anytime crude language is aired on television or radio, regardless of the context in which the word is used.

First Amendment protection of ISPs and websites

Section 230 of the Communications Decency Act, enacted in 1996, states that, "No provider or user of an interactive computer service shall be treated as the publisher or speaker of any information provided by another information content provider."[11] This legislation protects Internet Service Providers (ISPs) from liability for the material that ISPs' customers post online. For example, if someone uses his Comcast Internet account to post material online that is considered obscene or defamatory, the user may be held liable, but Comcast cannot be. Many First Amendment advocates praise Section 230, as it reduces the ISPs' interest in monitoring or blocking content transmitted online. Court decisions have also held that Section 230 shields websites from liability for the activities of website visitors or customers. As a result, MySpace, Google, eBay, and others have been ruled immune from liability for fraudulent, abusive, and offensive material posted by users.

Intellectual property: a brief history

According to the United Nations' World Intellectual Property Organization, intellectual property is:

> Industrial property, which includes inventions (patents), trademarks, industrial designs, and geographic indications of source; and Copyright, which includes literary and artistic works such as novels, poems and plays, films, musical

works, artistic works such as drawings, paintings, photographs and sculptures, and architectural designs. Rights related to copyright include those of performing artists in their performances, producers of phonograms in their recordings, and those of broadcasters in their radio and television programs.[12]

To simplify, the intellectual property of the mass media includes hardware, such as cameras, recording devices, and media playing devices, typically protected by patent laws. It also includes software, such as songs, games, writings, programs, and movies, which fall within copyright protection. A third type of intellectual property involves identifying names and marks, such as trademarks and service marks.

The U.S. Chamber of Commerce estimates that intellectual property contributes more than $5 trillion to the U.S. economy annually, and accounts for more than half of the U.S.'s exports.[13] The importance of intellectual property to the economy is reflected in the U.S. Constitution, which empowers Congress, "To promote the Progress of Science and useful Arts, by securing for limited Times to Authors and Inventors the exclusive Right to their respective Writings and Discoveries."[14]

Intellectual property: copyright

Congress has enacted a series of copyright laws during the nation's history. The first, the Copyright Act of 1790, borrowed heavily from British copyright law. As discussed in Chapter 6, the law only protected the works of American writers. Congress passed the International Copyright Act of 1891, which protected the works of foreign authors in the United States, and led to reciprocal agreements with other countries.

The Copyright Act of 1976, as amended, provides the basis of copyright law today. Copyright protection now extends to, "original works of authorship fixed in any tangible medium of expression, now known or later developed, from which they can be perceived, reproduced, or otherwise communicated, either directly or with the aid of a machine or device."[15] The term "fixed" means that a work enjoys copyright protection today once it is written, recorded, etc. You are probably familiar with the copyright symbol, which appears in Figure 11.2.

Copyright: what rights? whose rights?

Although the authors of a book, song, movie script, etc. may formally register their work, this is not required for legal protection. We will use the

Figure 11.2 Copyright law is evolving as communications technology evolves. *Source:* iStockphoto

example of a coat on a coat rack at a restaurant. Even if the coat has nobody's name on it, we know it belongs to somebody. Just as it is helpful to put a nametag inside one's coat, formally registering a work with the copyright office may help if there is later an ownership dispute.

However, the holder of the copyright may not be the person who created the copyrighted piece. Many copyrighted works are *works for hire*. In these situations, the firms that hire people to create material hold the copyright. For example, Disney employs a vast staff of creative artists to generate a wide assortment of intellectual property. These artists are creating work for Disney, not themselves.

Copyright and other types of intellectual property law can be complicated. Many of those who create copyrighted works have far more artistic skill than business acumen. Stories abound about shrewd, sometimes dishonest business people taking advantage of this fact. Many talented artists have unwittingly signed over some or all of their rights to profit from their creative activity.

Former Beatle Paul McCartney and the estate of John Lennon control only 50 percent of the performance, sales, and broadcast rights to their songs. The other half had been owned by their publisher, ATV, which sold its rights for $47.5 million in 1984 to Michael Jackson, who outbid McCartney. Although McCartney and Jackson were friends, McCartney later told the London *Daily Mirror*, "The annoying thing is I have to pay to play some of my own songs. Each time I want to sing 'Hey Jude' I have to pay."[16]

Similarly, John Fogerty does not own the rights to "Run Through the Jungle," one of the most popular songs he wrote while in Creedence Clearwater Revival. Refusing to do what Paul McCartney complained of, for years Fogerty did not perform old Creedence songs, as he did not want to have to pay royalties for songs he had written. However, when Fogerty released the song "The Old Man Down the Road" in 1985, Saul Zaentz, who headed Fogerty's old record label and owned the rights to "Run Through the Jungle" sued Fogerty—for plagiarizing *himself*, claiming that Fogerty's new song sounded too much like his old song. Fogerty won at trial.

Copyright in the twenty-first century

Changes in media technology on the eve of the new century necessitated a Congressional review of existing copyright law. The Digital Millennium Copyright Act of 1998 enhances protection of copyrighted materials that are transmitted on the Internet, while also limiting the liability of Internet service providers (ISPs) for infringement by ISP customers. Another piece of legislation, the Copyright Extension Act of 1998, named for the late entertainer and member of Congress, Sonny Bono, is commonly attributed to the successful efforts of lobbyists for Disney. (Lobbyists are individuals and firms that companies and interest groups pay to present their views to government leaders and try to influence government actions.) Some of Disney's works were approaching the end of their copyright protection under existing laws, and were about to phase into the public domain. This included the original *Winnie-the-Pooh* book, to which Disney had purchased the rights.

The Copyright Act of 1976 protected a work for the life of the author plus 50 years, or 75 years for a work of corporate authorship. The Copyright Extension Act lengthened protection to the life of the author plus 70 years. As works for hire, most of Disney's work fit into the category of corporate authorship. Corporate works are now protected for 120 years after creation or 95 years after publication, whichever occurs first. In addition, copyright protection for works published prior to the date the Copyright Act of 1976 took effect was increased by 20 years to a total of 95 years from their publication date. Critics say this is too long.

Copyright and fair use

U.S. copyright law permits *fair use* of copyright protected material. We may incorporate small portions of the copyright protected material of others in our own work for commentary, news reporting, educational purposes, and scholarship. For example, the publisher of this book tells writers that they must obtain permission to use the work of others when using:

- Text (prose) extracts of more than 400 words, or a total of 800 words from the same volume if there are several shorter extracts
- An article in a journal that comprises more than a third of the original
- More than one line of poetry
- More than one line of a song lyric, hymn, or dramatic work, including film scripts

The publisher believes that using less than this falls within permissible fair use.

As discussed in Chapter 10, passion communities and knowledge communities use a wide variety of media to share information, images, and music. Many people create "mashups," which are collages of the words, sounds, and images created by others. There are also genres of work known as fan fiction and fan films, in which individuals produce work based on characters and plotlines created by others. For instance, there are thousands of stories based on J. K. Rowling's *Harry Potter* series. There are also numerous videos based on the *Star Wars* series.

While some copyright holders have fought consumer-generated media based on their work, others have welcomed it. For example, George Lucas, the creator of the Star Wars series, has been recognizing fan films through an annual award, "The *Star Wars* Fan Movie Challenge" since 2002.[17] Many believe that fan fiction and fan films benefit the original work as they generate continued interest in that work.

Although copyright law allows fair use, the U.S. Copyright Office warns, "The distinction between fair use and infringement may be unclear and not easily defined. There is no specific number of words, lines, or notes that may safely be taken without permission."[18] The reality is that large media firms have more money and more lawyers than consumers do, and that a "cease and desist" letter from a large media firm scares people enough to stop activity that may fall within permissible fair use.

Copyright and piracy

New communication technology, including the Internet and digital file compression, has accelerated copyright infringement over the past decade.

As Internet connection speeds have improved, so has the ability to upload and download files that contain copyright protected material. The ease of file sharing has led to its widespread popularity, despite the legal issues involved.

Napster, created by 18-year-old Shawn Fanning in Boston in 1999, quickly rose as the best-known early source of *peer-to-peer* (*P2P*) file sharing. Challenged by the Recording Industry Association of America (RIAA) Napster was ordered to shut down by a federal appeals court in July 2001. Some believed that Napster's downfall came because it connected users through a central server that it controlled. Since Napster controlled the server, it was held responsible for those who shared files illegally.

Other firms thought they found a loophole. Grokster and similar firms used software that allowed members to connect directly to each other without a central server, using some members' computers for indexing files. This loophole was also challenged in court by companies that controlled music rights. In 2005, the U.S. Supreme Court unanimously agreed that Grokster, because it made money by selling advertising on its website, was commercially exploiting copyrighted material without permission, and the site closed immediately thereafter, as seen in Figure 11.3.

Recorded music industry figures hoped that forcing the shutdown of Napster and the successful effort to stop Grokster would lead to the end of illegal P2P music sharing. Today, however, BitTorrent technology that

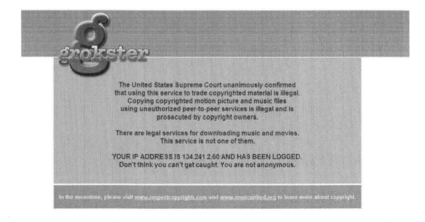

Figure 11.3 Grokster's website after the firm was shut down.

allows for easy P2P sharing using relatively low computing and bandwidth resources, coupled with foreign BitTorrent tracking services that assist those looking for specific files (including music and movies) means that it is still relatively easy to upload and download copyright-protected files. Although transmitting copyright-protected material without the permission of the copyright owner is illegal, the process continues, relatively unabated. The tracking services never actually "host" (possess) the copyright-protected material; rather, these services connect individuals who possess that material with those seeking the material. In some nations, this is enough to spare the tracking services from criminal liability.

Many of the firms that actually host copyright-protected material have set up operations in nations that have not entered into intellectual property treaties with the United States, or in nations where intellectual property law enforcement is weak (or nonexistent). Many of the P2P file-sharing servers are located in countries that most Americans would have trouble finding on a map. In a domestic case, the conviction of a American blogger in July 2009 for illegally uploading tracks from Guns N' Roses' "Chinese Democracy" was notable primarily for the fact that the blogger had acted so publicly. The RIAA, whose investigator initiated the case, estimated the loss to Guns N' Roses at over $3 million.[19]

Many observers blame the recorded music industry for some of its problems. As discussed in Chapter 5, the recorded music industry missed the paradigm shift that began in the 1990s, as consumer preference moved from buying packaged music at retail stores to downloading music from the Internet. The fact that much of the music available online was free only accelerated the shift. Belatedly, the recorded music industry has begun to embrace the Internet. However, many musicians realize today that because many consumers are obtaining musicians' recordings without those musicians receiving royalties, the surest way to make money through their music is concert touring.

One effort by the music industry to prevent unauthorized copying of music and video files uses various types of technology referred to as *digital rights management (DRM)*. Some of these efforts have been disastrous, with legal copies of music files rendered unplayable on certain playback devices. For its part, Apple announced in January 2009 that its iTunes music files would no longer be DRM protected, although its video files and iPhone applications still are. As Figure 11.4 symbolizes, protecting music ownership is a rigorous task.

Figure 11.4 Most efforts to prevent music sharing have failed.

Privacy

The interactivity of the Internet and other new media is a mixed blessing when it comes to privacy issues. Website operators can identify our IP (Internet Protocol) address when we visit their sites. They also may place cookies on our computer, which allow them to track our Internet usage. Advertisers on websites we visit may also place cookies on our computer. If we enter personal information or financial information at a site, whether it is a social networking site, our personal start page, an online marketplace, etc., that data is stored. If a website's privacy policy tells the visitor that the website operator plans to sell our personal data to any willing buyer, this is generally legal, as the website operator has published this information on its site, and we have effectively consented by continuing to visit that site. Although responsible website operators offer privacy policies, they know that relatively few Internet users actually read those policies.

In 1998, Congress passed the Children's Online Privacy Protection Act (COPPA).[20] The rule, enforced by the Federal Trade Commission (FTC), requires commercial websites and online services to get consent from a parent or guardian before they can collect personal information from children under the age of 13. Since COPPA was enacted, many website operators have decided that is simply easier not to allow visitors under the age of 13 to register at all.

Cybercrime

The FTC plays an important role in media regulation. Created by Congress in 1914, the FTC enforces rules about what information must be contained in advertisements and investigates claims of fraudulent and deceptive advertising. This enforcement spans all communications media. The advent of each new medium brings the opportunity for people to try to take our money through deceit. The FTC today warns consumers about Internet fraud, or what it calls "Dot Cons."

Most of the financial crimes that take place online are simply new versions of old scams. However, the Internet's speed and its reach have made it easier for criminals to practice their trade. Stolen goods, child pornography, and dangerous explosives can be obtained online by those who want them, and more easily now than ever before. Financial fraud existed long before the advent of the Internet, but criminals' ability to obtain our financial data has grown easier. To avoid U.S. law enforcement, many cyber criminals operate outside the jurisdiction of the United States.

One relatively new type of crime that is specific to the Internet is hacking. The primary federal anti-hacking law punishes someone who:

1. intentionally accesses without authorization a facility through which an electronic communication service is provided; or
2. intentionally exceeds an authorization to access that facility; and thereby obtains, alters, or prevents authorized access to a wire or electronic communication while it is in electronic storage in such system.[21]

Some hackers do it simply because they can—they enjoy flaunting their technical abilities. However, others may be engaged in foreign spying, industrial espionage, or other malicious activities. For example, a denial of service attack, in which a website is overloaded by fake communication requests, can effectively shut a website down for a few minutes or a few hours. For online retailers such as Amazon and eBay that have been the victims of such attacks, this can mean millions of dollars in lost sales.

Cyberstalking and cyberbullying

Cyberstalking is one of the more insidious forms of cybercrime. The National Center for Victims of Crime defines cyberstalking as "threatening behavior or unwanted advances directed at another using the Internet and other forms of online and computer communications."[22] As is true of stalkers in general, cyberstalkers tend to be male and the victims are most likely to be female. Most commonly, the stalking occurs after the termination of a relationship. However, the Internet and other new communication technology make it increasingly easy and thus more likely to stalk someone who does not know the stalker. Celebrities have found themselves particularly vulnerable to cyberstalking by mentally ill fans.

Cyberstalkers also use communication technology to encourage others to engage in threatening behavior against the victim. Some cyberstalkers are emboldened by the fact that they do not have to confront the victim directly, but can do so anonymously, or by using a false identity. Most states have added cyberstalking statutes to existing stalking statutes. Unfortunately, despite the presence of these laws, it is likely that you know someone who has been the victim of cyberstalking.

Among children and adolescents, educators and policymakers are concerned about cyberbullying, more formally known as "electronic aggression." The Centers for Disease Control define electronic aggression as, "Any type of harassment or bullying (teasing, telling lies, making fun of someone, making rude or mean comments, spreading rumors, or making threatening or aggressive comments) that occurs through email, a chat room, instant messaging, a website (including blogs), or text messaging."[23] In contrast to cyberstalking, both the victims and perpetrators of cyberbullying tend to be female.[24] While cyberstalking tends to be treated as a criminal matter, cyberbullying, because it occurs primarily among minors, is often viewed as an issue best addressed by parents and teachers.[25]

Mass communications and the legal environment: the future

Major media corporations rely on lobbyists to help shape media regulations in the United States and rely on communications lawyers to help them stay in compliance with existing laws. As discussed in the two previous chapters, there are many more voices in the media today. Every one of us can create a blog, start a website, and upload graphics, information, and opinions that will be available to millions of others. We can do all of these things without any knowledge of the laws that regulate the media, which means that some of us will find ourselves on the wrong side of the law.

Recent technological changes also make it easy for us to obtain the copyrighted works of others, including music, movies, television programs, and literary works, often without paying for them. The large corporations that hold the rights to this content have lobbied Congress to extend and strengthen copyright laws. The global nature of media today means that we will see continued efforts by the U.S. government to persuade other nations to enforce existing and future intellectual property laws.

Mass communications and the legal environment and careers

The U.S. Bureau of Labor Statistics predicts that jobs in the legal profession will grow at about the same rate as all occupations in general between 2006 and 2016. However, the Bureau warns that there will be significant competition for legal careers due to the high number of students graduating from American law schools.[26] Perhaps better opportunities exist for those seeking careers in computer engineering, as there is a strong demand among media firms for those who can develop technologies that deter or prevent unauthorized duplication and sharing of media content. The Bureau describes the job market for those seeking careers in computer software engineering between 2006 and 2016 as "excellent."[27]

Questions for critical thinking and discussion

1. This chapter discusses the different standard used in defamation cases for "ordinary" people and for public figures or public officials. The courts argue that public figures or public officials put themselves in the public light, and so they should be tolerant of criticism in the media. Thus, it is more difficult for public figures or public officials to sue successfully for defamation than it is for "ordinary" people.

    - Is this different treatment of famous people and ordinary people fair? Explain why or why not.

    (Continued)

Questions for critical thinking and discussion—Cont'd

2. Some people have argued that the Federal Communications Commission (FCC) does not have to regulate what we hear or see on broadcast radio and television. They believe that the marketplace should control that content; if some programming is too violent or obscene, consumers will look for alternatives. Advertisers will also place pressure on broadcasters to maintain certain standards of decency in order not to alienate consumers. Other people argue that the FCC provides an important governmental function by preventing broadcasters from pushing the envelope of sex and violence too far.

   • Do we need the FCC to regulate forbidden content on television and radio? Or should "the marketplace of ideas" control that content instead? Explain your answer.

3. In December 2008, the Recording Industry Association of America (RIAA) announced that after filing suit against more than 35,000 individuals for illegal music file sharing, it would stop bringing future suits. Instead, the RIAA said that it would work with Internet Service Providers to deny service to those who ignored RIAA warnings against unauthorized downloading and file sharing.[28] However, the RIAA's efforts have failed to deter thousands of individuals who regularly download and share music files daily.

   • Are the financial interests of musicians and the recorded music industry the same, or does each group have different financial interests? Explain.
   • If you were an executive with one of the major recorded music companies, what actions would you take in response to the unauthorized downloading and file sharing of your company's music? Explain.
   • If you were a professional musician, what actions would you take in response to the unauthorized downloading and file sharing of your music? Explain.

4. Most responsible website operators post a privacy policy at their website. Read the privacy policy of a website that you visit regularly. The link to the privacy policy can usually be found at the bottom of the website's front page.

   • Do you understand the privacy policy of the website?
   • Are you comfortable with or are you concerned about this privacy policy? Explain.

5. American journalist and press critic A. J. Liebling once famously said, "Freedom of the press is guaranteed only to those who own one."

   • Liebling died in 1963. Have technological developments occurred since then that make Liebling's statement more accurate or less accurate, or are things about the same? Explain.
   • Do the changes to copyright law since Liebling's death support his statement? Explain why or why not.

Additional resources

Center for Democracy & Technology, "Digital Copyright," www.cdt.org/copyright

Electronic Frontier Foundation, http://www.eff.org/

Federal Communications Commission, www.fcc.gov

Federal Trade Commission, www.ftc.gov

Global Intellectual Property Center, www.theglobalipcenter.com

Goldstein, Norm, *The Associated Press Stylebook and Briefing on Media Law* (New York: Basic Books, 2009).

Lasica, J.D., Darknet; *Hollywood's War against the Digital Generation* (Hoboken, NJ: Wiley, 2005).

Motion Picture Association of America, "Piracy and the Law," www.mpaa.org/piracy_AndLaw.asp

Privacy Rights Clearinghouse, www.privacyrights.org/netprivacy.htm

Recording Industry Association of America, "Piracy: Online and on the Street," www.riaa.com/physicalpiracy.php

Sadler, Roger L., *Electronic Media Law* (Thousand Oaks, CA: Sage, 2005).

U.S. Department of Justice, "Computer Crime and Intellectual Property Section," www.cybercrime.gov

12 Globalization

Chapter contents

Issues and trends in globalization

- Although North America has the largest percentage of Internet users per capita, Asia has three times as many total users.
- Many developing nations are using the latest forms of communication technology without going through the same stages of technological infusion as more developed nations have—a process called technological leapfrogging.
- Businesses are using communication technology to shift American jobs overseas and to increase collaboration of American employees with employees abroad.
- Many American advertisers rely heavily on foreign markets for sales growth.
- English remains the dominant language in global communications; there are more people speaking English as a second language than there are native speakers.
- Government censorship continues to be a significant problem in many parts of the world.

1973   Today

Figure 12.1 Old and new Pepsi logos.

Pepsi's logo has evolved over the years. Its current logo no longer includes the Pepsi name. Pepsi sells its products around the world, including many countries that do not use the Roman alphabet that English uses. It makes sense in a global market for Pepsi to emphasize a universal symbol rather than a language-specific name. Many other firms have branding that allows them to compete in an increasingly global business environment. Figure 12.1 shows the old and new Pepsi logos.

The globalization of mass media goes well beyond soft drink logos. The social medium Twitter provides evidence for the importance of social media in global political affairs. On June 16, 2009, the U.S. State Department asked Twitter to postpone a scheduled upgrade. The State Department believed that the upgrade would disrupt the efforts of dissident Iranians. These dissidents were using Twitter to protest against an allegedly corrupt election held several days earlier.[1]

When we discuss *globalization*, we mean "The increasing integration of economies and societies around the world, particularly through trade and financial flows, and the transfer of culture and technology."[2] Our discussion in this chapter focuses on the global transfer of electronic media technology and the resulting transfer of culture.

Bringing the Internet to the world

If information is power, then it is more difficult for the poor to attain power. You are probably familiar with domestic efforts to bring the Internet to impoverished areas of the United States. There are similar efforts abroad. The One Laptop per Child initiative's mission statement tells us that its goal is, "To create educational opportunities for the world's poorest children by providing each child with a rugged, low-cost, low-power, connected laptop with content and software designed for collaborative, joyful, self-empowered learning. When children have access to this type of tool they get engaged in their own education. They learn, share, create, and collaborate. They become connected to each other, to the world and to a brighter future."[3] A professor at the Massachusetts Institute of Technology, Nicholas Negroponte, founded the organization in 2006. The organization's laptop, the XO, sells for $175. So far, 900,000 laptops have been shipped to children in 31 countries.[4] Donors and governmental agencies have paid for the majority of the laptops.

The XO faces competition from netbooks—small and relatively inexpensive laptops that can sell for less than $300. Netbook users often rely on *cloud computing* rather than self-contained software and hardware. Cloud computing services offer certain types of software such as word processing and spreadsheets through Internet access. Cloud computing services also offer data storage, which reduces the hardware requirements for netbooks. Cloud computing is attractive to large corporations, which can save money by buying less powerful computers for their employees and paying for online services only when used. The goal of many humanitarian and educational organizations is to provide free cloud computing resources to those in developing nations. One of the best-known firms offering cloud computing resources is Google. It charges business users for its services, but offers those services free to educational and certain not-for-profit organizations.

Less expensive computers means that more people will have access to computers. The next issue becomes access to the Internet through those computers. According to Internet World Stats, less than seven percent of Africans are using the Internet and less than 20 percent of Asians, compared to nearly 75 percent of those in the United States and Canada.[5] In terms of numbers of users, however, over 738 million Asians currently use the Internet, compared to 252 million U.S. and Canada residents.[6]

Technological leapfrogging

Some developing nations rely more today on wireless phones than landline phones. Similarly, some developing nations have a more extensive system of satellite television than broadcast television. Broadband Internet access is available today in countries that never had dial-up access. In essence, these nations have skipped a step or two in their technological diffusion; this is *technological leapfrogging*. For example, in 2007, Cambodia, a small, poor nation in Southeast Asia, had 17.9 mobile phone subscriptions per 100 inhabitants, but only 0.3 landline phone lines per 100 inhabitants.[7]

An advantage of technological leapfrogging is the lack of pressure by owners of older technology to maintain that older technology's status. (Imagine what oil companies, which are among the largest and most powerful corporations in the United States, think about the development of electric cars.) There may also be resistance to new technology from users who have already made substantial investments in older technology. Thus, some developing nations are experiencing a more rapid diffusion of new communications technology than more economically advanced nations are.

Globalization and language

As you read this sentence, there are more people using English as a second language than there are using it as their first language. According to the Rosetta Project, linguists predict that up to 90 percent of the world's languages will disappear in the near future.[8] Why should we care? Many believe that the loss of language contributes to the loss of culture and identity. Anthropologists have found that many Americans consciously or subconsciously try to hold onto regional expressions and dialects as a means of maintaining an identity that is not homogenous with everyone else in the nation. Others have pointed to the relatively recent practice common among many African Americans to give their children names that can be clearly identified as "black" (LeBron James is just one example). This practice is thought to be the result of the Civil Rights Movement of the 1950s and 1960s, when African Americans firmly asserted their presence in American culture.

The impulse to maintain one's identity through language may be even more important in societies that find their native language threatened by the fact that only a handful of languages dominate most media. For some media content producers, it is cost effective to produce media in only a few dominant languages. Speakers of vanishing languages tend to be older. Older consumers tend to be less attractive to the advertisers who support mass media financially, as older consumers are less likely to change long-established buying habits. On an optimistic note, perhaps the trend toward disaggregation discussed in Chapter 10 may help individuals preserve threatened languages.

The Census Bureau estimates that the United States will be a "majority minority" nation by 2050.[9] This means that the majority of Americans will not consider themselves white. With increasing diversity come more speakers of languages other than English in American society. In many American cities, one can live and work reasonably well without fluency in English.

Some native English speakers have resisted the trend toward the use of other languages within the United States. The movement to have English established as the official language has generated debate among government leaders. According to ProEnglish, a group that advocates for recognition of English as the official language of the United States, 30 states have formally adopted English as their official language.[10] Polls have also found that only a third of Americans believe that it is important that American children learn a foreign language. By contrast, about half of those polled in Europe said that it was important for children to learn English.[11]

Regardless of sentiment in the United States regarding foreign languages, the Census Bureau estimates that 32.2 million U.S. residents speak Spanish at home.[12] This is more than ten percent of the total U.S. population. Many American firms advertise in Spanish-language media, as they want to appeal to the large number of Spanish speakers. For example, McDonalds operates MeEncanta.com, a website aimed at Spanish speakers in the United States.

Univision, a Spanish-language cable network, ranks among the top five television networks in the United States and also owns or provides programming for seventy Spanish-language radio stations in the United States.[13] Univision's television stations in Los Angeles, Houston, Miami, Dallas, Phoenix, Fresno, and Bakersfield enjoy the highest prime-time ratings in their respective markets, surpassing all English-speaking stations.[14] NBC Universal owns Telemundo, another Spanish-language cable network available in most of the United States.

Globalization, health, and welfare

Cigarettes advertisements are not allowed on television or billboards in the United States today. The cigarette advertisements that appear in magazines must include the Surgeon General's warning that smoking is a health hazard. The American tobacco industry today relies on exporting cigarettes to other nations for sales growth. Many developing nations lack the governmental infrastructure that more advanced nations have. It is easier to sell cigarettes in countries that have insufficient health regulations and inadequate health education. This is also true of food products and medications that fail to meet U.S. Food and Drug Administration standards, but can be sold legally in other countries. Advertising agencies, many of them based in the United States, develop advertising campaigns that help sell these products to unsuspecting consumers abroad. Even today, many developing nations have adult literacy rates of less than 50 percent. Television advertisements in those countries are often directed toward consumers who may be illiterate, and thus unable to read product safety warnings, ingredient lists, etc.

Globalization, poverty, and desire

You may have grandparents who were "children of the Depression." Many of those who lived through the Great Depression of the 1930s experienced tremendous poverty and deprivation. However, many of these individuals can be heard to say, "We were poor but we didn't know we were poor." Living in a time when all of those around them were experiencing the same impoverishment, it may have been difficult to realize what one lacked. Poverty may be relative; you are only poor when you know you are poor. So what happens when a community that previously lacked mass media gains access to mass media? If people did not know that they were impoverished before, only a few hours of watching television and its advertisements for numerous products and services can make viewers realize that there are many things out there that they do not have.

Advertisers strive to create a sense of lack. In order to sell something to somebody, advertisers need to create a desire among consumers to buy the advertised item. Of course, the advertised items are often produced by American or other Western firms. Some critics have argued that the media and the advertisers that support them are engaged in a new version of colonization.

European colonization of the Americas, Africa, Asia, and the Pacific Rim began hundreds of years ago. Most former colonies have since become independent nations. Colonization is an uneven exchange between the colonizing nation and the colony. More developed colonizing nations exploit the natural resources and cheap labor supply in the colony and treat the colony as a captive market for the manufactured goods of the colonizing nation.

Although political colonization has waned, many argue that what has been substituted is a process called "Coca-colonization," or "Coca-Cola Diplomacy," by which corporations attempt to exploit previously untapped or underserved markets. This process has included joint efforts between the U.S. government and Coca-Cola, as well as the U.S. government and Pepsi, among other advertisers, to enter trade agreements with previously hostile countries. Thus, Pepsi was introduced into the Soviet Union soon after President Richard Nixon's visit there in 1972.[15] Coke's re-introduction into China after 30 years followed a visit by U.S. President Jimmy Carter in 1978, and was announced on the same day that the United States formally announced it was normalizing diplomatic relations with China.

Globalization and the dissemination of American ideas

As American and European firms find their home markets saturated, they turn to developing nations for sales growth. For example, McDonalds now has a restaurant in just about every feasible location in the United States. Most new McDonalds restaurants are being built elsewhere, with locations in 118 nations so far. McDonalds is one of many American and European firms that maintain global operations. These firms must identify cultural differences in order to compete successfully in different nations. For example, Pizza Hut's pepperoni in India is all pork, and its pepperoni in Saudi Arabia is all beef, reflecting prevailing religious practices in those countries. Some of the stores McDonalds operates in Israel are closed on Saturday, in keeping with Orthodox Jewish beliefs. Pepsi sells a cucumber-flavored soft drink in Japan, and Coca Cola markets a cherry/plum flavored soft drink in Africa. Political, religious, and cultural issues affect not only what products or services are offered, but also the messages that are advertised. In 2009, Burger King used an in-store advertisement at its stores in Spain that depicted a Hindu goddess sitting atop a meat sandwich. Hindu people in India and elsewhere were greatly offended by the advertisement, and Burger King officials quickly apologized.[16]

Many societies resist what they see as Western cultural imperialism, and their political and religious leaders object to what they perceive as Western immorality. Of course, the discussion about immorality in the media also takes place within Western culture. Many Americans believe that there is too much sex and too much violence in American media, but sex and violence continue to exist in the media. In more conservative cultures, the presence of sex and violence in media exported from the Western world is often viewed as completely unacceptable. Many of those who create and distribute Western media say that they are merely meeting popular demand, both here and abroad.

Just as American media attempt to promote lifestyles based on heavy consumption of advertised goods and services within the United States, Western media attempt to promote those lifestyles in other nations. Accordingly, Western media portray Western cultures as positive, and often identify other cultures as lesser, or even evil. In particular, Islamic culture has been under attack, especially since the events of the two Gulf Wars. Critics cite Disney's animated film *Aladdin* (1992) for depicting a particularly brutal, stereotyped, and ultimately incorrect image of Islamic culture. These critics argue that what little most Americans know about Islam is often based solely on media depictions created by Westerners who themselves have little knowledge of Islamic culture and beliefs. Western media are so dominant that there is little cultural exchange through which non-Western cultures can inform Western cultures about what those other cultures, and the people who practice them, are really like.[17]

Americans do not tend to feel threatened by the imposition of other cultures in American life because American media are so predominant in the world. In Chapter 1, we discussed the fact that nine companies, six of which are based in the United States, control most television, music, and movie production in the world. The three firms that are not based in the United States each maintain a strong presence here and many are engaged in partnerships with the American firms.

The Motion Picture Association of America (MPAA) states that, "the American motion picture industry carries a positive balance of trade around the world and a $13.6 billion trade surplus."[18] In other words, American films do $13.6 billion more in business outside of the United States than do the films of all foreign countries imported into the United States. The U.S. motion picture and television industries rank among the nation's most successful exporters. The MPAA tells us that, based on reports from the U.S. Commerce Department, "The motion picture and television [international trade] surplus was larger than the combined surplus of the telecommunications, management and consulting, legal, and medical services sectors, and larger than sectors like computer and information services and insurance services."[19] As Benjamin Barber says in *Jihad vs. McWorld*, "American films dominate the world market in a manner that far outpaces its leadership in any other area."[20] U.S. films do particularly well in Europe; in the 1990s, American movies accounted for 85 percent of European film revenues.[21] The global popularity of American movies is apparent as one views Box Office Mojo's list of box office figures by nation. In 2008, *The Dark Knight* was the most popular movie in Bolivia, *Kung Fu Panda* was the top box office hit in Lithuania, and *Sex and the City* topped the charts in Croatia.[22]

A trip to an ethnic grocery store in the United States can help you understand the relationship of media and culture. Many Asian and Latin American grocery stores also offer rentals of movies made in their representative nations. The recent success of *Slumdog Millionaire*, although not truly an Indian film, introduced many Americans to Bollywood, the Indian film industry. *Slumdog*'s success in the U.S. reflects the fusion of Asian and American cultures, a process that is likely to expand in the future.

Global communications and the legal environment

Because communication media cross international borders, political and legal issues arise. Not only is the "marketplace of ideas" global; so is the marketplace of goods and services. This can create legal problems. If the purchaser is in one nation and the seller is in another, which nation's laws apply? Types of commerce that are legal in one nation may be illegal in another. For example, online sports gambling is illegal in the United States.

Yet millions of Americans place bets through online services located in other nations, wagering more than an estimated $100 billion annually.[23] At least one nation (Antigua and Barbuda) has challenged the American ban as a violation of trade agreements.

Intellectual property

The Congressional International Anti-Piracy Caucus's "Country Watch" identifies those nations that members of Congress believe pose the greatest threat to the rights of intellectual property owners. China and Russia, both on the list, are well known for inadequate protection of intellectual property rights. [24] The International Intellectual Property Alliance, an association of copyright industry groups, estimates that owners of copy-righted music, motion pictures, and games lost $3.5 billion to piracy in China and $2.7 billion in Russia in 2008.[25]

As discussed in Chapter 11, the global reach of the Internet facilitates the illegal uploading and downloading of copyright-protected items, including music, movies, and books. Computer software developers also suffer from piracy in other nations. The Business Software Alliance estimates that more than 40 percent of software used globally is pirated, costing software firms an estimated $50 billion annually in lost sales. According to the Alliance, the countries with the highest rate of business software piracy are Armenia, Bangladesh, Georgia, and Zimbabwe, where over 90 percent of software in use is thought to be pirated.[26]

Censorship

Another legal concern is the freedom of the press from censorship. We will use the term *censorship* to include deleting or altering of certain words or images or removing those words or images from public access entirely. Censorship evolves from several sources, including religious beliefs, political concerns, and the desire to protect children. Few object to protecting children from exploitation and shielding them from inappropriate material. Religious restrictions are more problematic and political censorship is even more so. Today, most discussions of global censorship focus on the Internet, but censorship has existed forever.

Many Americans believe that freedom of speech and the press from government censorship is a basic right, as demonstrated by their protection in the First Amendment of the U.S. Constitution. However, as has been discussed elsewhere in this book, U.S. courts have never interpreted freedom of speech and the press as an absolute right. For example, one can be sued for defaming someone else. In addition, the First Amendment only protects against unreasonable government censorship. Private censorship is permitted. For example, a newspaper's editor does not have to run an advertisement that is viewed as objectionable, and a retailer does not have to sell certain materials such as recorded music or movies that it finds distasteful.

Because it is the most populous nation in the world and due to its rigid governmental policies, China tops most commentators' lists when discussing government censorship. China has come into conflict with the World Trade Organization (WTO) over the Chinese government's efforts to keep certain books, magazines, movies, recorded music, and other material from entering the country. In order to maintain its control over what types of material enter China, the government has maintained a monopoly over importing, which violates the WTO's rules. Many publishers and others in the entertainment business have pointed out that the demand for their material exists in China. If the Chinese people cannot obtain this material legally, they will seek pirated material.

Amnesty International advocates on behalf of those people in various countries that have been imprisoned or otherwise persecuted for *cyberdissidence*, or speaking out against governmental policies and practices in those countries as symbolized in Figure 12.2. The organization identifies China, Vietnam, Tunisia, Iran, Saudi Arabia, and Syria among the "guiltiest" countries.[27] Furthermore, Amnesty International claims that Yahoo has supplied email users' private data to the Chinese authorities, which has led to the imprisonment of some Yahoo users. The organization also claims that Microsoft and Google have both complied with government demands to actively censor Chinese users of their services. In 2006, Google co-founder Sergey Brin acknowledged that Google did not make all information on the Internet available to Chinese users. Brin explained, "We ultimately made a difficult decision, but we felt that by participating there, and making our services more available, even if not to the 100 percent that we ideally would like, that it will be better for Chinese Web users, because ultimately they would get more information, though not quite all of it."[28] However, in early 2010, Google

Figure 12.2 Some governments view the Internet as a threat. *Source:* iStockphoto

announced that it would no longer censor its Chinese website. Told by the Chinese government that this was unacceptable, Google shut down Google. cn in March of 2010, and redirected visitors to its Hong Kong site.

For its part, the Chinese government is transparent about the issue. The China Illegal Information Reporting Centre's website is available in English at http://ciirc.china.cn. The Centre states, "CIIRC is mainly focused on contents harmful to the healthy growth of minors, such as obscenity and pornography, gambling, violence, terror, criminal abetting, and contents that spread ethnic hatred, libelling and insulting, violating the others' rights, and violating intellectual property rights." It goes on to identify "illegal and harmful information" as including information that "hinders national security and national unity."[29] The Centre maintains a website that solicits complaints about such information. The lack of Internet freedom in China was highlighted during President Obama's visit to Shanghai in November 2009. Responding to a question from a student, Obama said, "I've always been a strong supporter of open Internet use. I'm a big supporter of non-censorship." Obama's remark appeared on one of the major Chinese portals for only 27 minutes before censors removed it.[30] (Perhaps the most censored type of speech is criticism of censorship.)

Reporters sans Frontières (Reporters without Borders) is an organization of journalists that monitors and evaluates freedom of the press in

173 countries. The organization ranks China at 167th, with Turkmenistan, North Korea, and Eritrea rated the worst offenders against freedom of the press.[31] At the top of the list are Iceland, Luxembourg, and Norway. The United States is placed at the 36th position, with the organization objecting to court rulings that require reporters to reveal confidential informants in certain cases.

Globalization: convergence and disaggregation

Chapter 10 discusses *convergence* and *disaggregation*. Today's communication media promote global convergence, as they allow us to interact with those in nearly every other society. While the lack of a common language may present an obstacle, we can still communicate with others through visual imagery and musical expression. Although the English language and Western culture remain prominent in world media, there are also other cultures involved in the mix. In the process, cultures blend and infuse each other.

The process of disaggregation continues as well. Communication media are generating new media channels, and individuals are able to create channels of their own, based on their particular ideas, beliefs, and interests. Physical barriers and distance no longer control mass media to the degree that they once did.

Globalization and careers

As symbolized in Figure 12.3, new communication technology accelerates the process of globalization. Globalization causes employment shifts. Many of the communication devices that we use daily were designed and assembled outside of the United States. Many of us are driving Japanese or American branded cars that were built in Mexico. Manufacturing jobs are moving from countries with relatively high wages to those nations where the prevailing wages are lower.

Services are also shifting. If you have called a computer firm for technological support, it is highly likely that you have talked to a customer support

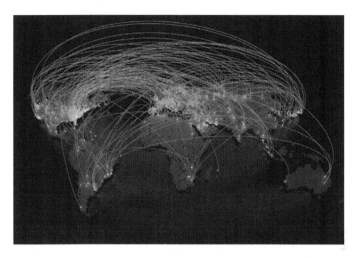

Figure 12.3 The wired world brings global change. *Source:* iStockphoto.

technician in India, China, or Taiwan. Some professional positions are also shifting globally. For example, your next x-ray may be read by a radiologist in India. Teleradiology, a relative new practice, sends x-ray images electronically from the radiology lab to the doctors who read them, and they submit their diagnoses electronically as well. Teleradiology can save the insurer money through lower fees paid to doctors who live in countries with a lower cost of living. It also allows patients and medical care providers to have emergency readings of x-rays in the middle of the night. Teleradiology is only one form of telemedicine expanding globally.

Most colleges now offer distance education, with students able to take classes wherever they are. Distance education is also *asynchronous*—students and faculty do not have to be online together at the same time, but can log on at anytime. Many American colleges and universities employ faculty members who live in other nations. This allows schools to have a broader base of teachers, and it may allow some American schools to pay lower wages to teachers, as some teachers may live in nations with a lower cost of living.

Global communications support the spread of just in time manufacturing. For example, this book was written on a computer that was ordered online in suburban Boston on a Sunday evening in the spring of 2008. The manufacturer was instantly able to verify the purchaser's credit card (issued by a bank in Colorado) online, and the order was sent directly to the computer firm's manufacturing facility in China. There, the computer was custom built and shipped to the United States, where it was available for pickup in Massachusetts on Friday of the same week, after the shipper had notified the purchaser by e-mail. The only direct communication that the purchaser had with a human being was with the shipping company's employee at the pickup counter.

Just as real goods can be manufactured globally, so can virtual items. According to the *New York Times*, there are at least 100,000 people in China who are paid to play video games twelve hours a day, seven days a week.[32] This may sound like fun, but the pay is poor and the working conditions are miserable. These workers are engaged in *gold farming*. The virtual money or virtual equipment that they acquire through their gaming is sold online, often to Americans. Higher playing levels are also offered for sale in a process called "power leveling." Although the business of selling virtual items in exchange for real currency is now officially illegal in China, a quick search for "gold farming" yields a large number of sites that are still in business. Richard Heeks at the University of Manchester (England) estimates that the gold farming industry generates $200 million to $1 billion annually for gold farmers' employers.[33]

Elsewhere in Asia, a team of 120 South Korean animators produces episodes of *The Simpsons*. The American creators of the show have been sending their storyboards and detailed instructions for each episode to a studio in Seoul since 1989. South Korean animators receive salaries estimated to be about one-third those of U.S. animators.[34]

Global communications also allows businesses to engage in a practice called *chasing the sun*. Imagine that you and two other individuals work on the same project for your employer. You do your work in the United States during the standard 8-hour workday. At the end of the day, as you shut down your computer, a co-worker in India logs-on. She picks up where you left off. Eight hours later, she logs off, and a co-worker in Europe logs on. The three of you have provided 24 hours of productivity to your employer. The European worker may be paid more than you and the Indian worker less, reflecting the different costs of living in each worker's home nation.

Questions for critical thinking and discussion

1. This chapter discusses American firms selling hazardous or potentially hazardous products in developing nations that lack adequate consumer protection laws.

   - If it is legal for a firm to advertise its products or services in a developing country, does that mean it is always also ethical to do so? Explain why or why not.

2. Many nations have more than one official language, including Canada, Belgium, Switzerland, and India.

   - Do you think it is important for the United States to adopt English as the sole official language of the nation? Explain your answer.

3. As discussed in this chapter, Google decided to stop censoring its search engine results in China, but other Internet search services still do so.

   - Is it ethical for media firms from the U.S. and elsewhere to do business in nations whose governments actively enforce censorship of information? Explain your answer.

4. Global advertising by American firms and the dominance of American mass media in the world affect how those in other nations perceive Americans.

   - If those who live in foreign nations identify the United States as primarily the land of Coke, McDonalds, and movie stars, is that a correct view of the United States or not?
   - Explain your answer and provide evidence for your argument.

5. Suppose that you wanted to get a better understanding about the activities, values, and interests of people in another part of the world. We will use the example of Afghanistan, a nation that is prominent in the American news media today.

   - Do you think that by conducting some Internet research that you would be able to develop a decent understanding of Afghanistan's history as well as Afghanistan today? Explain your answer.
   - Which method of learning about Afghanistan would you prefer—conducting Internet research on your own, or hearing a lecture by a person who is considered an expert on Afghanistan? Explain.

Additional resources

Barber, Benjamin R., *Jihad vs. McWorld; How Globalism and Tribalism are Reshaping the World* (New York: Ballantine, 1996).

Crothers, Lane, *Globalization and American Popular Culture*, 2nd ed., (Lanham, MD: Rowman & Littlefield, 2009).

Friedman, Thomas L., *The World is Flat 3.0* (New York: Picador, 2007).

Global Censorship in the Digital Age, http://library.thinkquest.org/07aug/02035/index.html

LinguaPax, www.linguapax.org/en

One Laptop per Child, www. laptop.org

Reporters without Borders, www.rsf.org

Rosetta Project, rosettaproject.org

Yang, Jeff, Dina Gan, and Terry Hong, *Eastern Standard Time; A Guide to Asian Influence on American Culture* (Boston: Mariner Books, 1997).

Notes

Chapter 1

1. Yahya R. Kamalipour and Theresa Carilli, eds., foreword to *Cultural Diversity and the U.S. Media* (Albany, NY: State University of New York Press, 1998), xv.

2. Wilbur Schramm, "How Communication Works," in *The Process and Effects of Communication*, ed. Wilbur Schramm (Urbana, IL: University of Illinois Press, 1954), 3–26.

3. Jill Sergeant, "Obama draws 37.8 million U.S. TV viewers," Reuters, http://www.reuters.com/article/televisionNews/idUSTRE50J15820090122. While this was fewer than 41.8 million people who watched Ronald Reagan's inauguration on television in 1981, Obama's inauguration actually drew far more viewers overall, due to the Internet, which was not available to the public during Reagan's presidency.

4. Ironically, although Hershey popularized the candy bar as we know it, his company did not engage in national advertising until many years after his death.

5. At the time this book was going to press, General Electric was negotiating the sale of NBC Universal to Comcast. For a more complete and updated list of the holdings of the Big Six, visit http://www.freepress.net/ownership/chart/main.

6. Raymond Williams, "Culture," *Keywords; a Vocabulary of Culture and Society*, revised edition (New York: Oxford Press, 1983), 87–93.

7. David Buckingham, *Media Education; Literacy, Learning and Contemporary Culture* (Cambridge, England: Polity, 2003), 1.

8. Bureau of Labor Statistics, "Occupational Outlook Handbook, 2008–2009 Edition, News Analysts, Reporters, Correspondents," United States Department of Labor, http://www.bls.gov/oco/ocos088.htm.

9. Bureau of Labor Statistics, "Appendix: Employment by occupation, 2006 and projected 2016," United States Department of Labor, http://www.bls.gov/emp/mlrappendix.pdf.

10. Bureau of Labor Statistics, "Industries at a Glance: Broadcasting (except Internet)," United States Department of Labor, http://www.bls.gov/iag/tgs/iag515.htm.

11. Bureau of Labor Statistics, "Industries at a Glance: Motion Picture and Sound Recording Industries," United States Department of Labor, http://www.bls.gov/iag/tgs/iag512.htm.

12. Bureau of Labor Statistics, "Industries at a Glance: Publishing Industries (except Internet)," United States Department of Labor, http://www.bls.gov/iag/tgs/iag511.htm.

13. Bureau of Labor Statistics, "Career Guide to Industries: Advertising and Public Relations Services," United States Department of Labor, http://www.bls.gov/oco/cg/cgs030.htm.

14. Bureau of Labor Statistics, "Career Guide to Industries: Publishing, Except Software," United States Department of Labor, http://www.bls.gov/oco/cg/cgs013.htm#outlook.

15. Bureau of Labor Statistics, "National Employment Matrix: Internet publishing and broadcasting," United States Department of Labor, ftp://ftp.bls.gov/pub/special.requests/ep/ind-occ.matrix/ind_pdf/ind_516000.pdf.

Chapter 2

1. Twitter, "About Twitter," Twitter, http://twitter.com/about#about.

2. US Aid, "Afghanistan: Education," US Aid, http://afghanistan.usaid.gov/en/Program.23a.aspx.

3. Media Awareness Network, "The Language of Media Literacy: A Glossary of Terms," Media Awareness Network, http://www.media-awareness.ca/english/resources/educational/teaching_backgrounders/media_literacy/glossary_media_literacy.cfm.

4. Josh Ozersky, "TVs Anti-Families: Married . . . with Malaise," *Tikkun* 6(1) (1991): 11–17.

5. United Nations Educational, Scientific and Cultural Organization, "Media Literacy," United Nations Educational, Scientific and Cultural Organization, http://portal.unesco.org/ci/en/ev.php-URL_ID=27056&URL_DO=DO_TOPIC&URL_SECTION=201.html.

6. National Association for Media Literacy Education, "Vision and Mission," National Association for Media Literacy Education, http://namle.net/about/vision-mission.

7. National Association for Media Literacy Education, "Core Principles Of Media Literacy Education in the United States," National Association for Media Literacy Education, http://www.amlainfo.org/uploads/r4/cE/r4cEZukacxNYaFFxlMONdQ/NAMLE-CPMLE-w-questions.pdf.

8. Center for Media Literacy, "About CML," Center for Media Literacy, http://www.medialit.org/about_cml.html.

9. Center for Media Literacy, "CML's Five Key Questions," Center for Media Literacy, http://www.medialit.org/pdf/mlk/14A_CCKQposter.pdf.

10. Associated Press, "Kellogg's to drop Phelps over marijuana picture," SI.com; Darren Rovell, "Phelps' Kellogg Deal Won't Be Renewed," CNBC, February 5, 2009, http://www.cnbc.com/id/29041954.

11. Sports Business Daily, "Turnkey Poll Examines Brand Loyalty Among Sports Fans," Sports Business Daily, December 10, 2008, http://www.sportsbusinessdaily.com/article/117156.

12. Bill Moyers Journal, "Buying the War," PBS.org, http://www.pbs.org/moyers/journal/btw/transcript1.html.

13. For example, a poll by the Pew Research Center for the People & the Press found that two-thirds of Republicans believe that the press is too critical of America. The Pew Research Center for the People & the Press, "Press Accuracy Rating Hits Two Decade Low," The Pew Research Center for the People & the Press, September 13, 2009, http://people-press.org/report/543/.

14. Anthony Ramirez, "Procter & Gamble Pulls Some TV Ads Over Slur to Coffee," *New York Times*, May 12, 1990, http://www.nytimes.com/1990/05/12/us/procter-gamble-pulls-some-tv-ads-over-slur-to-coffee.html?pagewanted=all.

15. Fairness and Accuracy in Reporting, "Health Debate in Quarantine," Fairness and Accuracy in Reporting, July/August, 1993, http://www.fair.org/index.php?page=1557.

16. Bureau of Labor Statistics, "Occupational Outlook Handbook, 2008–2009 Edition, Teachers—Preschool, Kindergarten, Elementary, Middle, and Secondary," United States Department of Labor, http://www.bls.gov/oco/ocos069.htm.

17. Bureau of Labor Statistics, "Occupational Outlook Handbook, 2008–2009 Edition, Teachers—Postsecondary," United States Department of Labor, http://www.bls.gov/oco/ocos066.htm.

Chapter 3

1. See for example, "How Many Advertisements is a Person Exposed to in a Day?" presented at the American Association of Advertising Agencies' website at http://www.aaaa.org/eweb/upload/FAQs/adexposures.pdf. Another discussion of the widely varying estimates of daily advertising exposure appears at http://answers.google.com/answers/threadview?id=56750.

2. Quoted in Cameron Zimmer, "Persuasion on the Prairies," *Explore* 2(1) (2009), http://www.usask.ca/research/communications/explore/vol2no1/persuasion-on-the-prairies.php.

3. "Marketer Trees 2009" *Advertising Age* http://adage.com/marketertrees09.

4. Ibid.

5. A.H. Maslow, "A Theory of Human Motivation," *Psychological Review* 50(4) (1943), 370–396.

6. Plunkett Research Ltd., "Advertising & Branding Industry Overview" http://www.plunkett-research.com/Industries/AdvertisingandBranding/AdvertisingandBrandingStatistics/tabid/70/Default.aspx.

7. "U.S. Ad Spending Trends: 2008," *Advertising Age*, June 22, 2009, http://adage.com/images/random/datacenter/2009/spendtrends09.pdf.

8. "Facts and Figures" Outdoor Advertising Association of America, http://www.oaaa.org/marketingresources/factsandfigures.aspx.

9. "Radio Revenue Trends," Radio Advertising Bureau, http://www.rab.com/public/pr/yearly.cfm.

10. John Consoli, "TargetCast: Prime Ad Rates Dip 11%" *Adweek* July 10, 2008, http://www.adweek.com/aw/content_display/news/e3i33fe2c109f8912f6c295191a72d35abc.

11. Aaron Smith, "How $3 million gets you 30 seconds," CNNMoney.com, February 3, 2009, http://money.cnn.com/2009/01/09/news/companies/superbowl_ads.

12. Plunkett Research Ltd., "Advertising & Branding Industry Overview," http://www.plunkettresearch.com/Industries/AdvertisingandBranding/AdvertisingandBrandingStatistics/tabid/70/Default.aspx. Nonlinear television viewing occurs when viewers use technology to watch a program at a time other than when it is originally broadcast.

Chapter 4

1. Newton N. Minow, "Television and the Public Interest" (speech delivered to the National Association of Broadcasters Washington, DC, May 9, 1961) found at http://www.americanrhetoric.com/speeches/newtonminow.htm.

2. "Industry: Faded Rainbow, *Time*, October 22, 1956. http://www.time.com/time/magazine/article/0,9171,824531,00.html.

3. Alexander B. Magoun, *Television; The Life Story of a Technology* (Westport, CT: Greenwood Press, 2007) 108.

4. Bill Carter, "Stunned CBS Now Scrambling for A.F.C.," *New York Times*, December 19, 1993, http://www.nytimes.com/1993/12/19/sports/pro-football-stunned-cbs-now-scrambling-for-afc.html.

5. "Industry Data," National Cable and Telecommunications Association, http://www.ncta.com/Statistics.aspx.

6. "Top 25 MSOs," National Cable and Telecommunications Association, http://www.ncta.com/Stats/TopMSOs.aspx. MSO stands for multiple system operator—a firm that owns more than one local cable system.

7. DTV.Gov, "United States Statistics," Federal Communications Commission, http://www.dtv.gov/dtv_stats.htm.

8. National Association for the Advancement of Colored People, "Out of Focus—Out of Sync Take 4; A Report on the Television Industry, December, 2008, http://www.naacp.org/news/press/2008-12-18/NAACP_OFOS_Take4.pdf.

9. Johnny Diaz, "1,400 New Englanders decided what you watched last night." *Boston Globe* March 28, 2009, G14–15.

10. "TV Basics: Television Households" Television Bureau of Advertising, http://www.tvb.org/rcentral/mediatrendstrack/tvbasics/02_TVHouseholds.asp.

11. In some major television markets, Nielsen conducts additional sweeps research.

12. Basil Katz, "New media upends TV ratings system" Reuters, October 1, 2009, http://www.reuters.com/article/entertainmentNews/idUSTRE59014820091001?pageNumber=2&virtualBrandChannel=11604.

13. Quoted in Tim Arango, "Broadcast TV Faces Struggle to Stay Viable" *New York Times*, February 27, 2009, http://nytimes.com/2009/02/28/business/media/28network.html.

14. Ibid.

15. Bureau of Labor Statistics, "Occupational Outlook Handbook, 2008–2009 Edition, Actors, Producers, and Directors," United States Department of Labor, http://www.bls.gov/oco/ocos093.htm.

16. Bureau of Labor Statistics, "Occupational Outlook Handbook, 2008–2009 Edition, Television, Video, and Motion Picture Camera Operators and Editors," United States Department of Labor, http://www.bls.gov/oco/ocos091.htm#outlook.

17. Bureau of Labor Statistics, "Occupational Outlook Handbook, 2008–2009 Edition, Announcers," United States Department of Labor, http://www.bls.gov/oco/ocos087.htm#outlook.

18. Marshall Sella, "The Remote Controllers," *New York Times*, October 20, 2002, http://www.nytimes.com/2002/10/20/magazine/the-remote-controllers.html.

Chapter 5

1. "Flashback: The 70th Anniversary of FDR's Fireside Chats," The Museum of Broadcast Communications, http://www.museum.tv/exhibitionssection.php?page=79.

2. "More Than 234 Million Listen to Radio Every Week Reports Arbitron," December 10, 2008, http://www.onlinepressroom.net/arbitron.

3. Ted Drozdowski, "Record Breaker," *Boston* Magazine, June 2006, http://www.bostonmagazine.com/arts_entertainment/articles/boston_magazine_record_breaker.

4. Recording Industry Association of America, Communication and Strategic Analysis Department, "The CD: A Better Value Than Ever," Recording Industry Association of America, August, 2007, http://76.74.24.142/F3A24BF9–9711-7F8A-F1D3–1100C49D8418.pdf.

5. "iTunes Store Top Music Retailer in the US" Apple, April 3, 2008, http://www.apple.com/pr/library/2008/04/03itunes.html.

6. In the case of iTunes and the iPod, the downloading service is a loss leader for the very profitable hardware. For approximately its first decade, the cell phone industry took the opposite approach from Apple; it priced the hardware (the phone itself) as a loss leader, while requiring customers to buy two-year service contracts. The cell phone industry later realized that it could charge higher prices for feature-loaded phones, and has moved away from its previous pricing model.

7. Recording Industry Association of America, "RIAA Parental Advisory Logo Standards Effective as of October 23, 2006," http://riaa.org/parentaladvisory.php#paladvisorylogostandards.

8. J. Freedom du Lac, "Green Day Adds Wal-Mart to List of American Idiots," "Post Rock," *The Washington Post*, May 22, 2009, http://voices.washingtonpost.com/postrock/2009/05/_headlines_video_of_the.html.

9. Chris Morris, "Korn Signs Broad-based Deal with EMI Music," *Hollywood Reporter*, September 13, 2005, http://www.redorbit.com/news/entertainment/238621/korn_signs_broadbased_deal_with_emi_music/index.html; "EMI Takes a Stake in Band," by Charles Duhigg, *Los Angeles Times*, September 12, 2005, http://msl1.mit.edu/furdlog/docs/latimes/2005–09-12_latimes_korn_emi.pdf.

10. Patrick Klepek, "Activision: 'Guitar Hero' A Bigger Money-Maker For Aerosmith Than Any Album," MTV Multiplayer Blog, http://multiplayerblog.mtv.com/2008/09/15/gh-money-for-aerosmith.

11. Bureau of Labor Statistics, "Occupational Outlook Handbook, 2008–2009 Edition, Broadcast and Sound Engineering Technicians and Radio Operators," United States Department of Labor, http://www.bls.gov/oco/ocos109.htm.

12. Bureau of Labor Statistics, "Occupational Outlook Handbook, 2008–2009 Edition, Musicians, Singers, and Related Workers," United States Department of Labor, http://www.bls.gov/oco/ocos095.htm.

Chapter 6

1. W. Joseph Campbell discusses the lack of credibility about this account of Hearst's actions in Chapter 3 of *Yellow Journalism: Puncturing the Myths, Defining the Legacies* (Westport, CT: Praeger, 2003).

2. Newspaper Association of America, " Daily Newspaper Readership Trend—Total Adults (1964–1997)," http://www.naa.org/docs/Research/Daily_National_Top50_64-97.pdf; Daily Newspaper Readership Trend—Total Adults (1998–2007), http://www.naa.org/docs/Research/Daily_National_Top50_1998-2007.pdf.

3. Audit Bureau of Circulations, "Top Media Outlets: Newspapers, Blogs, Consumer Magazines & Social Networks" found at BurrellesLuce.com, http://www.burrellesluce.com/top100/2009_Top_100List.pdf.

4. http://scarborough.com/press_releases/INA%20FINAL%203.25.pdf.

5. Larry Margasak, "Cardin proposes nonprofit status for newspapers," *Baltimore Sun*, March 24, 2009, http://www.baltimoresun.com/news/nation-world/politics/bal-cardin-newspapers0324,0,7631327.story.

6. David Kaplan, "Yahoo Newspaper Consortium Adds *Boston Globe* and *St. Petersburg Times*," *Washington Post*, March 10, 2009, http://www.washingtonpost.com/wp-dyn/content/article/2009/03/10/AR2009031003358.html.

7. John William Tebbel and Mary Ellen Zuckerman, *The Magazine in America, 1741–1990* (New York: Oxford University Press, 1991), 57–72.

8. "Edward William Bok," *Encyclopedia of World Biography*, Thomson Gale, 2004, Encyclopedia.com. http://www.encyclopedia.com/doc/1G2-3404707967.html.

9. Edward Bok, The Americanization of Edward Bok; The Autobiography of a Dutch Boy Fifty Years After, 1920, http://www.gutenberg.org/dirs/etext02/ewbok10.txt

10. Magazine Publishers of America, "A Magazine for Everyone," *Magazines; The Medium of Action*, 8, http://magazine.org/ASSETS/088C8564EB9E4E978A69B183881AEF58/MPA-Handbook-2009.pdf.

11. Magazine Publishers of America, "Historical Subscriptions/Single Copy Sales," www.magazine.org/CONSUMER_MARKETING/CIRC_TRENDS/1318.aspx.

12. *Reader's Digest*, "Circulation," http://www.rd.com/mediakit/rd/circulation.jsp. Recognizing that many of its members are not retired, the American Association of Retired Persons formally changed its name to the acronym AARP in 1999.

13. Magazine Publishers of America, "Top 100 ABC magazines by average Total Paid & Verified circulation" First Half 2009, http://www.magazine.org/CONSUMER_MARKETING/CIRC_TRENDS/FH2009Top100ABCTotalPaid.aspx.

14. Magazine Publishers of America, "Advertising Revenue, January–December 2008 vs 2007," http://www.magazine.org/advertising/revenue/by_mag_title_ytd/pib-4q-2008.aspx.

15. Magazine Publishers of America, "Editorial and Advertising Contribute to the Reader Experience," *Magazines; The Medium of Action*, 13, http://magazine.org/ASSETS/088C8564EB9E4E978A69 B183881AEF58/MPA-Handbook-2009.pdf.

16. Marketing Charts, "Share of Ad Spending by Medium," September 2008, http://www.marketingcharts.com/television/share-of-ad-spending-by-medium-september-2008-7477.

17. Magazine Publishers of America, "2008 Magazine Advertising Shows Effects of Soft Economy," January 13, 2009, http://www.magazine.org/advertising/revenue/by_ad_category/pib-4q-2008. aspx.

18. Gloria Steinem, "Sex, Lies, and Advertising," *Ms.*, July/August 1990, reprinted in *Ms.*, Spring 2002, 60.

19. Gail K. Smith, "The Sentimental Novel: The Example of Harriet Beecher Stow," in The *Cambridge Companion to Nineteenth-Century American Women's Writing*, eds. Dale M. Bauer and Philip Gould (Cambridge: Cambridge University Press, 2001), 221.

20. Sramana Mitra, "How Amazon Could Change Publishing," Forbes.com, May 16, 2008, http://www.forbes.com/2008/05/16/mitra-amazon-books-tech-enter-cx_sm_0516mitra. html.

21. Amazon.com, "Amazon.Com Announces Fourth Quarter Sales Up 18% To $6.70 Billion; 2008 Free Cash Flow Grows 16% To $1.36 Billion," January 29, 2009, http://media.corporate-ir.net/ media_files/irol/97/97664/consolidated_pressrelease_Q408.pdf.

22. Audio Publishers Association, "Audio Industry Holds Ground In 2008," June 23, 2009, http:// www.audiopub.org/resources-industry-data.asp.

23. Ralph Lombreglia, "Exit Guttenburg?" *The Atlantic*, November 16, 2000, http://www.theatlantic. com/unbound/digitalreader/dr2000–11-16.htm.

24. Bureau of Labor Statistics, "Occupational Outlook Handbook, 2008–2009 Edition, News Analysts, Reporters, and Correspondents," United States Department of Labor, http://www.bls. gov/oco/ocos088.htm.

25. Bureau of Labor Statistics, "Occupational Outlook Handbook, 2008–2009 Edition, Writers and Editors," United States Department of Labor, http://www.bls.gov/oco/ocos089.htm.

26. American Library Association, "Free Access to Libraries for Minors," http://www.ala.org/ala/ aboutala/offices/oif/statementspols/statementsif/interpretations/freeaccesslibraries.cfm.

27. USA Patriot Act of 2001, Public Law 107–56, 107th Cong., 1st sess. (October 24, 2001), §215.

Chapter 7

1. It is now preferred practice to refer to both males and females in the acting trade as "actors."

2. Joel W. Finler, *The Hollywood Story* (New York: Crown Publishers, 1988) 288.

3. Motion Picture Association of America, "Theatrical Market Statistics 2008," 2, http://www. mpaa.org/2008_Theat_Stats.pdf.

4. Pamela McClintock, "'Ice Age,' 'Transformers' tie for top spot" *Variety*, July 5, 2009, http://www.variety.com/article/VR1118005652.html?categoryid=13&cs=1.

5. Brandchannel, "Leading brand appearances this year . . ." http://www.brandchannel.com/brandcameo_brands.asp.

6. Crystal Ng and Bradley Dakake, "Tobacco at the Movies; Tobacco Use in PG-13 Films," 2, MASSPIRG, static.masspirg.org/reports/TobaccoattheMovies.pdf.

7. Robert B. Ray, *A Certain Tendency of Hollywood Cinema, 1930–1980*, (Princeton: Princeton University Press, 1985), 59.

8. Motion Picture Association of America, "Movie Attendance Study 2007," 2, http://www.mpaa.org/MovieAttendanceStudy.pdf.

9. Screen Actors Guild, "A Different America on Screen," *Screen Actor*, Winter 2007, 57, http://www.sag.org/files/documents/CastingDataReport.pdf.

10. "All-Time Box Office: USA," The Internet Movie Database, http://www.imdb.com/boxoffice/alltimegross; "All-Time Box Office: World-wide," The Internet Movie Database, http://www.imdb.com/boxoffice/alltimegross?region=world-wide.

11. "Domestic Grosses Adjusted for Ticket Price Inflation," Box Office Mojo, http://boxofficemojo.com/alltime/adjusted.htm.

12. Motion Picture Association of America, "Theatrical Market Statistics 2008," 6, http://www.mpaa.org/2008_Theat_Stats.pdf.

13. National Association of Theatre Owners, "U.S. Cinema Sites," http://www.natoonline.org/statisticssites.htm.

14. Motion Picture Association of America, "Theatrical Market Statistics 2008," 6, http://www.mpaa.org/2008_Theat_Stats.pdf.

15. National Association of Theatre Owners, "Number of U.S. Movie Screens," http://www.natoonline.org/statisticsscreens.htm.

16. National Association of Theatre Owners, "Top 10 U.S. & Canadian Circuits," July 21, 2009, http://www.natoonline.org/statisticscircuits.htm.

17. Cinema Buying Group, National Association of Theatre Owners, "Cinema Buying Group Selects AccessIT As Digital Integrator Provider," April 2, 2008, http://www.cbgpurchasing.com/news/news20080402.aspx.

18. National Association of Theatre Owners, "State of the Industry," http://www.natoonline.org/pdfs/Talking%20Points/TP-State%20of%20the%20Industry.pdf.

19. National Association of Theatre Owners, "Digital Cinema," http://www.natoonline.org/pdfs/Talking%20Points/TP-Digital%20Cinema.pdf.

20. Motion Picture Association of America, "Theatrical Camcorder Piracy," http://www.mpaa.org/piracy_theatrical_cam.asp.

21. Motion Picture Association of America, "Economies," http://www.mpaa.org/piracy_Economies.asp.

22. Bureau of Labor Statistics, "Occupational Outlook Handbook, 2008–2009 Edition, Television, Video, and Motion Picture Camera Operators and Editors," United States Department of Labor, http://www.bls.gov/oco/ocos091.htm.

23. Bureau of Labor Statistics, "Occupational Outlook Handbook, 2008–2009 Edition, Actors, Producers, and Directors," United States Department of Labor, http://www.bls.gov/oco/ocos093.htm.

24. Shaheen, Jack G., *Reel Bad Arabs; How Hollywood Vilifies a People*, (Brooklyn: Olive Branch Press, 2001), 2.

Chapter 8

1. The pets.com website address may have been worth more than the rest of the company's assets, and was purchased by PetSmart.

2. Benjamin Edelman, "Red Light States: Who Buys Online Adult Entertainment?" *Journal of Economic Perspectives*, 23(1) (2009): 210.

3. The State of Oregon has been particularly vigilant in identifying diploma mills. Oregon's Office of Degree Authorization maintains an excellent website: http://www.osac.state.or.us/oda/diploma_mill.html.

4. "Trend Data: Internet Activities," Pew Internet and American Life Project, http://pewinternet.org/Static-Pages/Trend-Data/Online-Activites-Total.aspx.

5. BBC News, "Wikipedia survives research test," December 15, 2005, http://news.bbc.co.uk/2/hi/technology/4530930.stm.

6. Federal Trade Commission, "FTC Publishes Final Guides Governing Endorsements, Testimonials," October 5, 2009, http://www.ftc.gov/opa/2009/10/endortest.shtm.

7. "Center for the Digital Future at USC Annenberg with 13 Partner Countries Release First World Internet Project Report," November 24, 2008, USC Annenberg School Center for the Digital Future, http://www.digitalcenter.org/WIP2009/WorldInternetProject-FinalRelease.pdf.

8. One should note that many of these hits take users to websites that *ridicule* those who make these claims about Obama and McCain's citizenship.

9. Anick Jesdanun, "Study: Arrests of online sexual predators rise; better enforcement credited" Chicago Tribune.com, March 30, 2009, accessed at Crimes Against Children Resource Center, http://www.unh.edu/ccrc/news/Internet_ChicagoTribune_3_30_09.pdf.

10. "Search Engine Strategies Conference: Conversation with Eric Schmidt hosted by Danny Sullivan," August 9, 2006, Google Press Center, http://www.google.com/press/podium/ses2006.html.

11. "Generational differences in online activities," January 28, 2009, Pew Internet and American Life Project, http://pewinternet.org/Infographics/Generational-differences-in-online-activities.aspx.

12. "Country-wise Total Domains Data as of 11/2/09," Webhosting.Info, http://www.webhosting.info/domains/country_stats.

13. "Internet Usage Statistics; The Internet Big Picture: World Internet Users and Population Stats,"June 30, 2009, Internet World Stats, http://www.internetworldstats.com/stats.htm.

14. "Top Sites; The top 500 sites on the web," Alexa, http://www.alexa.com/topsites.

15. Bureau of Labor Statistics, "Occupational Outlook Handbook, 2008–2009 Edition, Computer Scientists and Database Administrators," United States Department of Labor, http://www.bls.gov/oco/ocos042.htm.

16. Bureau of Labor Statistics, "Occupational Outlook Handbook, 2008–2009 Edition, Computer and Information Systems Managers," United States Department of Labor, http://www.bls.gov/oco/ocos258.htm.

17. Bureau of Labor Statistics, "Occupational Outlook Handbook, 2008–2009 Edition, Writers and Editors," United States Department of Labor, http://www.bls.gov/oco/ocos089.htm.

18. Bureau of Labor Statistics, "Occupational Outlook Handbook, 2008–2009 Edition, Graphic Designers," United States Department of Labor, http://www.bls.gov/oco/ocos090.htm.

Chapter 9

1. Matt Sussman, "Day 4: Blogging Revenues, Brands and Blogs: SOTB 2009," Technorati, State of the Blogosphere, October 22, 2009, http://technorati.com/blogging/article/day-4-blogging-revenues-brands-and.

2. Nielsen, "Global Faces and Networked Places; A Nielsen report on Social Networking's New Global Footprint," March, 2009, http://blog.nielsen.com/nielsenwire/wp-content/uploads/2009/03/nielsen_globalfaces_mar09.pdf.

3. Experian Hitwise, "Dashboards-'Top 20 Sites & Engines'" October 31, 2009, http://www.hitwise.com/us/datacenter/main/dashboard-10133.html.

4. Facebook, "Facebook Receives Investment from Digital Sky Technologies," May 26, 2009, http://www.facebook.com/press/releases.php?p=103711.

5. Amanda Lenhart and Susannah Fox "Twitter and status updating," Pew Internet and American Life Project, February 12, 2009, http://pewinternet.org/Reports/2009/Twitter-and-status-updating.aspx.

6. comScore, "Comscore Media Metrix Ranks Top 50 U.S. Web Properties for April 2009," May 14, 2009, http://comscore.com/content/download/2273/24215/file/comScore%20Inside%20the%20Ratings%20April%202009.pdf.

7. Jessi Hempel, "How Facebook is Taking over Our Lives," *Fortune*, March 2, 2009, 49–56.

8. Nielsen, "The Global Online Media landscape; Idnetifying Opportunities in a Challenging Market," April 2009, http://blog.nielsen.com/nielsenwire/wp-content/uploads/2009/04/nielsen-online-global-lanscapefinal1.pdf.

9. Twitter, "About Twitter; How do you make money from Twitter?" https://twitter.com/about#about.

10. Justin Smith, "Fastest Growing Demographic on Facebook: Women Over 55," *Inside Facebook*, February 2, 2009, http://www.insidefacebook.com/2009/02/02/fastest-growing-demographic-on-facebook-women-over-55.

11. Pattie Giordani, "Technology Influences the Profession," National Association of Colleges and Employers, Fall 2006, http://www.naceweb.org/50thanniversary/history_articles/megatrends3_fa06.htm.

12. Daily Hamster, "Your daily dose of cute hamsters," http://dailyhamster.com.

13. Facebook, "Privacy," http://www.facebook.com/privacy/?view=feeds&tab=ads.

14. MySpace, "Targeting," https://advertise.myspace.com/targetedadvertising.html.

15. Arlen Parsa, "Exclusive: Belkin's Development Rep is Hiring People to Write Fake Positive Amazon Reviews," The Daily Background, January 16, 2009, http://www.thedailybackground.com/2009/01/16/exclusive-belkins-development-rep-is-hiring-people-to-write-fake-positive-amazon-reviews/?ref=email.

16. Word of Mouth Marketing Association, "An Introduction to WOM Marketing with Definitions," http://womma.org/wom101.

17. Word of Mouth Marketing Association, "Ethics Code," http://womma.org/ethics/ethicscode.pdf.

18. Libby Quaid, "Poll finds sexting common among young people," Associated Press, December 3, 2009, hosted.ap.org/dynamic/stories/U/US_SEXTING_POLL.

19. The National Campaign to Prevent Teen and Unplanned Pregnancy, "Sex and Tech; Results from a Survey of Teens and Young Adults," http://www.thenationalcampaign.org/sextech/PDF/SexTech_Summary.pdf.

20. Guinness World Records, "Confirmed: Grand Theft Auto IV Breaks Guinness World Records With Biggest Entertainment Release Of All-Time," May 13, 2008, http://gamers.guinnessworld-records.com/news/130508_GTA_IV_break_record.aspx.

21. Entertainment Software Association, "Industry Facts," http://www.theesa.com/facts/index.asp.

22. Yankee Group, "Advertising and Games: 2007 In-Game Advertising Forecast," http://www.yankeegroup.com/ResearchDocument.do?id=16395. This revenue estimate was given before the economic crisis of 2008–2009, and will likely prove to be too optimistic.

23. Entertainment Software Rating Board, "ESRB Retail Council," http://www.esrb.org/retailers/retail_council.jsp.

24. Linden Lab, "1 Billion Hours, 1 Billion Dollars Served: Second Life Celebrates Major Milestones for Virtual Worlds" September 22, 2009, http://lindenlab.com/pressroom/releases/22_09_09.

25. There.com, "The Opportunity is There," http://www.there.com/info/opportunities.

26. Dian Schaffhauser, "Bryant & Stratton To Hold Graduation in Second Life for Online Students," Campus Technology, May 27, 2009, http://campustechnology.com/articles/2009/05/27/bryant-stratton-to-hold-graduation-in-second-life-for-online-students.aspx.

27. Apple, "Podcasting; A Better Messenger For Your Message," http://www.apple.com/business/podcasting/?cid=WWA-SEGO-BIZ080324G-A1BJR&cp=WWA-SEGO-BIZ080306G&sr=WWA-SEGO-BIZ080306G.

28. Bureau of Labor Statistics, "Tomorrow's Jobs," United States Department of Labor, http://www.bls.gov/oco/oco2003.htm.

29. "Economic Data," The Entertainment Software Association, http://www.theesa.com/facts/econdata.asp.

Chapter 10

1. Bill Carter, "Dismal Ratings for Networks in a Coveted Age Group," *New York Times*, June 24, 2009, B3.
2. YouTube, "YouTube Fact Sheet," http://www.youtube.com/t/fact_sheet.
3. "The Ten Biggest Technical Failures of the Last Decade," May 14, 2009, http://www.time.com/time/specials/packages/article/0,28804,1898610_1898625_1898631,00.html.
4. Gaywheels.com, "LGBT Auto Survey Results," April 7, 2009, http://www.gaywheels.com/lgbt_auto_survey_results.htm.
5. Henry Jenkins, "Convergence? I Diverge," *Technology Review*, June 2001, 93.
6. Billboard, "Remembering Michael Jackson: King of Charts," July 8, 2009, http://www.billboard.com/bbcom/news/remembering-michael-jackson-king-of-charts-1003991737.story.
7. Wikipedia, "Wikipedia: About," http://en.wikipedia.org/wiki/Wikipedia:About.

Chapter 11

1. *Gitlow v. New York*, 268 U.S. 652, 666 (1925).
2. Google, "Google Terms of Service," http://www.google.com/accounts/TOS.
3. *Schenck v. United States,* 249 U.S. 47, 52 (1919).
4. *New York Times v. Sullivan*, 376 U.S. 254 (1964).
5. *Miller v. California*, 413 U.S. 15 (1973).
6. *Luke Records v. Navarro*, 960 F2d 134 (11th Cir. 1992).
7. *Reno v. ACLU*, 521 U.S. 844 (1997).
8. Child Pornography Prevention Act of 1996, U.S. Code 18, §2256(8).
9. Federal Communications Commission, "Obscene, Indecent, and Profane Broadcasts," http://www.fcc.gov/cgb/consumerfacts/obscene.html.
10. *Federal Communications Commission v. Fox Television Stations*, 566 U.S. __(2009).
11. Communications Decency Act of 1996, U.S. Code 47, §230(c)(1).
12. World Intellectual Property Organization, "What is Intellectual Property?" United Nations, http://www.wipo.int/about-ip/en.
13. U.S. Chamber of Commerce, "U.S. Chamber Releases Comprehensive Study on the Importance of Intellectual Property in all 50 States," July 16, 2009, http://www.uschamber.com/press/releases/2009/july/090716_ip.htm.
14. U.S. Constitution, art. 1, sec. 8, cl. 8.
15. Copyright Act of 1976, U.S. Code 17 §102.
16. Steve Marinucci, "How Michael Jackson acquired the Beatles catalog: a short outline" examiner.com, June 27, 2009, http://www.examiner.com/x-2082-Beatles-Examiner~y2009m6d27-How-Michael-Jackson-got-the-Beatles-catalog.

17. The Official 2009 *Star Wars* Fan Movie Challenge, http://www.atom.com/spotlights/starwars/challenge.

18. U.S. Copyright Office, "Fair Use," http://www.copyright.gov/fls/fl102.html.

19. http://www.wired.com/images_blogs/threatlevel/files/linares.pdf.

20. Children's Online Privacy Protection Act, U.S. Code 15 §§6501–6506.

21. Unlawful Access to Stored Communications, U.S. Code 18 §2701(a).

22. The National Center for Victims of Crime, "Cyberstalking," http://www.ncvc.org/ncvc/main.aspx?dbName=DocumentViewer&DocumentID=32458.

23. Marci Feldman Hertz and Corinne David-Ferdon, *Electronic Media and Youth Violence: A CDC Issue Brief for Educators and Caregivers* (Atlanta: Centers for Disease Control, 2008), 3.

24. Stop Bullying Now, "Cyberbullying," United States Department of Health and Human Services, Health Resources and Services Administration, http://stopbullyingnow.hrsa.gov/adults/cyber-bullying.aspx.

25. In December 2009, MTV launched "A Thin Line" (www.athinline.org), a project aimed at preventing digital abuse, including cyberbullying.

26. Bureau of Labor Statistics, "Occupational Outlook Handbook, 2008–2009 Edition, Lawyers," United States Department of Labor, http://www.bls.gov/oco/ocos053.htm.

27. Bureau of Labor Statistics, "Occupational Outlook Handbook, 2008–2009 Edition, Computer Software Engineers," http://www.bls.gov/oco/ocos267.htm.

28. Eliot Van Buskirk, "RIAA to Stop Suing Music Fans, Cut Them Off Instead," *Wired*, December 19, 2008, http://www.wired.com/epicenter/2008/12/riaa-says-it-pl.

Chapter 12

1. Sue Pleming, "U.S. State Department speaks to Twitter over Iran," Reuters, June 16, 2009, http://www.reuters.com/article/rbssTechMediaTelecomNews/idUSWBT01137420090616.

2. Millennium Ecosystem Assessment, *Ecosystems and Human Well-Being* (Washington: Island Press, 2005), 99.

3. One Laptop per Child, "Vision," http://laptop.org/en/vision/index.shtml.

4. Vivian Yeo, "A Laptop for Every Poor Child," ZDNet Asia, July 17, 2009, http://www.zdnetasia.com/insight/hardware/0,39043471,62056166,00.htm.

5. Internet World Stats, "Internet Usage Statistics," September 30, 2009, http://www.internet-worldstats.com/stats.htm.

6. The population of Asia is ten times that of the U.S. and Canada.

7. Global Information and Communication Technologies Department and the Development Economics Data Group, *Information and Communications for Development 2009: Extending Reach and Increasing Impact* (Washington: World Bank, 2009) 181.

8. Rosetta Project, "Welcome to The Rosetta Project Digital Language Archive!" http://rosetta-project.org/about.

9. U.S. Census Bureau, "An Older and More Diverse Nation by Midcentury," August 14, 2008, http://www.census.gov/Press-Release/www/releases/archives/population/012496.html.

10. ProEnglish, "English in the 50 States," http://www.proenglish.org/issues/offeng/states.html.

11. Pew Global Attitudes Project, "A Global Generation Gap; Adapting to a New World," Pew Research Center, February 24, 2004, http://pewglobal.org/commentary/display.php?AnalysisID=86.

12. U.S. Census Bureau, "Hispanic Heritage Month 2007: Sept. 15 – Oct. 15," http://www.census. gov/Press-Release/www/releases/archives/facts_for_features_special_editions/010327.html.

13. Univision, "Media Properties," http://www.univision.net/corp/en/mp.jsp.

14. Univision, "Univision Announces 2009 First Quarter Results," May 15, 2009, http://files.share-holder.com/downloads/UVN/701155596x0x294906/35c4a24d-63b5–414d-befa-caaf1beadfab/294906.pdf.

15. In exchange, the Russian firm Stolichnaya began exporting vodka to the United States.

16. "Burger King apologises for ad offending Hindu sentiments," *The Times of India*, July 10, 2009, http://timesofindia.indiatimes.com/NEWS/India/Burger-King-apologises-for-ad-offending-Hindu-sentiments/articleshow/4759706.cms.

17. Jack G. Shaheen has written about Hollywood's representation of Arabs in the movies in *Guilty: Hollywood's Verdict on Arabs After 9/11* (Northampton, MA: Olive Branch Press, 2008) and *Reel Bad Arabs: How Hollywood Vilifies a People*, 2nd ed. (Northampton, MA: Olive Branch Press, 2009).

18. Motion Picture Association of America, "2009 Economic Impact of the Motion Picture and Television Industry," April 2009, 7, http://www.mpaa.org/EconReportLo.pdf.

19. Ibid.

20. Benjamin R. Barber, *Jihad vs. McWorld* (New York: Ballantine, 1996), 95.

21. Ibid., 93.

22. Box Office Mojo, "Yearly Index," http://www.boxofficemojo.com/intl/yearly/?page=yearcountry&yr=2008&sort=country&order=ASC&p=.htm.

23. Reuters, "New Internet Gambling Legislation to Be Introduced by Financial Services Committee . . ." May 5, 2009, http://www.reuters.com/article/pressRelease/idUS182614+05-May-2009+PRN20090505.

24. The Congressional International Anti-Piracy Caucus, "2009 Country Watch List," http://schiff.house.gov/antipiracycaucus/pdf/IAPC_2009_Watch_List.pdf.

25. International Intellectual Property Alliance, "International Intellectual Property Alliance (IIPA) Submits to the U.S. Trade Representative its Report on Copyright Piracy in 48 Countries," February 17, 2009, http://www.iipa.com/rbc/2009/2009SPEC301PRESSRELEASE.pdf.

26. Even in the United States, which boasts the world's lowest piracy rate, twenty percent of software in use is thought to be pirated. Business Software Alliance, "A Fifth of PC Software in United States is Pirated, Posing Challenges to High Tech Sector and Cyber Security," May 12, 2009, http://www.bsa.org/country/News%20and%20Events/News%20Archives/global/05122009-idc-globalstudy.aspx.

27. Irrepressible.Info, "About this Campaign," Amnesty International, http://irrepressible.info/about.

28. David Kirkpatrick, "Google founder defends China portal," *Fortune*, January 25, 2006, http://money.cnn.com/2006/01/25/news/international/davos_fortune.

29. China Internet Illegal Information Reporting Centre, "Illegal and Harmful Information," China Internet Information Service Commission, Internet Society of China, http://ciirc.china.cn/about/txt/2006–06/12/content_125592.htm.

30. Melanie Lee, "Obama visit arouses mistrust in China's Internet populace," Reuters, November 16, 2009, http://www.reuters.com/article/politicsNews/idUSTRE5AC0KV20091116.

31. Reporters without Borders, "Press Freedom Index 2008," http://www.rsf.org/en-classement794–2008.html.

32. Barboza, David, "Ogre to Slay? Outsource It to China," *New York Times*, December 12, 2005, http://www.nytimes.com/2005/12/09/technology/09gaming.html?ex=1291784400&en=a723d0f8592dff2e&ei=5090&partner=rssuserland&emc=rss.

33. Richard Heeks, "Current Analysis and Future Research Agenda on 'Gold Farming': Real-World Production in Developing Countries for the Virtual Economies of Online Games," (working paper 32, Development Informatics Working Paper Series, Institute for Development Policy and Management, University of Manchester, 2008) 9, http://www.sed.manchester.ac.uk/idpm/research/publications/wp/di/di_wp32.htm.

34. "'The Simpsons' Made in S. Korea," *China Daily*, March 5, 2005, 10, http://www.chinadaily.com.cn/english/doc/2005–03/05/content_421986.htm.

Glossary

360 deal contract in which a recording company receives part of musical artist's income from touring, merchandise sales, and licensing revenue, in exchange for marketing support from the recording company

advergame videogame that is essentially an advertisement; examples include Burger King's King Game series

advertiser firm that uses media to sell goods or services, not to be confused with an *advertising agency*

advertising agency firm that contracts with advertisers to create and place advertisements in the media

advertising kit information provided by media to advertisers regarding rates, technical requirements, deadlines, etc.

affiliate owner of a broadcasting station that contracts with a major broadcasting firm for content; compare with *owned and operated*

antagonist the "other" character, often the "bad guy," in a story plot; compare with *protagonist*

asynchronous not at the same time; for example, most online education today does not require students to be logged on at the same time as others in the class

auteur movie from the French word for author, a movie that bears signs of the director's cinematic style; auteurs include Alfred Hitchcock and Quentin Tarantino

avatar computer-generated character that represents a participant in a video game or virtual world

behavioral targeting placement of online advertising based on the identified interests or web surfing habits of individuals; compare with *contextual targeting*

blockbuster traditionally, a movie that earns over $100 million in box office receipts

boutique firm advertising agency specializing in particular services (such as media buying) rather than a full-service agency

brand	name or icon used to identify a product or service
censorship	restriction of the free expression of ideas, either by governmental or private entities
channel effect	effect that consumers' positive or negative perception of the medium in which an advertisement appears has on consumers' perception of the advertised item
chasing the sun	using communication technology to create a 24 hours a day work cycle, with workers in different parts of the world cooperating on a project
circulation	average number of copies of a print publication sold per edition; compare with *readership*
classified advertisement	print advertisement, typically relying on text rather than graphics, organized by subject matter; compare with *display advertisement*
click-through rate	percentage of viewers exposed to an advertisement that click on the advertisement for more information
cloud computing	using online software, replacing the need for software loaded on a user's computer
cocooning	Faith Popcorn's term for aging baby boomers' desire to spend more time at home in the evenings and on weekends than they did when they were younger
communication	encoding information through sounds, symbols, and actions in order to transmit that information to others
complementary copy	print media's placement of editorial content that helps advertisers sell their goods and services
concept album	music recordings in which each song is part of an album's central theme
contemporary hit radio	modern term for *top 40 radio*
contextual targeting	matching advertising to the content of a medium. For example, a site that features photos of puppies will have ads for dog food and supplies; compare with *behavioral targeting*
convergence	media's move to electronic platforms that allow users to interact with many others, creating and sharing content, often without the participation of media content firms

copy	the printed or spoken words in an advertisement
cost per click (CPC)	advertising charge based on how many web users click on an online advertisement; compare with *cost per thousand*
cost per thousand (CPM)	advertising charge based on how many thousands of web users are exposed to an online advertisement; compare with *cost per click*
crowdsourcing	when users generate content for a medium; content may be information (Wikipedia), music (MySpace), photography (Flickr), or video (YouTube)
culture	ways in which people develop shared meaning and ideals, through material production (houses, furniture, clothing) musical and artistic creation, which often vary, based on ethnic, geographic, religious, and economic factors
cyber-dissidence	use of interactive media to criticize the actions of the government and other institutions that hold power
demographics	statistics about people based on quantifiable factors such as age, income, education attained, and geographic location; compare with *psychographics*
digital rights management (DRM)	file encryption that limits which types of devices can play those files
disaggregation	shift from a few large media audience groups into much smaller groups, each with its own specific media preferences
display advertisement	print advertisements that take any form other than that of a *classified advertisement*
dog whistle marketing	marketing campaigns aimed at very specific target audiences without the larger audience understanding the advertiser's message. For example, Hollister stores attract young people although they have no exterior signage.
drive time	"rush hours," when the most motorists are on the road; period of highest radio listenership

fair use permitted use of a limited amount of copyright protected content in order to comment on, review, or satirize it

feature story non-news story in a news medium

focus groups people gathered to help researchers predict public reaction to media content or advertising

franchise movie movies based on the same characters or plotlines; examples include the Star Wars films and the Harry Potter series

frequency emphasis on repeating advertisements regularly, a practice commonly used on *low involvement* media; compare with *reach*

genre classification of a medium by type; genres of magazines include "shelter publications" (home decorating); genres of movies include "buddy films"

globalization increasing integration of economies and societies around the world, particularly through trade and financial flows, and the transfer of culture and technology

gold farming practice in which individuals are paid to play some of the more monotonous parts of *MMORPGs*, then selling their advance game status to others

high involvement when consumers are actively engaged in consuming a medium, such as a video game or movie; compare with *low involvement*

icon symbol or image representing a *theme*

impressions measurement of the number of people exposed to a medium, multiplied by times they are exposed; a combination of *reach* and *frequency*

imprints publishing brands; for example, Simon & Schuster's imprints include Pocket Books, Scribner, and Free Press

information cascades multiple sources of information from many people using a variety of media technologies

knowledge community	groups of people who use interactive media to record and distribute information to others; Wikipedia is among the best known creations of a knowledge community
long tail	term popularized by Chris Anderson, who argues that the future of business is selling less of more; in other words, consumers will have more choices and thus will buy fewer of any single choice
low involvement	when consumers pay little attention when exposed to a medium; examples include radio and billboards. Compare with *high involvement*.
market segmentation	dividing a market into *niches* based on *demographics* and *psychographics*
mass communications	communicating with many people, perhaps millions of people, often simultaneously, through *mass media*
mass marketing	using *mass media* to sell a product or service to a large audience
mass media	media engaged in *mass communications*
MMORPG	massively multiplayer online role playing game
narrowcasting	identifying a relatively small but carefully identified audience for a television network, such as Lifetime (for women) or Spike (for men)
newsreel	short documentary movie that provided moving visual images of important contemporary events before the arrival of television
niche	carefully identified consumer base that results from *market segmentation*
owned and operated	broadcast station owned by a major broadcaster; compare with *affiliate*
p2p, peer-to-peer	individuals sharing audio, video, graphic, and text files online
paradigm	prevalent way of doing or thinking about something
paradigm shift	when a new paradigm replaces an existing one
participation	when an actor receives a percentage of box office receipts in addition to a salary

passion community group of people who share a common interest, such as a celebrity fan group

production values media coding designed to increase audience appeal

protagonist main character, often the "good guy" in a story plot; compare with *antagonist*

pseudo-event Daniel Boorstin's term for events created primarily to generate publicity

psychographics categorization of people based on attitudes, beliefs, and habits (including buying habits); compare with *demographics*

public domain not protected by intellectual property law, such as when a novel is older than its period of copyright protection

puffery use of advertising terms that sound impressive but cannot be objectively measured, such as "the hottest"

pull content media content that consumers ask for, such as local weather reports or sports scores; compare with *push content*

push content media content that consumers have not asked for, such as advertisements; compare with *pull content*

qualitative research evaluation of consumers' perceptions and attitudes rather than numerical factors; compare with *quantitative research*

quantitative research evaluation based on audience size, sales, and other numerical factors; compare with *qualitative research*

rate card document containing advertising prices, technical requirements, and submission deadline provided by a medium to advertisers

reach total audience that an advertising message reaches rather than how often; compare with *frequency*

readership total number of readers exposed to a particular print publication rather than the number of copies sold; compare with *circulation*

recto right hand page of a print medium; compare with *verso*

sandbox game	video game without a definite end, allowing players to engage in the game as they like
selective exposure	process by which individuals decide which media messages to read, watch, or listen to based on their point of view
selective perception	process by which individuals interpret information based on their point of view
selective retention	process by which individuals remember or forget information based on whether that information conforms with or contradicts their point of view
shock jock	radio personality who relies on provocative material to build listenership, such as Howard Stern
spot advertisement	broadcast advertising purchased directly from a local broadcast outlet rather than a network
stealth marketing	sales tactic designed to make a consumer think that the seller is not really selling anything
strip program	television programming, typically a syndicated program that is broadcast daily or Monday through Friday
studio system	old practice by which an actor agreed to work only for a particular movie studio for a period of time
syndicated program	program generated from a source other than a television network, such as "Dr. Phil" or "Jeopardy"
synergy	coordinated action between two or more entities creating a combined effect greater than the results those entities could have individually
technological lag	when society is able to invent technology before society is able to effectively control that technology
technological leapfrogging	when rapidly developing nations shift from a primitive technological state to a more advanced state without moving through the intermediate technologies of more developed nations
terrestrial radio	term that distinguishes broadcast (AM/FM) radio from satellite or Internet radio
theme	idea or ideal, often represented by an *icon*
third-person effect	belief that advertising affects others, but not oneself

top 40 radio format that played only the forty most popular songs of the day; now called *contemporary hit radio*, it relies on less than 30 songs today

verso left hand page of a print medium; compare with *recto*

virtual retailer seller that relies exclusively on online sales for revenue

wire story news story distributed to news outlets by a news gathering agency such as the Associated Press

work for hire creative work by an employee who agrees to allow the employer to own the intellectual property rights to that work

yellow journalism sensationalist newspaper journalism of the 1800s designed to boost circulation, often inaccurate and unethical

Index

Made in the USA
Lexington, KY
26 September 2013